ISBN 978-0-282-00413-2
PIBN 10200734

FB &c Ltd, Dalton House, 60 Windsor Avenue, London, SW19 2RR.
Company number 08720141. Registered in England and Wales.

Edith Daley Parkhurst.

PUBLICATIONS OF SOWER, POTTS & CO., PHILADELPHIA.

Brooks's Normal Geometry and Trigonometry.

By the aid of Brooks's Geometry the principles of this beautiful science can be easily acquired in one term. It is so condensed that the amount of matter is reduced one half, and yet the chain of logic is preserved intact and nothing essential is omitted. The subject is made interesting and practical by the introduction of Theorems for original demonstration Practical Problems, Mensuration, etc., in their appropriate places. The success of the work is very remarkable. Key, $1.10*.

Brooks's Normal Algebra.

The many novelties, scientific arrangement, clear and concise definitions and principles, and masterly treatment contained in this quite new work make it extremely popular. Each topic is so clearly and fully developed that the next follows easily and naturally. Young pupils can handle it, and should take it up before studying Higher Arithmetic. Like the Geometry, it can be readily mastered in one term. It only needs introduction to make it indispensable. Key, $1.10*.

Peterson's Familiar Science. 12mo.
Peterson's Familiar Science. 18mo.

This popular application of science to every-day results is universally liked, and has an immense circulation. No school should be without it. Inexperienced teachers have no difficulty in teaching it.

Griffin's Natural Philosophy.

BY LA ROY F. GRIFFIN,

PROF. OF THE NAT. SCIENCES AND ASTRON., LAKE FOREST UNIVERSITY, ILL.

Professor Griffin presents his subject so simply, clearly and logically, his definitions are so brief and yet clear, and his experiments so vivid and impressive, that the subject is easily mastered and firmly impressed on the student. All the latest applications of the science to Electric Lights, Telephone, Phonograph, Electro-Plating, Magnetic Engines, Telegraphing, etc. are lucidly explained.

Griffin's Lecture Notes on Chemistry.

Roberts's History of the United States.

Short, compact and interesting, this History is admirably arranged to fix facts in the memory. These only are dealt with, leaving causes for more mature minds. It ends with the close of the late war.

Sheppard's Text-Book of the Constitution.
Sheppard's First Book of the Constitution.

The ablest jurists and professors in the country, of all political denominations, have given these works their most unqualified approval. Every young voter should be master of their contents.

Montgomery's Industrial Drawing.

This consists of a series of Drawing Books, comprising a Primary and Intermediate Course. The system is self-teaching, is carefully graded and is easily taught.

Fairbanks's Bookkeeping.*

Edith Daley Parkhurst

Seattle,

W. T.

How to Write Letters:

A MANUAL OF

CORRESPONDENCE,

SHOWING

THE CORRECT STRUCTURE, COMPOSITION, PUNCTUATION, FORMALITIES, AND USES OF THE VARIOUS KINDS

OF

Letters, Notes, and Cards.

BY

J. Willis Westlake, A. M.,

PROFESSOR OF ENGLISH LITERATURE IN THE STATE NORMAL SCHOOL, MILLERSVILLE, PA.

PHILADELPHIA:

SOWER, POTTS & CO.

1883.

WESTCOTT & THOMSON,
Stereotypers and Electrotypers, Philada.

SHERMAN & CO.
Printers, Philada.

PREFACE.

NEARLY all the writing of most persons is in the form of letters; and yet in many of our schools this kind of composition is almost entirely neglected. This neglect is probably due in some measure to the fact that heretofore there has been no complete and systematic treatise on the subject of letter-writing. When it is considered, that in the art of correspondence there is much that is conventional, requiring a knowledge of social customs, which, if not early taught, is obtained only after many years of observation and experience; and that the possession or want of this knowledge does much to determine a person's standing in cultured society,—the value of this art, and of a thorough text-book by which it may be taught, will be duly appreciated. For many years the author, in common with many other teachers, has felt the need of such a work, in the instruction of his own classes, and it is to this want that the present treatise owes its origin.

In plan the work is broad and comprehensive, embracing as it does the whole field of letters—their classification, structure, rhetoric, and literature—as well as the forms and uses of the various kinds of notes and cards. It is designed, both in matter and in method, to meet the wants, not only of schools of various grades, but also of private learners and of society at large.

Most of the materials employed have been gathered from original sources, and now appear in print for the first time. This is especially true of the articles on *Notes and Cards*, *Titles*, and *Forms of Address* and *Salutation*. No pains have been spared to ascertain the best present usage in regard to all the subjects presented. Concerning official and professional titles and forms, information has been sought and obtained from various Heads of Departments of our National and State Governments, from military and naval officers, from the leading colleges, and from other high sources; and on social matters the author has been kindly favored with the advice and suggestions of many ladies and gentlemen in the principal cities, who, if he were permitted to name them, would at once be recognized as persons of the highest culture and refinement. To these, and to all others who have in any way afforded him assistance and encouragement in his labors, he proffers his grateful acknowledgments. His special thanks are due, and are hereby cordially tendered, to Mr. William S. Schofield of Philadelphia, whose tireless zeal, sound judgment, and excellent taste, constantly and variously exercised in the interest of the work, have added greatly to its value and completeness.

And now, with many hopes and a few fears, the author submits his little book to the great tribunal of public opinion, adding only the assurance that, whatever may be its merits or its faults, it is the result of an earnest desire to promote the literary and social culture of our schools and people.

MILLERSVILLE, PA., February 2, 1876.

CONTENTS.

[A GENERAL INDEX MAY BE FOUND ON PAGE 263.]

LETTER-WRITING.

INTRODUCTION.

OUTLINE.

- I. Importance.
  - 1. Business.
  - 2. Social.
  - 3. Intellectual.
- II. Plan of the Work.

Importance.—As letter-writing is the most generally practiced, so also it is the most important, practically considered, of all kinds of composition. This will more fully appear from the following considerations:—

1. *Letter-writing is indispensable in business.* All persons have business of some kind to transact, and much of it must be done by means of letters. To be able to write a good letter is greatly to a person's advantage in any occupation. Many good situations are obtained by teachers, clerks, and others, on account of this ability; and quite as many are lost for the want of it.

2. *It is a social obligation.* We are naturally social beings; and pleasure, interest, and duty equally demand that our friendships and other social ties should be maintained and strengthened. In many cases this can be done only by means of letters. No one would willingly lose out of his life the joy of receiving letters from absent friends, nor withhold from others the same exquisite pleasure.

It may be stated, also, that a person's social, intellectual, and moral culture are indicated in his letters, as plainly as in his manners, dress, and conversation; and it is as great a violation of propriety to send an awkward, careless, badly written letter, as it is to appear in a company of refined people, with swaggering gait, soiled linen, and unkempt hair.

3. *It gives intellectual culture.* Letter-writing is one of the most practical and interesting exercises in English composition—one that is suitable for persons of all grades, from the child just learning to write, to the man of highest attainments. It affords exercise in penmanship, spelling, grammar, diction, invention—in short, in all the elements of composition, and gives ease, grace, and vivacity of style. Many who have become distinguished in other kinds of writing, have acquired much of their power and fluency of expression by their practice of writing letters. Of these Robert Burns is a notable example. In fact the letters of distinguished men and women form a distinct and important department of literature; and some who are recognized as standard authors would long ago have been forgotten but for their admirable correspondence. Of the latter it is sufficient to mention Madame de Sévigné, Lady Mary Wortley Montagu, and Horace Walpole.

Plan of the Work.—For convenience, this treatise is divided into three parts:—

PART I. LETTERS, NOTES, AND CARDS.

PART II. ORTHOGRAPHY AND PUNCTUATION.

PART III. MISCELLANEOUS, containing Titles, Forms of Address and Salutation, Abbreviations, Foreign Words and Phrases, Postal Information, and Business Forms.

Suggestion to Teachers.—In view of the great educational and literary value of letter-writing, teachers should to a great extent substitute this exercise for the writing of ordinary "compositions." They will thus secure greater ease and freedom of expression than by the old method, and will at the same time give their pupils a practical acquaintance with the forms and peculiarities of letters.

PART I.

LETTERS, NOTES, AND CARDS

Special Notice.

Owing to the rapidly increasing use of the **type-writing machine** *in correspondence, the author has thought proper to insert in the present edition of this work some special directions applicable to type-written letters, which may be found on pages 66 and 67.*

10

LETTERS.

IN discussing the subject of Letters, we shall treat, *first*, of the various kinds of letters; *secondly*, of the materials required and the formalities to be observed in writing them; *thirdly*, of their language, style, and other rhetorical requirements; and *fourthly*, of their value and characteristics as a department of literature. This division of our work will therefore consist of four chapters, as follows:—

CHAPTER I. THE CLASSIFICATION OF LETTERS.
CHAPTER II. THE STRUCTURE OF LETTERS.
CHAPTER III. THE RHETORIC OF LETTERS.
CHAPTER IV. THE LITERATURE OF LETTERS.

To the Teacher.—It is suggested that each pupil be required at the beginning of the course in letter-writing, and without consulting the book, to hand in a *specimen letter* to represent his present style. It may answer, in narrative form, the following questions:—

1. Where do you live?
2. Where did you last attend school?
3. What literary advantages have you enjoyed?
4. What studies are you now pursuing?

This letter the teacher will do well to keep till the close of the course, that he may then compare it with another specimen letter, and thus be able to measure the pupil's progress in this branch.

CHAPTER I.

Classification of Letters.

OUTLINE.

- I. PRIVATE.
  - 1. Social
    - Domestic,
    - Introductory, etc
  - 2. Business.
    - Personal,
    - Official.
  - 3. Miscellaneous.
  - 4. Postal Cards.
- II. PUBLIC, OR OPEN.

Definition.—A Letter is a prose composition addressed to some person or persons.

Letters may be divided into two general classes,—1. Private, or Personal; 2. Public, or Open.

PRIVATE LETTERS.

Private Letters are those that are intended only for those to whom they are addressed. They may be divided into three classes,—Social, Business, and Miscellaneous.

Social Letters are letters of sentiment. They include the great mass of familiar correspondence, to which belong Domestic or Family letters, letters of Introduction, of Congratulation, of Condolence, of Advice, of Affection, and, in a word, all letters that are prompted by love or friendship. The names of the various classes are so plainly descriptive as to render formal definitions unnecessary.

A **Business Letter,** as its name implies, is a letter on business.

NOTE.—A business letter should be exclusively such. Matters of a social or domestic nature should generally be in a separate letter.

Business letters are of two kinds,—Personal and Official.

A *Personal* business letter is one on personal or private business.

To this class belong the letters written by merchants, manufacturers, lawyers, bankers, and others, whether as individuals or as firms or companies, in connection with their trade or occupation.

An *Official* business letter is one written to or by a person holding a public office, on business pertaining thereto.

To this class belong letters to the executive or heads of departments of a national, state, or municipal government, letters of army and navy officers, etc.

Miscellaneous Letters include those letters of an accidental or unusual character, to which our complicated relations to society give rise; in short, all letters not elsewhere classified.

Postal Cards.—The Postal Card is a letter in the form of a card. But little need be said of it, and that little may as well be said now. In the postal card many of the formalities of letters are dispensed with, and no attention is paid to style, except as to clearness and condensation. In this respect it resembles a telegram. The following directions should be observed :—

1. A card should be dated either on the upper right-hand corner, or on the lower left-hand corner.

2. The writer's full name should be signed to it.

3. If an answer is required, the writer's full post-office address should be given, unless it is well known by the person to whom the card is directed.

4. Important matters should not be entrusted to a postal card, as it is open to inspection, and as the law does not provide for its return to the writer in case of failure to reach its destination. Nor is it allowable to use postal cards for notes of invitation, etc., in which society prescribes certain polite forms to be observed.

5. Write on the face nothing but the name and directions. These are to be written as on the envelope of an ordinary letter (see page 57).

Public Letters.

Public Letters are letters in form only. They are essays or reports intended for the public, but addressed to some individual. The writers adopt this form because it gives a personal interest to what they say, and because it admits of a more familiar style of treatment than a formal essay.

To this class belong most of the letters published in the newspapers addressed either to the editor or to some distinguished public man.

How Prepared for the Press.—In preparing manuscript for the press, the following directions should be observed: 1. Write plainly. 2. *Write on only one side of the paper.* This rule is imperative. 3. Attend carefully to the spelling, capitals, paragraphing, and all the minor details of composition. This is the author's duty, not the printer's. 4. Number the pages.

CHAPTER II.

STRUCTURE OF LETTERS.

OUTLINE.

1. **Materials.**—Paper, Envelopes, Ink.
2. **Heading.**—Place, Date.
3. **Introduction.** — Address.* (Name and Title, Residence.); Salutation.
4. **Body.** — Beginning, Margin, Paragraphs, Miscellaneous Suggestions.
5. **Conclusion.** — Complimentary Close, Signature, Address (if not at the top).*
6. **Folding.**
7. **Superscription, or Outside Address.**
8. **Stamp.**

SECTION I.—Materials.

OUTLINE.

1. **Paper**—Size, Color, etc.
2. **Envelopes**—Size, Color, etc.
3. **Ink**—Color.

Paper.—The paper used should be such as is suitable and intended for the purpose. It may now be had in infinite variety, adapted to all tastes and wants.

---

* The Address is always written at the top of a business letter, and always at the bottom of a domestic letter (that is, a letter to a near

...erly the kind known as *letter-paper* ... inches) was used exclusively; and it ... some extent, but mainly in business correspondence. Nine-tenths of the letters written now-a-days are on *note-paper*. This is of a great variety of styles and sizes. The most popular size is that known as "commercial note," which is about 5 by 8 inches. A kind much used by gentlemen is "packet note," which is about 5¾ by 9 inches.

Never write a private letter on foolscap paper: to do so is awkward, clumsy, and generally inexcusable. If compelled to use it, for want of any other, an apology should be offered.

Never send a half-sheet letter, except on business: and never send less than a half-sheet under any circumstances. For a social letter, even if you write only a line or two, use a whole sheet. To use part of a sheet looks mean and stingy, and is disrespectful to the receiver.

COLOR.—No color is more elegant and tasteful than white, for any kind of letter, and gentlemen should use no other. Ladies may use delicately tinted and perfumed paper if they choose, but for a man to use it is, to say the least, in very bad taste. For business letters, no color is allowable but pure or bluish white.

Persons who have lost a near relative may use "mourning paper"—that is, paper with a black border

relative). In other letters it may be written at the top or bottom, to suit the taste or convenience of the writer. (See Sec. III., p. 30 also Sec. V., p 48.)

—and envelopes to match; the width of the border corresponding somewhat to the nearness of the relationship and the recentness of the bereavement.

LINES.—A person, without violating good taste, may use either ruled or plain paper; but plain or unruled paper is decidedly to be preferred, both because it is more stylish, and because it is more convenient, enabling one to write close or open—to put much or little upon a sheet. Any one by diligent practice may learn to write straight without a guiding line, and the ability to do so is a valuable acquirement. Some persons who use unruled paper put "lines" under it. This practice is not to be commended, as it is inconvenient, and prevents that discipline of the hand which renders the writer independent of such help; and besides, the best note-paper is too thick to allow lines to show through.

Envelopes.—The envelope should be adapted, both in size and color, to the paper.

SIZE.—If note-paper be used, the envelope should be a little longer than the width of the page. Letter-paper requires the same size of envelope as commercial note; that is, about 3¼ by 5½ inches.

Fine imported papers are cut into note-sheets for ordinary correspondence, to fold twice for an envelope 2⅞ by 5¼, and once for an envelope 3¾ by 4⅝. Smaller sizes may be used for notes of invitation, etc.

Official letters, manuscripts for newspapers, legal documents, and all large communications sent by mail, should be enclosed in what are called *official* envelopes, which are about 9 inches long—long enough to take in the full width of letter or foolscap paper.*

COLOR.—Gentlemen may use either white or buff† envelopes in writing to each other; but it is not allowable to send a buff envelope to a lady, nor do ladies use that kind at all. If tinted paper is used, the envelope must have the same tint.

NOTE.—The sizes of paper and envelopes above given are those that are regarded as standard—those that are always in fashion among sensible people. The styles of fine papeterie at a modern stationer's are as capricious and variable as the figures of a kaleidoscope.

QUALITY.—Both paper and envelopes should be of fine quality. It conduces to fine penmanship, and perhaps inspires the writer with fine thoughts. Coarse paper, coarse language, coarse thoughts,—all coarse things seem to be associated.

Ink.—Never write a letter with red ink. Indeed, it is in better taste to discard all fancy inks, and use simple black. It is the most durable color, and one never tires of it. At one time purple ink was used in the War Department at Washington; but the discovery was afterwards made that this color would fade, and an order was issued that all the records that

* The sizes and designations of Government envelopes, which are generally taken as the standard, are as follows: Note Size, 2¾ by 5¼ inches; Ordinary Letter Size, 3$\frac{1}{16}$ by 5½ inches; Full Letter Size, 3⅝ by 5½ inches; Extra Letter Size, 3½ by 6⅜ inches; Official Size, 3$\frac{15}{16}$ by 8⅞ inches: Extra Official Size, 4⅜ by 10¼ inches.

† By "buff" envelopes are meant all those colored envelopes (often of coarse quality) that are used by business men, whether described as light buff, dark buff, yellow, cream, or amber.

had been made with purple ink should be recopied with black ink.

Wax.—A few years ago sealing-wax was an indispensable article of stationery, but it has been rendered nearly obsolete by the almost universal use of gummed envelopes. It is now principally used on packages or letters containing money and other valuable enclosures, as an additional protection against their being feloniously opened, it being difficult to open a sealed letter without breaking the seal. Money packages sent by express are always sealed; so too are foreign despatches. A lady of fine culture (to whom the author is indebted for many valuable suggestions) remarks as follows:—

"Although the use of the tongue is admirably adapted to the hurry and press of business, it is not, if one thinks of it, a very elegant manner of closing a letter to a friend. A neat little seal of red wax for a gentleman, and of gold, blue, or other fancy color for a lady, will give a much more refined appearance to a note, than simply closing it with adhesive gum. Sealing is an art, however; and to do it handsomely will require considerable practice."

SECTION II.—The Heading.

OUTLINE.

- 1. Parts.
  - 1. Place.
    - Post Office (or No. and Street),
    - County (or City),
    - State.
  - 2. Date.
    - Month,
    - Day of the Month,
    - Year.
- 2. Position and Arrangement.
- 3. Punctuation.
- 4. Models.

The Heading consists of the *Place* and the *Date.* In other words, it is a statement of the place where, and time when, the letter is written.

Place.—When a person is answering a letter, he generally looks at the heading of it to see how his answer is to be directed. Hence, if the letter is written elsewhere than in a large city, the "place" should embrace *at least* two items,—the name of the post-office and the name of the state. The heading of a business letter should also embrace the name of the county. Indeed, in all letters the county should be named, either at the top or the bottom, unless the writer is perfectly sure that it is well known to his correspondent. In a city, the number and street, city, and state should be given. If the city is very large, such as Philadelphia, New York, Chicago, the state need not be given. It would seem absurd to write, "530 Broadway, New York, N. Y."

A person writing from a large school, a college, a hotel, or any well-known institution, generally writes the name of the institution at the head, as in Model 3.

NOTE.—On fine paper it is fashionable to have the writer's monogram, crest, or coat of arms printed near the top of the first page. The place of residence is also frequently printed at the head of the sheet—a practice which, for neatness and accuracy, is to be much commended. Business men almost always use paper with printed heading.

Date.—The **date** consists of the month, day of the month, and year; as, "Sept. 14, 1874." It may also include the day of the week; as, "Wednesday, Aug. 4, 1875." In social letters and notes of transient interest the day of the week is more important than the year; and the latter, in such cases, is often omitted.

NOTE.—Business men sometimes write the number of the day before the month, instead of after it; thus: "Boston, 2 Sept., 1875." Something is gained in clearness, perhaps, by separating the numbers. "Sept. 2, 1875" might, if poorly written or hurriedly read, be taken for "Sept. 21, 1875."

Position and Arrangement.—On ruled paper, the heading should begin on the first line, a little to the left of the middle; and it may occupy one, two, or three lines (never more than three), according to circumstances. If the paper is not ruled, the positions should be the same.

NOTE.—The first line is generally about an inch and a half below the top of the page. A letter should never begin much higher than that; but if the letter is to consist of but a few lines, it should be commenced lower, so that the spaces below and above the letter may be about equal.

If the heading is short, it may be written on one line, as in Model 1; and it may be laid down as a rule, that *the heading should occupy as few lines as possible, consistent with neatness and legibility.*

NOTE.—The number of lines will depend, of course, on the length of the heading, the style of the writing, and the size of the paper. On note-paper, the heading will rarely require more than two lines; on letter-paper, seldom more than one.

If the heading occupies two lines, the second should begin about an inch farther to the right than the first, as in Model 2.

If it occupies three lines, the second should begin farther to the right than the first, and the third than the second, as in Model 3; so that a line drawn through the initial letters will slope from a horizontal at an angle of about thirty degrees.*

CAUTION.—If the "place," or post-office address, occupies two or more lines, care must be taken not to put part of a word, name, or date on one line, and part on the next. For example, in writing "Broadway, New York," it would not do to write "New" in one line, and "York" in the next.

LETTERS WITHOUT HEADING.—Social letters are often dated at the bottom. This form is not so generally adopted as to establish a rule; but it has the sanction of some highly cultivated people, and may therefore be used if it is preferred. Letters written in the third person are generally dated at the bottom (see form on page 33). Business letters, however, are always dated at the top.

When the place and date are written at the bottom, they must be begun near the left edge of the paper, on the next line below that on which the signature is written (see Model 6), and the parts arranged as above directed (page 21). Observe, too, that in this case the name of the person addressed must be written in the introduction, as in Model 4, Sec. III., page 35.

Punctuation.—The parts of the heading should be separated by commas, and a period should be placed at the end of the heading, and after each abbreviation.

The parts of the heading are grammatically related. Thus, "Millersville, Pa., Sept. 15, 1874," is equal to "This is written at *Millersville*, which is in *Pa.*, on *Sept. 15th*, in the year *1874*." This indicates the

* A similar slope must be given to the parts of the introduction, the conclusion, and the superscription, reference being in all cases had to the *beginning*, not the end, of the parts.

proper order of the parts. "Lancaster County, Millersville," would imply that Lancaster County is *in* Millersville.

It is not customary at the present day to write *st*, *th*, or *d* after the number denoting the day of the month, when the year is expressed. Write Jan. 21, 1874, not Jan. 21st, 1874. When the year is not expressed, however, the letters must be suffixed; as, "Yours of the 21st inst." When the letters are used, write them *on the line*. The ordinals *1st*, *2d*, etc., are not abbreviations, and are not followed by a period.

MODELS OF HEADING.

Model 1.

Troy, N. Y., Aug. 5, 1875.

Model 2.

Gettysburg, Adams Co., Pa.,
Monday, Sept. 20, 1875

Model 3.

Mt. Holyoke Seminary,
South Hadley, Mass.,
July 22, 1875

Model 4.

222 Madison Av., New York,
June 28, 1875.

If preferred, this heading may be arranged as follows:—

Model 5.

222 Madison Avenue,

New York, June 28, 1875.

NOTE.—When the residence occupies more than one line, it should be so divided as to give each line a kind of completeness. (See Caution, p. 22.) It would not be well, for example, to write *79 N. Greene St., Baltimore,* on the first line, and *Md., July 5, 1875,* on the second, for the reason that the latter part when standing alone seems imperfect.

Model 6.

Residence and Date at the bottom.

(Place of Signature.)

17 Nahant Street,

Lynn, Mass., May 1, 1875.

EXERCISE I.

Copy the models neatly and accurately on note-paper, taking care to give to all the parts their proper place and proportion.

DIRECTION.—These headings may be written on the same sheet Divide the sheet into sections of about six lines each, by means of black or red horizontal lines, and regard each section as the top (or the bottom, as the case may be) of a page.

After the exercises have been corrected by the teacher, they should be copied in a book. This direction will apply to all exercises of this kind.

If the pages of the book are not of the proper size and shape, the pupil may mark out on them, with black or red ink, rectangular figures to represent pages of note-paper. These spaces can then be divided into sections, and the exercises written in them as above described. In ruling with pen and ink, be *sure to lay the bevelled side of the ruler on the paper.*

EXERCISE II.

Write the following headings, arranging and punctuating them as they should be in a letter :—

1. Conn New Haven Feb 3 1875
2. 1874 July 27 New York 96 Pearl street
3. Easton Pa Lafayette College Oct 4 1875
4. Phila Chestnut St Continental Hotel Feb 24 1876
5. Box 1077 Ill Evanston Nov 11 1873. [The box takes the place of house and street.]
6. The heading of a letter written at your own home.

SECTION III.—THE INTRODUCTION.

OUTLINE.

1. PARTS.
   - Address.
     - Name and Title,
     - Residence.
   - Salutation.
2. POSITION AND ARRANGEMENT.
3. PUNCTUATION.
4. MODELS.
   - Business,
   - Social and Miscellaneous.

The Introduction, in business and other formal letters, consists of two parts,—the *Address* and the *Salutation* ;* in familiar letters; of the *Salutation* alone.

The Address, in its fullest form, consists of the *Name and Title* of the person written to, and his *Residence* (that is, the place where he receives his mail).

---

* For convenience the long or business form of introduction is treated of first, but the learner should be made to understand clearly that *this form must in no case be used in a familiar letter.* (See p. 91.)

REMARK.—The Address as here described is the same as the Superscription, or what is put upon the envelope. Indeed the latter is often called "the address" of the letter. To distinguish the two. the former (that at the head or foot of the letter) may be designated as "the *inside* address;" the latter (that on the envelope), as "the *outside* address."

The word *Residence*. which generally means *private* residence, or home, is here used (for want of a more appropriate term), to mean the place where the person addressed receives his mail, whether his home, boarding-place, post-office, or place of business. The term "post-office address" is sometimes used in the same sense.

NAME AND TITLE.—The name should be written plainly and in full. And politeness requires that some title should be added to the name, unless the person is a member of the society of Friends. The ordinary titles are *Miss*, *Mrs*., *Mr*., and *Esq*. A boy is addressed as *Master*.

Two of these titles of courtesy cannot be joined to the same name; nor can they be used in connection with literary, professional, and military titles, such as Prof., Dr., Col., Hon., A. M., M. D., Ph.D., D. D., LL.D. To the latter part of this rule, however, there are one or two exceptions. When writing to a clergyman whose surname alone is known to us, we may write "*Rev. Mr*. Blank," the *Mr*. being in this case regarded as a substitute for the Christian name; and if a married man has a professional or literary title prefixed to his name, *Mrs*. may be used before it to denote his wife; as, *Mrs. Dr*. Baker, *Mrs. Secretary* Stanton. Such combinations as "*Mr*. John Smith, *Esq*.," "*Dr*. Sawbones, *Esq*.," and "*Mr. Dr*. Brown," are not to be tolerated.

Two literary or professional titles may be added

to one name if one does not include or presuppose the other; thus: *Prof.* Edward Brooks, *A. M.; Rev. Dr.* Hall; *Rev.* L. P. Hickok, *D. D., LL.D.*

When two or more titles follow a name, they must be written in the order in which they are supposed to have been conferred, so as to form an ascending series, or climax. The following, for example, are arranged in the proper order: A. M., M. D., Ph.D., D. D., LL.D., F. R. S.

In writing to two or more persons, if they are men, the proper title is *Messrs.* (for *Messieurs*, gentlemen); if young ladies, *Misses;* if married or elderly ladies, *Mesdames* (pronounced *mā-dahm'*). If none of these apply (if, for instance, the firm is composed of men and women), use no title.

RESIDENCE.—The Residence *must* comprise the name of the *post-office* nearest the person addressed, and the *state* in which it is situated. If the post-office is not in a city, the name of the *county* should also be given. If it is in a city, the *number* of the house, the *street*, the *city*, and the *state* should be given; but if the city is a very large one, such as Baltimore or Cincinnati, the name of the state is not essential. (See Section II., page 20.)

The address should not be omitted. The envelope being a mere wrapper, liable to be torn or lost, the letter itself should be self-explaining. It should contain not only the name and residence of the writer, but also the name and residence of the person to whom it is written. In business letters, indeed, the full address is almost indispensable, and it is generally given in full, as in Models 5, 6, 7, 8, and 9. In other letters an abbreviated form of address, consisting of the name alone, is much used. (See Model 4.) This form of address is appropriate in social letters written to mere acquaintances or strangers; also in brief or informal business letters; but no form of address should be used at the beginning of a familiar letter. In this case the address should be written at the end, for the reason stated on page 31.

The Salutation.—The Salutation is the term of politeness, respect, or affection, with which we introduce a letter; such as, *Dear Sir*, *My dear Friend*, *My dear and honored Father*, etc.

In business letters, the term generally employed in writing to a gentleman is *Sir*, *Dear Sir*, or *My dear Sir*.* In writing to a firm, *Sirs* may be substituted for *Sir* in the above expressions, or the much-abused term, *Gentlemen*, may be employed. (See Models 1, 2, and 3.) *Never use the vulgar contraction, "Gents" for "Gentlemen," nor "Dr." for "Dear."*

A military officer is saluted as *Captain*, *Colonel*, *General*, etc., as the case may be, or simply as *Sir;* a naval officer, as *Sir;* a governor of a state, as *Your Excellency*, *Governor*, or *Sir;* the mayor of a city as *Your Honor*, or *Sir*, etc., etc.

Reference.—A full classified list of official titles and salutations will be found in Part III., pages 216, 223.

---

* *Dear Sir* is a more familiar term than *Sir*, and implies previous acquaintance or correspondence; *My dear Sir* is more familiar than *Dear Sir*, and implies not only acquaintance but friendship.

In a business letter addressed to a married woman or a single woman not young, the proper salutation is *Madam*, *Dear Madam*, or *My dear Madam* (Model 4); to two or more, married or single, *Ladies.* In a business letter to a young unmarried lady, the salutation is generally omitted to avoid the repetition of *Miss*, the address alone being used as introduction (as in Model 9); or else the address is reserved for the bottom of the letter, and the salutation *Miss Blank* is used ("Blank" standing for the lady's surname).

REMARK.—In writing to a lady who is a stranger or a mere acquaintance, persons often feel a delicacy (unnecessarily so, it seems to us) about saying "Dear Miss Blank" or "Dear Madam." *Dear* does not mean any more in this case than it does in "Dear Sir." Surely no lady would hesitate to use the latter form of address in writing to a gentleman of her acquaintance; and the gentleman would be a fool to suppose she intended to make love to him by so doing.

When Miss or Dear Miss is used in the introduction, it must be followed by the lady's name; as, "Miss Flora May," "Dear Miss Barnes."

Most of the forms of salutation used in business letters are equally appropriate in many other letters. It would be absurd to attempt to prescribe set forms for all the varieties of social correspondence: the particular expression to be used depends, of course, upon the feelings or fancy of the writer, and his relation to the person addressed. Strangers may be addressed as *Sir*, *Miss Clark*, or *Madam;* acquaintances, as *Dear Sir*, *Dear Miss Brown*, or *Dear Madam;* friends, as *Dear Friend*, *Friend Mary*, *Friend Smith*, *My dear Smith*, etc.; near relatives and other very dear friends, by such terms as *My dear Father*, *My dear Daughter*, *My precious Child*, *Beloved Husband*, *Darling Wife*,

Dearest Mary, *My good-for-nothing Brother* (playful style), *My dear Charles*, *My dear Blanche*, etc., etc.

NOTE.—Young and sentimental persons are apt to indulge in extravagant and "gushing" salutations, such as "Sweetest and best of Girls," "Darlingest of Darlings," etc. Such expressions sound very flat and silly to sensible people. Those who express their feelings in this way are generally too shallow to be capable of entertaining a really strong and lasting affection.

Position and Arrangement.—The Introduction, as already stated, may consist of the address and salutation, or of the salutation alone. In the latter case the address is placed at the end of the letter, forming part of the Conclusion (see page 50). Hence the question arises, *When should the address be written at the beginning of a letter, and when at the end?* This question we proceed to answer.

PLACE OF THE ADDRESS.—In *business letters* not official, the address is always written at the top.

In military and other *official* business letters, the address is sometimes written at the top and sometimes at the bottom.

For example, General Grant writing to General Lee, under date of April 7, 1865, uses the following introduction, thus placing the address at the beginning of the letter:—

General R. E. Lee, commanding C. S. A.
General: etc.

General Lee in his answer of same date introduces the letter simply with the salutation, "General," and writes the address at the bottom in the following words:—

To Lieutenant General U. S. Grant,
Commanding Armies of the United States.

In another letter to General Grant, dated April 9th, General Lee places the address at the beginning.

In *ordinary letters* the address may, in many cases, be put at the beginning or at the end, as the writer may prefer. It is better, however, in writing to a stranger or to a person with whom we are but slightly acquainted, to put the address at the top, as in a personal business letter; there being a certain distance and formality implied in this method. And for this reason it is obviously improper to use this form in a *domestic letter*; that is, in a letter to a near relative or very intimate friend. In this case the address should be written at the bottom. (Model 3, p. 51.)

ARRANGEMENT OF THE ADDRESS.—The address should begin at the marginal line—that is, from one-fourth of an inch (on ladies' note-paper) to one inch (on letter-paper) from the left edge of the sheet—and on the first line (or the second) below the date. (See remarks on "Margin," p. 39.)

It may occupy three lines, two lines, or one line. The first line of the address should contain the *name and title alone*; because the name of the post-office, if written after the name of the person, on the same line, may be mistaken for the person's surname.

For example, "Mr. M. Blair, Fleming," may easily be mistaken for "Mr. M. B. Fleming," especially if, as is often the case, the punctuation is neglected.

The residence, or post-office address, may occupy one line or two, according to length. It should neither be strung across the page on one line, nor run down the page like cellar-stairs.

If the last item of the residence is a short word, such as Ohio, or an abbreviation, such as Pa., Va., Ky., or N. Y., it should be written on the same line as the preceding item, not on a separate line. The following forms will illustrate our meaning:—

1. Faulty Arrangement.	2. Correct Arrangement.
John G. Saxe, Esq., *Albany,* *N. Y.*	*John G. Saxe, Esq.,* *Albany, N. Y.*

The first arrangement is the proper one for the *outside* address. (See page 60.)

If the address is written in two or three lines, their initial letters should be in a line sloping downward to the right, at about the same angle as that of the heading. (See Models 4 to 10; also refer to page 21.)

Place of the Salutation.—If the address makes *three lines*, the salutation should begin under the initial letter or figure of the second line, as in Model 5; or under that of the first, as in Model 6. The former arrangement is preferred, as it makes a more effective and pleasing display than any other.

If the address makes *two lines*, the salutation should begin about an inch farther to the right than the second line, as in Model 7; or else under the initial letter of the first, as in Model 8. The former is preferable on a wide sheet, the latter on a narrow one.

If the address makes but *one line*, the salutation should begin about an inch to the right of the marginal line, as in Model 4.

Caution.—Take care that no two successive lines, in the heading, the introduction, the conclusion, or the superscription, begin at the same vertical line.

If there is no address at the top (as in *domestic* letters), the salutation should begin at the marginal line, as in Model 1.

In familiar letters, the salutation is often incorporated in the first sentence of the letter, as in Model 2. In that case the letter begins a little to the right of the marginal line—that is, at the paragraph line—and a blank line should be left under the heading.

Letters without Introduction.—A very formal letter is generally written in the third person; that is, the person to whom it is sent is spoken *of* instead of *to*. A letter so written has neither address nor salutation. The following is an example:—

Will Mr. Clarke oblige Mrs. Sumner by loaning her, until to-morrow, the last number of the Atlantic Monthly *(if he is not using it), as it contains an article which she very much desires to read. Her own copy has been mislaid.*

Laurel Hill, Friday, Nov. 20.

Letters in the third person may be properly styled "notes," and they will be treated of under that head. The place and date, in such letters, are generally (not always) written at the bottom, as in the above example. (See page 155.)

Punctuation.—A period should be placed at the end of the address, whether it consists of the name alone (Model 4), or the name and residence (Model 5). If the residence is given, place a comma after the name, and after each item of the residence except the last.

If a title follows the name, it must always be separated from it by a comma; and if two titles are used, a comma must be placed between them; thus: John McClintock, D. D., LL.D.

Every abbreviation must be followed by a period; as, Millersville, Lanc. Co., Pa.

The salutation, being in the nominative case independent, should in general be followed by a comma;

or, if the letter begins on the same line, by a comma and a dash. In a letter to a very high and dignified personage, or to any one with whom we are not on familiar terms, a colon is preferable.

NOTE.—Great irregularity prevails in the punctuation of the introduction. Many persons put a comma after the address, thinking, perhaps (if they think about it at all), that the address and salutation are in apposition. This is not the case. They are not, in fact, in the same grammatical person. The address is in the third person, while the salutation is in the second. Take the following example:—

Rev. Thomas D. Wheeler,
Lancaster, Pa.
Dear Sir,— etc.

Here *to* is understood before the name; and the construction is, "This is written to *Rev. Thomas D. Wheeler*. living at *Lancaster*, which is in *Pennsylvania*." Having written this down, as a sort of memorandum, we turn to our correspondent and say *Dear Sir,*— etc. The address is obviously in the same construction when at the beginning as when at the end of a letter—and of its construction in the latter case there can be no question. The word *to* is often *expressed* before the name, thus clearly indicating the grammatical person; as,—

To the Editor of the Tribune.
Sir:— etc.

When the address consists of the name alone, many persons place a colon after it, thus:—

Mr. Ralph Waldo Emerson:
My dear Sir,— etc.

There is very respectable authority for this punctuation; but with due respect for the opinion of those who use the colon, we decidedly prefer the period, for the reason stated above.

Never use a semicolon after any part of the address.

Please notice carefully the punctuation of the models on pages 35, 36 and 37.

CAPITALS.—Every important word of the address must begin with a capital; also the first word and every noun in the salutation Consult the models; also see Rules for Capitals in Part III

MODELS OF INTRODUCTION.

Model 1.—*Social Form (Familiar).*

My dear Daughter,

Since I last wrote to you, strange things have occurred, etc.

Model 2.—*Social Form (Unconventional).*

Your welcome letter, my very dear friend, arrived to-day, etc.

Model 3.—*Social Form.*

Respected Friend,

Thy kind favor was very gratefully received, etc.

When the name of the correspondent is not given at the top (as in Models 1, 2, and 3), it should be written at the bottom, as directed on pages 31 and 50. In addressing a member of the religious society of Friends, no title is used.

Model 4.—*Social Form (Formal).*

Mrs. Hannah More.

Dear Madam,

Accept my sincere thanks for the beautiful book, etc.

Model 5.—*Business Form.*

Messrs. Franklin & Hall,

53 Market St.,

Philadelphia.

Dear Sirs,—Your favor, etc.

NOTE.—The body of the letter usually begins under the end of the salutation, but when the address is long, as in the above and the following model, it should begin in the same line as the salutation, in which case a dash must precede it.

Model 6.—*Business Form.*

Messrs. Tiffany & Co.,

550 Broadway,

New York.

Dear Sirs,—Please send by return, etc.

NOTE.—It will be observed that in Model 5 the salutation begins under the initial figure of the second line, while in Model 6 it begins under the initial letter of the first. (See page 32.)

Model 7.—*Business Form.*

Messrs. Samuel Gilbert & Sons,

Boston, Mass.

Gentlemen,—I have the honor to acknowledge the receipt, etc.

Or the parts may be arranged as follows:—

Model 8.—*Business Form.*

Messrs. Samuel Gilbert & Sons,

Boston, Mass.

Gentlemen,

I have the honor, etc.

Model 9.—*Business Form (to a Lady).*

Miss Clara F. Abbott,

Newport, R. I.

We acknowledge with pleasure the receipt of your manuscript, etc.

Or the introduction, "Miss Clara F. Abbott," without the residence, may be used: or simply, "Miss Abbott." If the lady were married, *Madam*, or *Dear Madam*, would follow the address, as in Model 4.

Model 10.—*Official Form.*

Major-General M. C. Meigs,

Quartermaster-General,

Washington, D. C.

General,—I have the honor to transmit herewith my report, etc.

EXERCISE III.*

Copy carefully the 1st, 2d, 4th, 5th, 7th, and 9th of the foregoing models. [Copy *all* the models if there is time.]

EXERCISE IV.

Write in proper form, and punctuate, the following introductions, using capital letters where they are required (see models):—

1. dear Friend Your favor, etc.

2. my Dear friend Your letter, etc.

3. Mr john smith my dear sir Please, etc.

4 dear miss Jackson do tell me, etc.

5. prof Charles Thompson Kirkville Mo Dear sir please send me a catalogue, etc.

6. hon J. P. Wickersham superintendent of public instruction Pa Harrisburg dear sir the information you require, etc.

EXERCISE V.

Write and punctuate the following headings and introductions, rearranging when necessary :—

1. Cambridge Mass Feb 10 1874 Mr James F Hammond 421 Broadway New York Dear Sir in reply, etc.

2. Fifth avenue The Windsor N Y May 25 1875 my dear miss Adams I owe you a thousand thanks, etc.

3. Monday Hawthorne cottage June 15 1876 Your letter my dear friend is a new proof of the goodness of your heart [The order of the words "Your letter, my dear friend," etc., is not to be changed.]

4. Jan 2 1844 London Devonshire terrace my very dear

* *See Direction* on page 24, under Exercise I.

felton you are a prophet and had best retire from business straightway.

5. Pa Wyoming Seminary Kingston March 15 1875 Dr Noah Porter Pres of Yale College Sir Allow me commend to your special care, etc.

SECTION IV.—The Body of the Letter.

OUTLINE.

1. The Beginning.
2. Margin.
3. Paragraphing.
4. Penmanship.

The Body of the letter is the communication itself, exclusive of the heading, introduction, and conclusion.

Remark.—In this place we propose to speak merely of the *form*, or mechanical execution, of letters. Their style and characteristics as a species of composition will be treated of in a separate chapter. (See Chap. III., p. 70.)

The Beginning.—The Body of the letter should generally begin, as already stated (page 36), under the end of the salutation; but when the address is long, as in Models 5, 6, 7, and 10 (pages 36, 37), it may begin on the same line.

Note.—When this is the case, a comma and a dash (or colon and dash) must be placed between the salutation and the first word of the body of the letter, as in Model 3, already referred to.

Margin.—A blank margin should always be left on the *left-hand* side of each page—not on the right. The width of this margin should vary with the width of the page. On large letter-paper it should be about three-fourths of an inch; on note-paper about one-fourth of an inch—nearly equal to the thickness of a common lead-pencil. A margin that is too wide looks worse than one that is too narrow.

The margin should be perfectly even. If necessary, draw a light pencil-mark with a soft pencil, parallel with the edge of the paper, as a guide to the writing; but *be sure to erase it* after the letter is written.

Another way is to rule a heavy black marginal line on a separate piece of paper or cardboard, and lay this under the page to be written on, so that the line will show through. A paragraph line may be drawn on the same sheet. Two or three of these blanks may be kept on hand for different sizes of paper. All these helps should be dispensed with, however, as soon as possible. They are but crutches, at best, and should be thrown away as soon as you can walk without them.

Paragraphing.—Letters, as well as other compositions, should be divided into paragraphs, if they speak of different and disconnected things. For example, if, after speaking of affairs at home, the writer turns to speak of himself, he should make a new paragraph.

Do not make too many paragraphs. Sometimes persons make the mistake of making a paragraph of every sentence. It is a matter that depends wholly on the sense. A letter may consist of only a single paragraph.

Some persons suppose that a new paragraph should begin directly under the end of the old one. This is a mistake, as any one may see by opening a printed book. All the paragraphs after the first (which, in a letter, is an exception) should begin at the same distance from the edge. This distance varies somewhat, according to the width of the paper. On a large letter-sheet, the paragraphs should begin about an inch to the right of the *marginal line*, that is, the line of writing; on note-paper, they should begin about three-fourths of an inch to the right of this line. Some persons draw two lines—a marginal line and a paragraph line—as guides. If lines are drawn, let them be erased before the letter is sent. If preferred, "lines" may be placed under the leaf, as described in a previous paragraph (see under Margin).

REMARK.—The blank space at the beginning of a paragraph is called an *indentation*.

Penmanship.—Letter-writing presupposes the ability to write a legible hand. But we should not be satisfied with mere legibility: we should endeavor to attain to neatness and elegance. The practice of correspondence, if care be used, will greatly conduce to this end; but a careless habit of writing letters not only fails to improve the hand, but actually spoils a good hand already formed.

Many persons write letters so hurriedly as to slur over the words, half-forming or *de*forming many of the letters, and sometimes leaving half of the word represented by a sort of wavy line. This way of writing is injurious to the writer and disrespectful to the recipient of the letter. A letter so written is vexatious and unsatisfactory to the reader; as much so as an oral communication would be in which the words were uttered with a mumbling and indistinct articulation. It is true that some great men write a very bad hand, so that their letters are almost indecipherable; but if their letters are valuable *with* such a defect, how much more so they would be without it! It should be remembered, too, that a man of established reputation can better *afford* to be indifferent to the minor proprieties than one who has his reputation to make, for defects which in the former are scarcely noticed, are in the latter conspicuous and intolerable. A person who prides himself on his bad writing, thinking it a sign of smartness, is unconsciously a witness to the truth of Pope's couplet,—

> "Pride, where wit fails, steps in to our defence,
> And fills up all the mighty void of sense."

This, then, is our advice: Take pains; write as plainly and neatly as possible—rapidly if you can, slowly if you must. Good writing affects us sympathetically, giving us a higher appreciation both of what is written and of the person who wrote it. Don't say, I haven't time to be so particular. Take time; or else write fewer letters and shorter ones. A neat and well-worded letter of one page once a month is better than a slovenly scrawl of four pages once a week. In fact, bad letters are like store bills: the fewer and the shorter they are, the better pleased is the recipient.

1. *Style of Writing.*—All flourishing is out of place in a letter. The writing should be plain and, if possible, elegant, so that it may be both easy to read and gratifying to the taste. The most fashionable style for ladies is what is called the English running-hand. A rather fine hand is preferable for ladies, and a medium one for gentlemen. A person who writes a large hand should use large paper and leave wide spaces between the lines.

2. *Skipping Pages.*—After reaching the bottom of the first page, it is generally better to continue the letter on the second, instead of passing to the third; because the writer may find more to say than he at first thought of, and after having filled the first and third pages, may be compelled to go back to the second, and thence to the fourth.

If by accident or otherwise it becomes necessary to write on the second page after the third, the lines should run lengthwise of the sheet. Some cultivated ladies write in this way from choice; but, with due respect for their taste, we decidedly prefer the other method; namely, that of writing on successive pages, with lines running the same way on all, as they are in a printed book.

3. *Crossing.*—Many persons, ladies especially, have a habit of crossing their letters. It is better not to do it. If one sheet is not large enough to hold all you have to say without crossing, take an extra half-sheet, or a sheet if need be. Crossing does not *seem* to be entirely respectful to your friend; for it implies (though he may not so understand it) that you do not think enough of him to use any more paper on his account. Besides, crossed writing is hard to read; and you have no right to task your friend's eyesight and tax his time by compelling him to decipher it. Cross-lining came into use when paper was dear and postage high. Then there was some excuse for it. Now there is none.

4. *Blots and Interlineations.*—Of course no blots are allowable. Better rewrite the letter than send a blotted one. And avoid, as far as possible, interlineations and erasures. A few words may be interlined in

a very small hand, but even a single interlined word mars the beauty of a page. A letter should be regarded not merely as a medium for the communication of intelligence, but also as a work of art. As beauty of words, tone, and manner adds a charm to speech, sc elegance of materials, writing, and general appearance, enhances the pleasure bestowed by a letter.

SECTION V.—The Conclusion.

OUTLINE.

1. Parts.
   1. Complimentary Close,
   2. Signature,
   3. Address.*
2. Position and Arrangement.
3. Punctuation.
4. Models.

What is technically known as the **Conclusion** of a letter is that which is added after the communication itself is finished. It consists of the *Complimentary Close*, the *Signature*, and sometimes (when not at the top) the *Address* of the person written to.

Complimentary Close.—The Complimentary Close is the phrase of courtesy, respect, or endearment used at the end of a letter.

As in the salutation, the particular words used vary according to circumstances.

---

* See foot-note on page 15; also the remarks on the position of the address on pages 30 and 31.

Social letters admit of an almost infinite variety of forms of complimentary close. The following are a few out of many examples that might be given :—

Your friend; Your sincere friend; Yours with esteem; Yours very respectfully; Your loving daughter; Your affectionate father; Ever yours; Yours affectionately and for ever (Jefferson); Ever, my dear Fields, faithfully yours (Dickens); Ever your affectionate friend (Dickens); Yours heartily and affectionately (Dickens); Now and always your own; Ever, my dear Mr. ——, most gratefully and faithfully yours (Miss Mitford); I am, my dearest friend, most affectionately and kindly yours (John Adams to his wife); Believe me always your affectionate father (Sir Walter Scott); Yours very sincerely (Hannah More); Your obliged and affectionate friend (Bishop Heber); Sincerely and entirely yours.

REMARK.—In familiar letters the form of close used is generally that prompted by the feeling at the moment. It is proper that the language should seem spontaneous and natural, but at the same time it should be nicely adapted to the relation of the parties—not too familiar nor too formal. It should also have some reference to the form of salutation used, so that it may not seem tautological or inconsistent. For example, after having written at the beginning, *My dear Friend*, it would not be well to write, *Your friend* or *Yours respectfully* at the close. Having already called him "friend," the phrase "your friend" is tautological; and having called him "*dear* friend the word "respectfully," being somewhat cold and formal, is inconsistent. It would be better to write "Yours very truly," "Ever yours," or something equally familiar.

In *business* letters, or letters of any kind written to strangers or mere acquaintances, the customary form is "Yours truly," or "Yours respectfully." These may be emphasized by *very*, as "Yours very truly;" or varied by inversion, as "Truly yours."

Official letters have a more stately and formal close

than any other. The following are approved forms—the first being in the diplomatic style:—

I have the honor to be, Sir,
With the highest consideration,
Your obedient servant,
A—— B——.

I have the honor to be (or remain),*
With much respect,
Your obedient servant,
C—— D——.

I have the honor to be (or remain),
Your obedient servant,
E—— F——.

I have the honor to be (or remain),
Very respectfully,
Your most obedient servant,
G—— H——.

I am, Sir,
Your obedient servant,
I—— K——.

Very respectfully your obedient servant,
L—— M——.

These forms of strict official etiquette are often abbreviated, however, to "Yours very respectfully," "Very respectfully," or "Respectfully."

Remark.—The form "Your obedient servant," once so common, is now mostly confined to official letters. It is too undemocratic to suit the taste of our people. In writing to a patron or superior, however, it is a very appropriate form of complimentary close.

* *Remain* implies previous correspondence.

Signature.—On this subject the following directions should be carefully observed :—

1. *Every letter should be signed.*

This direction seems superfluous; and yet it is not so, for many a letter is carelessly sent without signature, leaving the receiver to guess, if he can, by whom it was written.

2. *If the letter contains anything of importance, the name should be written in full.*

The reason of this is, that otherwise the letter is liable to be lost. A letter that, on account of the death or absence of the person to whom it is written, or for any other cause, fails to reach its destination, is sent to the Dead Letter Office. There it is opened, and if it contains the name and residence of the writer, it is returned to him. Many thousand dollars enclosed in letters are thus returned to the senders every year; and many thousands are retained by the Post Office Department, because the writers did not sign their names in full or did not give their post-office address. If letters contain nothing but sentimental twaddle or idle gossip, they may be signed "Hattie," or "Fannie," or "Tom;" but if letters are worth anything, both the name and the residence of the writer should be written in full.

3. *The name should be plainly written.* A person's signature may be plain enough to himself, and yet be to a stranger worse than a Chinese puzzle.

Such a signature often drives business men and printers almost to distraction. Sometimes, in addressing the reply, a person is compelled to cut out the signature and paste it on the envelope.

4. If the writer is a lady, she should, in writing to a stranger, so sign her name as to indicate not only her sex, but also whether she is married or single.

If a letter written by Miss Wilson, for example, is signed J. E. Wilson, how is one to know whether to begin the answer with *Sir*, *Miss*, or *Madam*, and whether to address it to *Mr.*, *Miss*, or *Mrs.* J. E. Wilson? A person is thus placed in an unpleasant dilemma: he must either commit the apparent rudeness of addressing the lady without a title, or else run the risk of making a mistake.

The last direction may be complied with by prefixing *Miss* or *Mrs.* to the name; thus: *Miss Alice Earle.* There is no indelicacy in doing so in this case; but should there seem to be, the title may be enclosed in curves; thus: (*Miss*) *Anna Ward.* A married lady generally uses her husband's name, if he is living, with the title Mrs. before it; thus: Mrs. Edward Brooks. She *may*, however, use her own name, and if she is a widow, she *should* do it. (See *Social Titles*, p. 208.)

REMARK.—A lady must not prefix the title to her name, except in writing to *a stranger* or to *an inferior*. It would be disrespectful to do so in writing to a friend of equal or superior social position.

In a strictly *official* letter, the writer's official designation is written after or below his name, and forms part of the signature; thus:—

J. EATON,
Commissioner of Education.

The Address.—This subject having been fully treated of in Section III. (see page 25), it is unnecessary to do more in this place than call attention to what is there said. It may be further remarked, however, that the address is not only a safeguard and convenience, but also, to some extent, a matter of courtesy. To omit it, even in a letter to a near relative, savors of disrespect.

In writing to a father, for example, after having satisfied the claims of affection and kinship by the use of such terms as "Dear Father," "Your affectionate Daughter," etc., it is proper to satisfy the claims of politeness and the pride of manhood by giving his full name, together with any title or titles of courtesy or distinction that are justly his due. One should be as polite to his father as to any one else. How many of the boys and girls of to-day forget this!

Position and Arrangement.—The *complimentary close* is written on the next line below the end of the letter proper. If too long to look well in one line, it may occupy two or even three lines.

The *signature* is written on the next line below the complimentary close, near the right-hand edge of the sheet.

The close and signature must be arranged similar to the parts of the heading and introduction; that is, they must present a regular slope downward and to the right. To effect this, observe the following—

RULE: *Begin the complimentary close on a line conceived to be drawn from the beginning of the last line of the letter, to the beginning of the signature.*

If the close consists of two or three parts (as in the official forms given on page 46), each part should begin on this imaginary line.

An exception must be made to the above rule when the signature is very long: in that case it may begin a little farther to the left than the close; thus:—

Yours respectfully,
CARRINGTON, LESLIE & BLANCHARD.

CAUTION.—The close and the signature should never begin at the same vertical line.

The *address*, when it forms part of the conclusion, is written on the next line below the signature, near the left-hand edge, and the parts of it are arranged the same as when written at the top of the letter.

If the writer's post-office address is not fully given at the top of the letter, it may be given at the bottom. When this is the case, it should be written under the signature; thus:—

Yours respectfully,
FRANKLIN A. SCOTT,
Honesdale, Wayne Co., Pa.

Or the words *Please address*, or simply *Address*, may be substituted for the complimentary close; thus:—

Please address—
WM. D. HONEYWELL,
Salem, Ohio.

Or (if the space is not otherwise occupied) the residence may be given at the left; thus:—

Yours truly,
JOHN WALKER.

Please direct the answer to—
Union College,
Schenectady, N. Y.

Punctuation.—A comma is required after the complimentary close, and a period after the signature. If the close is long, other points may be required, as may be seen by consulting the examples given above, and the models given below. The Address, when placed at the bottom, is punctuated the same as when placed at the top of the letter. (See page 33.)

MODELS OF CONCLUSION.

(The dotted line stands for the last line of the letter.)

Model 1.

---.

Yours respectfully,
Henry F. Adams.

Model 2.

---------------------------------.

We remain, dear Sir,
Your obedient servants,
John Hancock & Co.

Model 3.—*With Address*

--.

Your loving daughter,
Evelyn Williams.

Dr. John Williams,
Providence, R. I.

Model 4.—*Official.*

----------------------.

Very respectfully,
Your obedient servant,
Oliver Warren,
Secretary of the Commonwealth.

Model 5.—*With Date.*

--.

Very truly yours,
Clara Hawthorne.
The Arlington, Washington, D. C.,
Sept. 20, 1875.

EXERCISE VI.

Write the following conclusions, punctuating and capitalizing as in the foregoing models:*—

1. Very respectfully Yours H Graham.

2. I am sir very respectfully your obedient humble servant Benj Franklin.

3. Your ever faithful Husband James Willis (to) Mrs Eliza Willis Bedford Pa

4. Eternally yours Evelyn Hope Cosey cottage may 1 1876. (See Model 5.)

* Represent the last line of the letter by a dotted or a wavy line.

ORAL EXERCISE.—Analyze each conclusion, pointing out the complimentary close, the signature, and, if given, the address.

EXERCISE VII.

[As a preparation for this exercise it is well to review Sections I., II., III., and IV. One of the letters may be written on the first page and the other on the third page of a sheet of note-paper.]

Write, in accordance with all the preceding directions, the following letters:—

1.

Heading: State Normal School Albany N Y Oct 5 1874

Introduction: Messrs Jas R Elliott & Co Boston Mass Gentlemen.

Body: Enclosed find P. O. order for Four Dollars ($4), for which please send me the *Literary Monthly* for one year, beginning with the September number.

Conclusion: Yours very respectfully (Sign your own name.)

2.

Heading: Wyoming seminary Kingston Pa Dec 20 1875.

Introduction: My dear brother.

Body: This is to be a business letter, and therefore it must be, as the book says, "brief and to the point." Well, the point is this: I start for home on Thursday next (the 23d), and would be pleased to have you meet me at the depot at 6:15 P.M. Oh, I can hardly wait for the time to come; I am so eager to see you all. [Write the "body" precisely as printed.]

Conclusion: Yours Lovingly Caroline May (to) Mr. Thomas May Binghamton N Y.

SECTION VI.—Folding.

OUTLINE.

1. Note-Paper—Four Ways.
2. Letter-Paper—Two Ways.
3. The Insertion of the Letter.

Having given directions for the heading, introduction, body, and conclusion of a letter, we are now ready to fold it. This is a very simple matter, yet it is often very awkwardly done.

It is here presupposed that the envelope is adapted to the paper, as directed on page 17; if it is not so, the writer must exercise his own ingenuity in the matter, as no directions can be given to cover such cases.

Note-Paper.—We will first suppose that the sheet lies upon the table, the first page up, and the bottom toward us. There are now four ways in which it may be folded; the method depending on the size and shape of the envelope. Each way requires two operations.

First Way.—If the envelope is of the proper length—that is, a little longer than the width of the sheet—we proceed thus:—

1. Turn the bottom up about one-third the length of the sheet;

2. Turn the top down in the same manner, and press the folds down neatly.

In this way are folded nearly all the letters that are written on note-paper.

Second Way.—If the envelope is shorter than the width of the sheet, the letter should be folded thus:—

1. Turn the bottom up to meet the top;

2. Bring the right and left edges together.

Third Way.—Under the last supposition, if the paper is thick, the following is the better way:—

1. Fold lengthwise, bringing the right and left edges nearly or quite together; then,

2. Bring top and bottom together, or as nearly so as necessary to fit the envelope.

Fourth Way.—A large square envelope, such as ladies sometimes use, requires only one operation; namely, to bring the bottom and top of the sheet together.

Letter-Paper.—A sheet of letter-paper may be folded in two ways,—*first*, to fit an ordinary letter envelope (the same size that is required for commercial note); *second*, to fit an official envelope. (See sizes, page 17.)

First Way.—In folding for an ordinary envelope, there are three operations:—

1. Turn the bottom edge up so as to meet the top (or as nearly so as necessary to fit the envelope);

2. Turn the right edge over one-third the width of the sheet;

3. Turn the left edge over it, and press the folds down neatly.

The first operation reduces the sheet externally to the exact size and shape of commercial note; and probably the most convenient way to perform the second and third operations is to swing the sheet around so as to bring the right-hand edge next to the body, and then proceed the same as for that kind of paper.

Second Way.—If the letter is to be enclosed in an official envelope, it must be folded thus:—

1. Turn the bottom up so as to form a lap about one-third the length of the sheet;

2. Fold the top down over it.

NOTE 1. The folds may be pressed down by the thumb or fingers, if they are perfectly clean and free from moisture; but the best way is to use an ivory or pearl paper-knife for this purpose. The folds should be pressed down flat enough to give the letter a snug, neat appearance, but not close enough to crack the paper, so that it will tear on being opened.

NOTE 2. Great care should be taken to have the edges of the letter, when folded, exactly even. The best way to secure this result is this: when you turn a fold, make the left edge of it exactly even with the edge of the under part, then hold a finger of your left hand firmly on the loose or free corner on that edge, and press down the fold with the thumb or paper-knife, bearing gently outward; that is, away from the finger. The stiffer the paper, the more difficult to fold. Indeed very thick paper is not suitable for letters. The paper should be of medium thickness, but of very fine quality.

The Insertion of the Letter.—There is a right way and a wrong way of doing even so simple a thing as this, and, as is usually the case, the right way is the easier. It is this:—

Take the envelope in the left hand, back up, and opening toward the right; then take up the folded letter with the other hand, and insert it, putting in the last folded edge first.* If you put it in the other way, the corners will be apt to catch.

* This direction does not, of course, apply to note-paper folded in the *third way*. In that case the folded *side* is first inserted.

The letter should be inserted in such a manner that when taken out in the usual way and unfolded, it will be right end up.

EXERCISE VIII.

(This exercise may be omitted if the teacher thinks it unnecessary.)

1. Let each pupil fold, in the presence of the teacher, a sheet (or half-sheet) of note-paper, in each of the first three ways.

2. Let each fold a sheet (or half-sheet) of letter-paper in each of the two ways described above.

3. Let each folded sheet be inserted in an envelope.

SECTION VII.—THE SUPERSCRIPTION.

OUTLINE.

1. PARTS.
   - Name and Title.
   - Residence.
     - Post Office,
     - County,
     - State.
2. POSITION AND ARRANGEMENT.
3. LEGIBILITY.
4. CONVENIENCES.
   - Addressed Envelopes.
   - Special-request Envelopes.
5. PUNCTUATION.

The Superscription, or Outside Address, is the address that is put upon the envelope.

Parts.—The Superscription consists of the Name and Title of the person who is expected to receive the letter, and his Residence, or post-office address.

Name and Title.—These being the same that are given in the inside address, but little need be added to what is said in Section III. (See "Address," page 25; also the same subject, page 48.) But let it be borne in mind that what in the inside is merely convenient and important, is here indispensable.

Be sure to put the right name on the envelope. Very ludicrous and awkward misunderstandings have sometimes occurred on account of sending a letter to the wrong person.

To avoid such a mistake, it is better, when we write several letters at the same sitting, to enclose and address each letter as soon as written.

As stated elsewhere (page 26), some title should be used with the name of the person addressed, because politeness requires it. But there is another reason for it; namely, that the title often aids in identifying the person. There may be two or more persons of the same name in the same place, and the title may be the only means of knowing, from the envelope alone, for which person the letter is intended.

If the person addressed is acting in an official capacity, the designation of his office must be given, in addition to his customary title; as, "Thos. A. Scott, Esq., *Pres. of the Pa. R. R. Co.*"

Official etiquette prescribes that in writing to the President of the United States, the words "To the President" be substituted on the envelope for the customary name and title; thus:—

To the President,
Executive Mansion,
Washington,
D.C

REFERENCE.—For proper titles and styles of address to be used in writing to persons holding official positions in church or state, see Part III., pages 216, 223.

Residence.—This consists of the name of the *post-office** nearest the person written to, and the *county* and *state* in which it is situated. If the person lives in a large city, the *number* and *street* should be given, but the county may be omitted. If the city is very large, both county and state may be omitted.

In writing to the city of New York, for example, it would be entirely superfluous to add the name of the state. At the same time, when there is doubt, it is better to err on the safe side—better to put too much on the envelope than too little. (See remarks on "Residence." page 27.)

Many letters go wrong because the name of the post-office is not correctly written. For example, it happens that there is a *Millersville* in Lancaster county, Pa., a *Millersburg* in Dauphin county, and a *Millerstown* in Perry county; and as these names are nearly alike and mean the same, one is often written for the other. If the county is given, the letters reach their destination; if not, they go to the Dead Letter Office.

Position and Arrangement.—The writing on the envelope should be in straight lines, parallel with the upper† and lower edges.

---

* The name of the post-office is not always the same as that of the place in which it is situated. Thus, the name of the post-office at Waynesburg, Chester co., Penn., is Honeybrook. Therefore be sure to give, in all cases, the name of the *post-office*.

† The *upper* edge is the open one. Have that edge *from you* when you direct the letter, otherwise the direction will be upside down.

Avoid the foolish affectation of writing diagonally across the corner. The watered lines of the envelope sometimes run in that direction, but they are not intended to be written upon.

Do not rule the envelope. Black lines look worse than crooked writing, and marks made with a pin or other sharp-pointed instrument are still worse. If you cannot write straight without lines, draw very faint lines with a soft pencil, and afterwards erase them; or, better still, slip a heavily ruled piece of paper or card-board into the envelope, so that the lines will show through. Such a piece may be kept on hand for that purpose.

The name should be a trifle below the middle of the envelope, and should begin near the left edge—sometimes close to the edge, sometimes one or two inches from it, according to circumstances; and the other parts should be written at equal distances under it, each a little farther to the right, so that the last part (city or state) shall come near the lower right-hand corner.

If the person addressed lives in the country, the proper order is,—

Name and Title,
Post-office,
County,
State.

If the person lives in a city, the order is,—

Name and Title,
Number and Street,
City,
State.

Sometimes it is desirable to address a letter to one person in care of another. When this is done, the words "Care of," etc., form the second line; thus:—

Miss Annabel Lee,
Care of Edgar A. Poe, Esq.,
Baltimore,
Md.

In writing to the Governor of a state, the term "His Excellency" is used, and forms a line by itself, above the name; thus:—

His Excellency,
Governor John A. Andrew,
Boston.

When a person's official designation is given in full, it forms the next line below the name; thus:—

Roberts Vaux, Esq.,
Pres. of the Board of Education,
Philadelphia.

NOTE.—Lately some have maintained that the items of the superscription should be given in the inverse order, thus:—

Pennsylvania,
Wayne Co.,
Honesdale,
Wm. M. Dimmick, Esq.

It is claimed that this is the order in which items are read by post-masters. In reply to this it may be stated, that whatever would be gained by this arrangement at the office of mailing, would be lost at the office of delivery. Both the post-master and the carrier at the latter would be subjected to great inconvenience.

6

Each part of the superscription (as in the following models) *should stand alone, forming a line by itself,* and the parts should be so arranged that a line drawn from the initial letter of the first to that of the last will pass through the initials of the others.

To avoid crowding, however, the name of the county may be written in the lower left-hand corner, as in Model 2. Sometimes the number of the post-office box is written in that corner; but it may be written next to the name, taking the place of the door-number and street.

Legibility.—The superscription should be plainly and legibly written, especially the name of the post-office and the state. If the name of the state is short, write it in full; and if abbreviations are used, take care to form the letters correctly. Pa. and Va., Penn. and Tenn., N. Y. and N. J. are particularly liable to be confounded. Hundreds of letters are sent to Trenton, N. Y., that were intended for Trenton, N. J., and *vice versa.*

Often letters are missent on account of sheer carelessness on the part of the writer. Of the three or four million letters that go to the Dead Letter Office every year, about seventy thousand are not properly directed, and between three and four thousand have no direction whatever!

Conveniences.—Safety and rapidity of correspondence may be promoted by the use (1.) of *Addressed Envelopes,* which prevent the misdirection of replies; and (2.) of *Special-Request Envelopes,* which secure the prompt return of the writer's own letters, in case of their non-delivery.

Addressed Envelopes.—By an Addressed Envelope is meant an envelope on which is printed or written the writer's own address. One of these may be enclosed in every business letter to which a reply is expected. If a person asks a reply for his own exclusive benefit, he should put a stamp on the enclosed envelope.

Special-Request Envelopes.—These are envelopes on which are printed, in the upper left-hand corner, the address of the sender, with a request to return if not called for in a certain time. They may be obtained (stamped) of the Post Office Department, through any post-master, without extra charge for printing. If the address is given without a request to return, it is understood as an implied request, and the letter will be returned if not called for in thirty days. The special request may be either printed or written.

The advantage of using such envelopes is, that letters enclosed in them are not sent to the Dead-Letter Office, in case of non-delivery; but are returned directly to the writers, thus frequently preventing great uncertainty, embarrassment, and loss. (For the form of a special request, see Model 2, page 64.)

Punctuation.—First, put a period after every abbreviation, and after the last word. Second, put a comma after each item (that is, each line, if properly written), except the last. If a title is added to the name, put a comma between the name and title; if two titles are added, put a comma between them. (Notice carefully the punctuation of the following models.)

CAPITALS.—Begin all important words and all abbreviations with capital letters. In ordinary superscriptions every word is capitalised. (Notice the capitalization of the models.)

MODELS OF SUPERSCRIPTION.

Model 1.

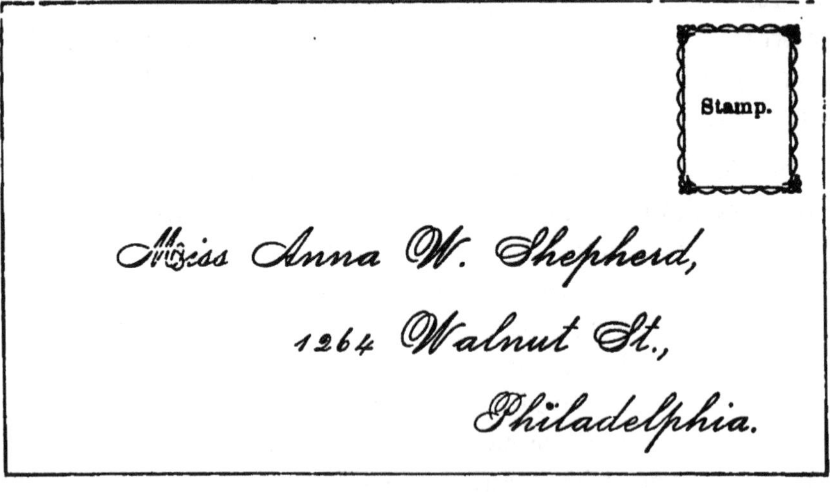

When the name of the county is necessary, it may be written in the regular place (see page 60), or as in Model 3. When a letter is sent by a friend, the name of the *bearer* is written in the lower left-hand corner.

Model 2.—*Special-Request Business Envelope.*

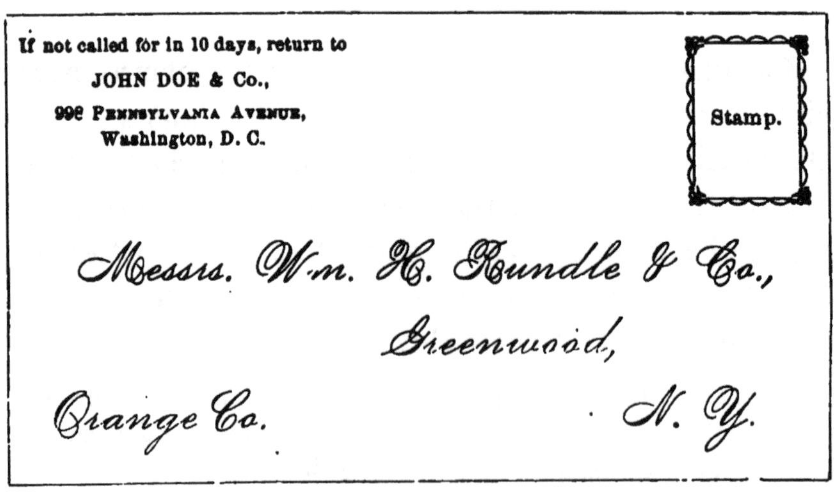

EXERCISE IX.

DIRECTION.—Envelopes may be used, but it will be more convenient to draw on a sheet of paper, figures of the proper size and shape, and write the superscriptions in them. The figures may be drawn by laying an envelope down and marking around it. Use unruled paper, or draw the figures so that the writing may be across the lines, not on them.

1. Copy the models on the preceding page.
2. Address an envelope to some absent friend.
3. Address an envelope to the President of the United States.
4. Address an envelope to the Governor of your state.
5. Address an envelope to the State Superintendent, County Superintendent, or some other leading educator.
6. Address an envelope to J. E. Caldwell & Company, who carry on business at 902 Chestnut Street, Philadelphia.

SECTION VIII.—THE STAMP.

Be sure that you affix the proper stamp to every letter before you mail it. A letter will not be forwarded unless it is prepaid at least one full rate, which is three cents.*

Position.—The stamp should be placed on the upper right-hand corner of the face of the envelope, at about an eighth of an inch from the end and half as far from the top. It does not look well close to the edge. And it should be put on right-end up, and with the edges of the stamp parallel with those of the envelope. Putting on a stamp upside down or awry indicates carelessness, and is disrespectful to the person addressed.

Amount.—Be sure that the stamp is sufficient. If you are in doubt, put on an extra stamp. A three-cent stamp is sufficient for two sheets of ordinary note-paper, or one sheet of letter-paper.*

* *Two cents* after July 1, 1883. For rates of postage, see p. 253.

SUPPLEMENT TO CHAPTER II.

Type-writer Correspondence.*

DURING the last few years the type-writing machine has been much used in correspondence, especially by business and professional men. Letters may be written in this manner much more rapidly and easily than with the pen; and if proper attention be paid to the position and arrangement of their several parts, letters so written are very neat and legible. Most of the instructions given in the preceding pages of this work apply to type-written as well as to pen-written letters; but, owing to the greater condensation of the former and to certain mechanical necessities, it is necessary to give a few special directions for this kind of correspondence.

Heading.—The experienced operator can readily calculate, from the number of words in the heading of a letter, where it should begin, and how the lines (if more than one, as is rarely the case) should be arranged. For type-written letters, printed letter-heads are generally used, with a blank for the date. These letter-heads are generally of the usual size of letter-paper, and for the note size are printed across the side instead of the end of the paper, so that the paper fills the whole of the printing-scale on the type-writer. The size of paper for letter-heads is usually eight by eleven inches; for note-heads, eight by five and a half inches.

Introduction.—In the address (see p. 25), the *name* should begin at printing-space 1 on the type-writer, two line-spaces below the line of the heading, the name and title constituting one line. The *residence*, or direction, should begin at space 5, one line below the name, and should all be included in one

---

* These valuable suggestions were kindly furnished by Messrs. Brown and Holland, Principals of the Brown & Holland Practical School of Short-hand and Type Writing, Chicago, Ill.

line if not too long. The *salutation* should begin at space 10, one line below the residence. This gives the three lines of the introduction a uniform slope from left to right, as directed for pen-written letters. If the introduction consists of four lines, the fourth line should begin at space 5, or under the first letter of the second line.

Paragraphs.—The first paragraph of the letter should begin at the printing-space immediately following the salutation, and one line below it. It may begin, however, on the same line as the salutation, in which case a dash (which is two hyphens on the type-writer) should separate it from the salutation. Each new paragraph after the first should begin at space 5. If narrow paper is used, the lines running the narrow way of the paper, the lines of the introduction may begin at spaces 1, 3, and 6, instead of 1, 5, and 10, and the paragraphs may begin at space 3.

Conclusion.—In closing a letter always begin the *complimentary close* (see p. 44) at printing-space 20, no matter at what point the letter ends; and if there is more than one line in the close, use the same relative spacing as in the introduction. The *signature*, if written with the type-writer, should fill the right-hand portion of the line next below the complimentary close.

Punctuation.—The punctuation should be the same in type-writing as in long-hand, except that when a period and a comma properly follow an abbreviation, the comma may be omitted, for a mechanical reason. After a comma no printing-space should be left in type-writing; but after a semicolon, colon, or exclamation, a space should be left, as these points nearly fill the printing-space, and the omission of a space would give the writing a crowded appearance. After a period at the close of a sentence leave four spaces.

Accuracy.—In type-writing especial care should be taken to avoid incorrect spelling and bad punctuation, as such errors are more conspicuous in print than in ordinary writing.

Form of Social Letter.

Urbana, Pa., May 4, 1876.

My dear Brother,

Your beautiful birthday gift almost reconciles me to the fact that I am to-day a year older than I was last May.

How did you know what I wanted? Surely some good angel must have whispered the secret to you. However that may be, you exactly suited my taste, and I thank you with my whole heart.

Your loving sister,

Mary Hamilton.

Mr. Henry Hamilton,
New Haven, Conn.

Form of Business Letter.

New Athens, Mass.,
Sept. 24, 1876.

Prof. Henry W. Russell,
Everett College,
Eton, Pa.

Sir,—It gives me pleasure to inform you that at a stated meeting of the Linnaean Society, held on the 20th inst., you were unanimously elected an honorary member.

Enclosed you will find a certificate of membership, duly signed and sealed, of which the Society begs your acceptance.

Yours respectfully,
William Darwin,
Corresponding Secretary.

CHAPTER III.

THE RHETORIC OF LETTERS.

OUTLINE.

1. GENERAL PRINCIPLES.
2. SPECIAL APPLICATIONS.

Definition.—The Rhetoric of Letters is the art of expressing thought and feeling in letters with clearness, force, and elegance.

REMARK.—For convenience we divide the present chapter into two sections. In the first, we shall consider the principles of rhetoric that apply to letters in general; in the second, those that apply to particular kinds of letters.

SECTION I.—GENERAL PRINCIPLES.

OUTLINE.

1. INVENTION.
2. EXPRESSION.
   - Orthography,
   - Diction,
   - Construction,
   - Punctuation,
   - Style.

The general principles applicable to the composition of letters will be discussed under two heads: 1. INVENTION; 2. EXPRESSION.

SUB-SECTION I.—INVENTION.

Invention is the action of the mind that precedes writing. In all kinds of composition, there are two things necessary: first, to have something to say; second, to say it. Invention is finding something to say. It is the most difficult part of composition, as it is a purely intellectual process, requiring originality, talent, judgment, and information; while expression is to some extent a matter of mechanical detail, and subject to rules that can be easily understood and applied. A person can write out in a few weeks or months a work the invention of which required the thought and labor of many years. Yet both parts of composition are equally essential. It is certainly a noble thing to have great thoughts, but without the power of expressing them the finest sentiments are unavailable.

Invention includes two operations: (1.) The collection of materials; and (2.) their proper and orderly arrangement.

In the composition of letters, the process of invention is simpler and easier than in most kinds of writing. Except in a letter of information, but little preparation is necessary; and yet it is proper in every case to think over beforehand what you want to say, so that no important thought or fact may be omitted, or tacked on to the end as an afterthought or postscript. Having done this, the mind should be given a pretty free rein, and be allowed to run along as easily and naturally as possible, glancing aside here and there to follow the butterfly flights of fancy, or pausing in shady nooks of sentiment and reflection. But in letters of great importance, on public or private business, we should not only think over beforehand the subjects to be attended to, but should make a memorandum of them, and arrange them in the proper order of presentation. This will be found to be a more methodical, safe, and convenient way than to trust to the memory alone. In an answer, the proper order is generally determined by the original letter. In fact it may be stated as a general rule, that the reply should correspond in length, subjects, arrangement, and style, with the letter that calls it forth. This, however, does not exclude the presentation of new subjects. Almost every answer is something more than an answer. (See Answers, page 85.)

SUB-SECTION II.—EXPRESSION.

Expression as here used is the presentation of thoughts in writing. It embraces the following subjects: Orthography, Diction, Construction, Punctuation, and Style.

Orthography treats of letters—the elements of written words, Diction treats of words—the elements of sentences; Construction treats of sentences—the elements of discourse; Punctuation treats of the division of discourse into its various grammatical elements: and Style treats of the special properties of discourse, and the means by which it is made to convey the moods and emotions of one mind to another.

Orthography is generally treated of as a separate branch, or as belonging to grammar; but in the present work it is more convenient and appropriate to regard it as a part of rhetoric.

ORTHOGRAPHY.

Orthography includes Spelling and the Use of Capitals.

Spelling. 1. *Importance.*—Thomas Jefferson, in one of his admirable letters to his daughter Martha, says:—

"Take care that you never spell a word wrong. Always, before you write a word, consider how it is spelt, and if you do not remember it, turn to a dictionary. It produces great praise to a lady [or gentleman] to spell well."

And Lord Chesterfield, a noted authority in the polite world, writes to his son as follows:—

"I must tell you that orthography, in the true sense of the word, is so absolutely necessary for a man of letters, or a gentleman, that one false spelling may fix ridicule upon him for the rest of his life; and I know a man of quality who never recovered [from] the ridicule of having spelled *wholesome* without the *w*."

But it needs not the authority of Jefferson or Chesterfield to convince any one of the importance of correct spelling. Not long since a young man of our acquaintance was refused a desirable situation because in his letter of application he wrote *wether* for *whether;* and such cases are of frequent occurrence. There are few persons of fine culture who do not know from experience what a chill of disappointment or disgust is produced by the receipt of a badly-spelled and ridiculous letter from one who has the appearance and pretensions of a refined gentleman or lady. Such a letter is no discredit to a person who has enjoyed no educational advantages; but to one who bears a seminary, normal-school, or college diploma it is nothing less than a disgrace.

It is claimed by some, to excuse their own deficiency, that spelling, like poesy, is a natural gift. This is true only to the extent that some learn it more readily than others. It may be that some are so constituted that they can never become good spellers. But even this defect does not excuse them for sending a badly-spelled letter. Let them, as Jefferson advises, consider how every word is spelt, and if they do not remember it with certainty, let them turn to a dictionary. In writing an important letter, especially to a stranger, it would be better to consult the dictionary for every word, than run the risk of misspelling a single one.

How Learned.—We learn words as we do faces—by their looks. Those that are frequently met with in reading and writing become, as it were, photographed upon the memory; and spelling is in most cases a mere description of this mental picture as we see it. Knowing how these words should look on paper, we readily notice when they are misspelled. If, therefore, we would become good spellers, we must read much and write much. There is no better exercise, not only in spelling, but also in capitals, punctuation, and grammar, than copying extracts from correctly-printed books. And if there are words that we especially wish to impress upon the memory, we should write them over and over—fifty or a hundred times, if necessary—until their forms are as familiar to us as are the features of our intimate friends. Close and careful attention, however, in this as in every other process of education, is essential to our success.

Common Words.—Most of the mistakes in spelling are in the use of simple, common words; such as *untill* for *until*, *to* for *too*, *of* for *off*, *there* for *their*, *loose* for *lose*, *except* for *accept*, *wile* for *while*, *wite* for *white*, *pleas* for *please*, *respectively* for *respectfully*, *proffessor* or *proff.* for *professor* or *prof.* These are for the most part errors of carelessness rather than ignorance, and the remedy is greater watchfulness and deliberation.

Rules.—There are other mistakes that might be avoided by attention to a few simple rules. The most important of these rules relate to the formation of derivatives by the addition of a suffix—

1. To words ending in silent *e*.
2. To words ending in *y*.
3. To words ending in a *single consonant*.

In the first class of derivatives we find such mistakes as *moveing* for *moving*, *loveable* for *lovable*, *changable* for *changeable*. In the second class, such as *mercyful* for *merciful*, *monies* for *moneys*. In the third, such as *runing* for *running*, *commited* for *committed*, *regreted* for *regretted*; or *benefitted* for *benefited*, *profitted* for *profited*.

Many mistakes are made, also, in the use of words containing *ei* or *ie*; for example, *recieve* for *receive*, *beleive* for *believe*, *acheive* for *achieve*, *greive* for *grieve*, etc. These may be avoided by remembering that *ei* is used after a letter having the sound of *s*, and *ie* in other cases. [This rule and the others referred to above may be found on pages 171—174 of this work.]

Numerals.—Arithmetical figures should not be used in letters, except in writing dates or very large numbers. For example, "He worked 5 days for $10," is not allowable; it should be, "He worked five days for ten dollars." It is proper, however, to write, "He sold his farm, May 5, 1875, for $100,000" (or "100,000 dollars"). In business letters, numbers that are written in words are also expressed, parenthetically, in figures; as, "Enclosed find my check for five thousand dollars ($5000)."

Abbreviations.—Abbreviations should be used very sparingly, especially in social letters; and none are allowable anywhere, except such as are sanctioned by custom. [A list of abbreviations may be found in Part III. of this book, page 242.]

Capitals.—A very common fault, in letters as well as every other kind of composition, is the improper use or omission of capital letters. In some cases we find too many capitals, especially in the letters of those who like to display their skill in penmanship; but it is much more frequent to find nearly all capitals discarded. It is not by any means rare to find (probably owing to the excessive modesty of the writer!) a small letter (*i*) used for the personal pronoun *I*. Persons liable to such mistakes should study diligently the rules on the subject (see Rules for Capitals, page 175), and then carefully apply them. Directions for capitalizing the heading, introduction, conclusion, and superscription, are given in the sections treating of these parts.

An excellent way to learn the correct use of capitals is to observe how they are used in the best books and papers.

Diction.

A man's Diction is his choice and use of words. It should have three qualities,—Purity, Propriety, and Precision. Purity is the use of words that are good English; Propriety is the use of words in their proper meaning; Precision is the use of words that express the exact meaning—no more and no less. For a full discussion of these properties the reader is referred to works on rhetoric.

The diction of letters is not so stately as that of books: it is that used in good conversation. The following are a few of the directions to be observed:—

Foreign Words.—Indulge sparingly, if at all, in the use of foreign words and phrases. They are characteristic, not of the scholar, but of the smatterer.

Slang Words.—Avoid slang words and phrases, such as "too thin," "won't wash," "over the left," "you bet," etc. Young people are apt to pick them up in the street and elsewhere and use them unconsciously. In such cases they indicate simply a want of taste; but in most cases they mark the man or woman of low associations and vulgar ideas.

Simple Words.—As in our talk, so in our letters, we should not use too many "dictionary words"; that is, long Latinized words. They give our language a pedantic air, and make it cold and formal. We should give preference to the "home words" of the language—the words used in the family and in the best standards of English. *Love*, for example, is preferable to *affection; motherly*, to *maternal; see*, to *perceive; tired*, to *fatigued; go*, to *depart; come*, to *arrive; have*, to *possess; do*, to *perform; begin*, to *commence; Sunday*, to *Sabbath; pray*, to *supplicate* or *implore*,—and so on to almost any extent.

Construction.

By Construction we mean sentence-building. The chief things to be aimed at in this, are Grammatical Accuracy and Clearness. Unity, strength, and harmony, so essential in essays and orations, are in letters of minor importance.

Grammatical Accuracy.—Persons are generally unable, in the necessary rapidity of correspondence, to prune and dress their sentences as in other kinds of composition, hence they cannot be held to a strict compliance with all the rules of rhetoric; but nothing will excuse a violation of the ordinary rules of grammar. Such expressions as "he *done*" for "he *did*," "he *come*" for "he *came*," "I *seen*" for "I *saw*," "he *laid* in bed" for "he *lay* in bed," "he *set* down" for "he *sat* down," "*knowed*" for "*knew*," "*blowed*" for "*blew*," "you *was*" for "you *were*," etc., etc., are intolerable, and fix upon the writer the stamp of illiteracy.

Clearness.—A sentence that is not clear is either obscure or ambiguous.

Use of Pronouns.—Ambiguity often arises from the unskilful or careless use of pronouns. In the sentence, "John told William that his book was in his room," for example, it is impossible to tell *whose* book or *whose* room is meant. The fault may be removed by reporting the speech in the first person; as, "John said to William, *Your* book is in *my* room;" or by repeating the noun parenthetically after the pronoun; as, "John told William that his (William's) book was in his (John's) room." The latter construction is awkward, but even awkwardness is preferable to want of clearness.

Bad Arrangement.—Ambiguity or obscurity is often caused by a misplacing of words, phrases, or clauses. For example, the sentence, "I only saw two boys," is rendered ambiguous by the wrong position of "only." The meaning may be, "I only *saw* two boys"—did not hear them, or speak to them; or, "I saw only *two* boys"—no others.

Again, in the sentence, "I saw an old woman darning stockings with a Roman nose," a ridiculous ambiguity is produced by the misplacing of the phrase "with a Roman nose": it should be placed close to the word *woman*, which it limits. In the sentence, "The figs were in small wooden boxes which we ate," the same effect is produced by placing the clause "which we ate" at a distance from its proper antecedent.

The rule in all such cases is, Place all modifying adjuncts as near as possible to the words which they limit.

Above all, have a clear conception of what you want to say. "Clear thinking," says Lowell, "makes clear writing"; and this, in most cases, is true. Muddy sentences indicate a muddy brain. A frank, earnest man, whose head and heart are full of his subject, will rarely fail to make himself clearly understood.

Length of Sentences.—Short sentences are easier to write and easier to read than long ones, and are therefore more suitable for correspondence. It is a common fault, especially in young people, to run several sentences together; or, in other words, to crowd several disconnected things into one long, loose-jointed, ungainly sentence. For example, a boy at school writing home to his mother would be likely to say:—

> Dear Mother,—I arrived here late last night, and I am much pleased with the place and the people, and to-morrow I shall be classed and shall begin my studies, and I want you to write to me often, for I know I shall be very lonely until I get well acquainted," etc.

In this there are four distinct statements, each requiring a separate sentence. It should be expressed thus:—

> Dear Mother,—I arrived here late last night. I am much pleased with the place and the people. To-morrow I shall be classed, and shall begin my studies. I want you to write to me often; for I know I shall be very lonely until I get well acquainted."

A very useful rule to bear in mind is this: Express every distinct thought or fact in a distinct sentence; and be very sparing in the use of *and's* and *but's*.

PUNCTUATION.

The proper punctuation of the heading, introduction, conclusion, and superscription has been given in Chapter II.: the body of the letter is subject to the same rules of punctuation that apply to other kinds of composition.

Neglect of It.—Punctuation, though a valuable art, and easily acquired, is neglected by many letter-writers, much to the detriment of their letters and the vexation of their correspondents. With some, especially with business men, it seems to be a foolish affectation to despise points, as something beneath their notice. Others omit to punctuate through ignorance or carelessness; or, if they make any attempt at pointing, throw in a dash here and there, making it do duty for all the other points. We have seen beautifully written letters, some of them from graduates and professors, without a single point in them from beginning to end.

Importance.—Punctuation is very closely connected with the construction of sentences; so closely, indeed, that without it a clear expression of thought in writing is next to impossible. Its importance may be illustrated by the following example:—

"The party consisted of Mr. Smith a clergyman his son a lawyer Mr. Brown a Londoner his wife and a little child."

Here it is impossible to tell how many persons were in the party, or how they were related. Let us insert a few commas and note the effect:—

"The party consisted of Mr. Smith, a clergyman, his son, a lawyer, Mr. Brown, a Londoner, his wife, and a little child."

This makes the party consist of eight persons. Now let us substitute semicolons for some of the commas:—

"The party consisted of Mr. Smith, a clergyman; his son, a lawyer; Mr. Brown, a Londoner; his wife, and a little child."

Mr. Smith is now a clergyman, his son is a lawyer, Mr. Brown is a Londoner, and the number of the party is reduced to five. Various other changes may be made in the same way. [Let the reader see how many meanings he can make the sentence express.]

Hundreds of similar illustrations could be given, showing conclusively that in letters, as well as in every other kind of written composition, a knowledge of the use of points is absolutely necessary to the clear expression of thought.

Punctuation is too important to be disposed of in a few sentences: we shall therefore make it the subject of a distinct treatise (see Part II., page 177); thus giving it greater prominence, and rendering it more readily accessible to persons who wish to make it a special object of study.

A Suggestion.—We will suggest, however, before passing to the next topic, that an excellent way to improve in this art is to notice carefully the points used in books and newspapers, endeavoring at the same time to ascertain why they are used as they are. Copying extracts, as already suggested, also conduces to the same end.

STYLE.

Letters, as a class, are distinguished from other kinds of composition by an easy, natural mode of expression—half colloquial, half literary—which we designate as the *epistolary style.* But in this apparent unity there is infinite variety; beneath this general style, we find a large number of special styles. In fact, every kind of letter—we may almost say every letter—has a style of its own. Some of these special styles will be examined and illustrated in a separate division of this chapter (Section II., page 91). All that we shall attempt to do in this place is to lay down a few general principles relating to the subject, leaving their application to particular cases to the taste and judgment of the writer.

Adaptation.—The style of a letter should be adapted to the person and the subject. To superiors it should be respectful and deferential; to inferiors, courteous; to friends, familiar; to relations, affectionate; to children, simple and playful: on important subjects it should be forcible and impressive; on lighter subjects, easy and sprightly; in condolence, tender and sympathetic; in congratulation, lively and joyous. It would be absurd to write to a schoolboy in the stately phrases of an official letter; and equally absurd to use the familiar language of love and friendship in a communication on business.

Figures of Rhetoric.—Public and descriptive letters admit of such rhetorical ornament as is appropriate to the subject; but in ordinary familiar letters only such figures are allowable as would naturally be used under like circumstances in conversation. In business letters no figures whatever should be used. The language should be plain, simple, direct.

Redundancy.—Tautology, repetition, and all sorts of redundancy, should be avoided. Do not insult the intelligence of your friend by stringing out vapid nothings for the purpose of filling the sheet.

> "Words are like leaves; and where they most abound,
> Much fruit of sense beneath is rarely found."

The value of a composition is not always in proportion to its length. As elsewhere remarked, a good short letter is better than a poor long one. But while the language of a letter should not be too diffuse, neither should it be too dry and abrupt. It should be easy, flowing, graceful; neither magnifying trifling things nor belittling great ones.

Cultivation of Style.—Style, being simply the mode of expression, can be cultivated, like music, painting, or any other art. This may be done: 1. By the study of rhetoric; 2. By judicious practice; 3. By the careful and extensive reading of good letters. (See Literaure of Letters, page 121.)

Plagiarism.—It is allowable to imitate an author's felicities of expression, and to adopt his sentiments; but it is base to copy his language as our own. Some persons, finding it difficult to express their feelings on paper, resort to what are called "Complete Letter-Writers"—books containing forms of letters for a variety of occasions. An instance is related of a young man who copied a letter of proposal from one of these books, and received in reply a note in these words: "You will find my answer on the next page." It was a polite refusal—and served him right. Discard all such "Letter-Writers," or if you use them, simply read the letters for the cultivation of your style and language. There are few of them, however, that can be recommended as models in any respect.

Italicizing.—Italicizing in writing is done by underlining. Persons of ardent temperament are apt to indulge in this to excess. It is like over-seasoning,—it cloys the appetite and fails of its intended effect. If sentences are properly constructed, the reader will know where to place the emphasis without any such help. Italicizing should be resorted to only when a word is used simply as a word (as, *advise* is a verb), or belongs to a foreign language (as, *au revoir*, adieu), or is used in some peculiar manner (as, "I said, a '*model* school,' not a model *school*").

Answers.—If a letter is not insulting, it should be answered; if it *is* insulting, it should be either returned to the writer or treated with silent contempt. The former is the better way, as silence might invite a repetition of the offence.

And letters that are to be answered should be answered promptly. Punctuality in this respect prevents misunderstandings and alienations, facilitates business, promotes good feeling, confirms friendships, and is in many ways advantageous to both parties to the correspondence.

The answer should correspond somewhat, so far as it *is* an answer, in style, length, and arrangement, to the letter that calls it forth. The answer to a short letter is generally short; to an affectionate letter, affectionate; to a formal letter, formal. Of course there are many exceptions, but this is the general rule.

Recapitulation.—The answer should generally begin with some reference to the letter to which it responds. In fact, the answer to a business letter should briefly recapitulate the points to be replied to; thus: "Your esteemed favor of the 12th inst., inquiring on what terms, etc., etc., was duly received. In reply," etc. Such a recapitulation connects the letter with the one it answers, and makes it a history of the whole transaction. It derives additional importance from the fact that all letters to a business house are filed, and constitute an important record.

Care of Letters.—Answered and unanswered letters should be kept separate, so that no mistakes may be made; and it is well to keep answered letters—if they *are* kept—tied up in bundles, and properly assorted and endorsed.*

Enclosing Stamp.—When you write requesting an answer exclusively for your own benefit and interest, be sure to enclose a stamp for return postage; or, still better, a stamped and addressed envelope.

Postscripts.—Postscripts are generally mere afterthoughts, and should generally be avoided. If, how-

* Of course there are other ways of filing letters, that are more suitable for persons having a very large correspondence.

ever, new information is received after the letter is finished, it may very properly be added. Never send a message of compliment or affection in a postscript: it is a glaring impropriety to do so, as it is a confession that the matter is of so slight consequence as to have escaped the writer's mind. What in the body of the letter would be a compliment, may become a positive insult in the postscript.

Beginning and Ending.—The most perplexing parts of a letter, to most persons, are the first and last sentences. In private letters, at least, the opening should be as free and natural as possible, by all means avoiding such set phrases as "I take my pen in hand," etc. Whatever is uppermost in the mind should generally be said first. In business letters, especially official ones, however, there is more formality. A letter should generally close with some expression of compliment or affection. Sometimes this is confined to the "complimentary close," but generally it embraces also the last sentence or two. To show how easily and naturally the best letters begin and end, we append a number of examples:—

Hannah More to Mr. Wilberforce.

MY DEAR FRIEND,—I was glad to receive, etc. * * * Adieu, my very dear friend. Do not forget to include in your prayers not the least affectionate of your friends,

H. MORE.

Charles Dickens to Lady Blessington.

Milan, Wednesday, Nov. 20, 1844.

Appearances are against me. Don't believe them. I have written you in intention fifty letters, etc. * * *

CHARLES DICKENS.

Mary Lamb to Miss Stoddart.

MY DEAREST SARAH,—I will just write a few hasty lines to say that Coleridge is setting off sooner than we expected, etc. * * *

God bless you and send you all manner of comforts and happiness.

Your most affectionate friend,

MARY LAMB

(*Note added by her brother Charles.*)

How do? how do? No time to write. S. T. C. going off in a great hurry

CH. LAMB.

The same to the same.

MY DEAR SARAH,—Do not be very angry that I have not written to you. I have promised your brother to be at your wedding, and that favor you must accept as an atonement for my offences. * *

I come with a willing mind, bringing nothing with me but many wishes, and not a few hopes, and a very little fear—of happy years to come.

I am, dear Sarah,

Yours ever most affectionately,

MARY LAMB.

Mrs. Barbauld to Miss Taylor.

Tunbridge Wells, Aug. 7, 1804.

I may call you dear Susan, may I not? For I can love you, if not better, yet more familiarly and at my ease under that appellation than under the more formal one of Miss Taylor, etc. * * *

That all your improvements may produce you pleasure, and all your pleasures tend to your improvement, is the wish of

Your ever affectionate friend,

LETITIA BARBAULD.

Charles Dickens to Mr. Felton.

Regent's Park, London, 2d March, 1843.

MY DEAR FELTON,—I don't know where to begin, but plunge headlong with a terrible splash into this letter, on the chance of turning up somewhere.—Hurrah! up like a cork again, with the "North American Review" in my hand. * * *

Faithfully always, my dear Felton,

CHARLES DICKENS.

Thomas Jefferson tc his daughter Martha.

Aix en Provence, March 28, 1787.

I was happy, my dear Patsy, to receive, on my arrival here, your letter informing me of your good health and occupation. * * * * * Continue to love me with all the warmth with which you are beloved by, my dear Patsy,

Yours affectionately,

TH. JEFFERSON.

Charles Lamb to P. G. Patmore.

DEAR PATMORE,—Excuse my anxiety—but how is Dash?* (I should have asked if Mrs. Patmore kept her rules and was improving—but Dash came uppermost. The order of our thoughts should be the order of our writing.) Goes he muzzled, or *aperto ore?* [And so on through pages of the most delightful drollery.] * * *

Let us hear from you concerning Mrs. Patmore's regimen. I send my love in a —— to Dash.

C. LAMB.

Wm. Penn to his family on embarking for America.

MY DEAR WIFE AND CHILDREN,—My love, which neither sea nor land nor death itself can extinguish or lessen toward you, most endearedly visits you with eternal embraces, and will abide with you for ever, etc. * * *

So farewell to my thrice dearly beloved wife and children.

Yours, as God pleaseth, in that which no waters can quench, no time forget, nor distance wear away, but remains for ever.

WILLIAM PENN.

WORMINGHURST, 4th of 6th mo., 1682.

Deliberation.—We should never write a letter when strongly excited; if we do, we shall almost certainly say things that we shall repent the next day. Persons have sometimes, in the heat of passion, written things that they would afterwards have given worlds, if pos-

* A large, handsome dog.

sible, to recall. This applies to the excitement of affection as well as to that of anger. A young person will sometimes, under a temporary spell of fascination, write words that will commit him (or her) to a life of regret and wretchedness.

If, when writing letters, we would keep before our minds the question, "How will this look a year or ten years hence?" we would save ourselves from writing a great many foolish things. In cases of excitement we should consult some judicious friend, if there is one within reach; if not, we should *wait*—sleep over the matter, as Webster did over his great speech.

Copies.—It is advisable to keep copies of all important letters, as a protection against possible misrepresentation, fraud, or malice.

Truthfulness.—Above all, in our letters as in everything else, we should be *perfectly truthful*, remembering that written words are sometimes more enduring than marble; and that years hence, if foolish or false, they may cause our own cheeks or those of our friends to tingle with shame.

Moderation.—Perfect truthfulness, as well as refined taste, demands moderation in the use of words. Exaggerated expressions, such as "perfectly splendid," "awful tired," etc., instead of strengthening the language, actually weaken it. "Splendid" means "shining," and "awful" means "awe-inspiring"; how absurd, then, such expressions as "a splendid bath," "an awful cold"! The strongest and best word, in any case, is the word which most perfectly fits the thought.

SECTION II.—SPECIAL APPLICATIONS.

OUTLINE

1. STYLE AND SPECIMENS OF SOCIAL LETTERS. — Familiar, Introduction, Congratulation, Condolence.

2. STYLE AND SPECIMENS OF BUSINESS LETTERS. — Introduction, Credit, Application, Recommendation, Mercantile, Miscellaneous.

REMARK.—Having in the preceding part of this chapter laid down the principles of rhetoric applicable to letters in general, we propose to consider in the present section the application of these principles to particular kinds of letters. The specimen letters printed under the several heads are designed merely to give an idea of the style appropriate in such cases; not to supply the lack of originality on the part of writers. (See the remark on "Plagiarism," page 84.)

SUB-SECTION I.

STYLE AND SPECIMENS* OF SOCIAL LETTERS.

The social letters of most frequent use are the following: 1. Familiar Letters, under which we include Domestic, or Family Letters, and ordinary Letters of Friendship; 2. Letters of Introduction; 3. Letters of Congratulation; 4. Letters of Condolence.

---

* It will be noticed that in the printed specimens the body of the letter begins on the same line with the salutation. This arrangement is proper in print, but not in writing. *In all written letters, the parts should be arranged in strict conformity with the directions and models given in Chapter II.*

Familiar Letters.

Supreme Excellence.—The supreme excellence of a familiar letter is naturalness. Such a letter should be unstudied, free from affectation, and as nearly as possible like good conversation. And it should be perfectly characteristic of the writer, so that the recipient may feel when reading it, as if his friend were actually present and speaking. When you are about to write a letter to a friend, think what you would say to him if he were at that moment with you, and then write it. We all like *talking* letters—good talking, of course.

Little Things.—Don't be afraid to write of little things. To one who loves us, nothing that concerns us is trivial or uninteresting.* Things that are worth talking about are worth writing about. When absent from home, we gloat over the simplest details,—what the baby says and does; how our favorite horse or cat or dog or canary is getting along; how the old familiar trees and vines and flowers look—when they blossom, how they grow, etc.; anything and everything that calls up the picture of home with all its dear associations, and makes us forget for the moment that we are scores or hundreds of miles away.

Affection.—The best domestic letters are dictated by the heart rather than the head. A loving heart naturally imparts a glow to the written page, and this warmth is communicated, by the mysterious power

* They are as dear to us from those we love, as they are tedious and disagreeable from others.—*Madame de Sévigné.*

of words, to the heart of the reader. It is wrong to indulge in strained and artificial expressions of affection; and it is equally wrong to suppress those that are prompted by genuine feeling. To a fond mother, an affectionate sister, a devoted wife, whose every breath is laden with a prayer for your safety and happiness,—a loving word is inexpressibly precious, filling the soul with sunshine, and making it for a time oblivious of the pain of separation.

"Such" words "have power to quiet
The restless pulse of care,
And come like the benediction
That follows after prayer."

Specimen Letters.—To afford a practical illustration of the style appropriate for familiar letters, a few specimens are given below. We have not in all cases chosen such as we would, but such as we could. The best letters are too long for reproduction in these pages.

1. *Emily Chubbuck* (*Fanny Forrester*) *to Mrs. Dr. Nott.*

Utica Female Seminary, October, 1842.

My dear M——— There it is again! I cannot write "Miss Sheldon," and I am sure such a bashful body as I could not be expected to address so dignified a personage as Mrs. Nott. So what shall I do? I am very lonely just now, and feel inclined to be somewhat sentimental; for I have been up the hall, and found a certain corner room, looking—not desolate—oh, no; it is wondrous cosy and comfortable—but as though it *ought* to be desolate. Yet I will spare you all the things I could say, and turn to some other subject. * * *

T——— sits studying close by; somebody is thumping Miss F.'s piano over our head tremendously; M. B. is passing the door—there! the bell rings—study-hour is over; there is a general increase of sound in the house, and I know by the voices in the hall that many a door has been flung open within the last half minute. How I wish—but no, there is no use in wishing! I will go to bed and dream (I have few day-dreams now) of pleasant things, and wake in the morning and see every thing pleasant; for this is a happy world, in spite of its perplexities. Fine dreams to you too, both waking and sleeping; yet now and then intermingling may there come a little (though it were the least in the world) thought of

Your truly affectionate

EMILY.

2. *Goethe's Mother (Frau Rath) to Bettine Brentano.*

Frankfort, May 12, 1808.

DEAR BETTINE,—Thy letters give me joy, and Miss Betty, who recognizes them in the address, says, "Frau Rath, the postman brings you a pleasure." Don't however be too mad about my son; everything must be done in order. The brown room is new-papered with the pattern which you chose; the color blends peculiarly well with the morning twilight, which breaks over the Catharine-tower and enters into my room. Yesterday our town looked quite holiday-like, in the spotless light of the Alba.

Except this, everything remains as it was. Be in no trouble about the footstool, for Betty suffers no one to sit upon it.

Write much, even if it were every day.

Thy affectionate friend,

ELIZABETH GOETHE.

3. *John Quincy Adams, when seven years old, to his Father*

Braintree, October 13, 1774.

SIR,—I have been trying ever since you went away, to learn to write you a letter. I shall make poor work of it; but, sir, mamma says you will accept my endeavors, and that my duty to you may be expressed in poor writing as well as good. I hope I grow a better boy, and that you will have no occasion to be ashamed of me when you return. Mr. Thaxter says I learn my books well. He is a very good master. I read my books to mamma. We all long to see you.

I am, sir, your dutiful son,

JOHN QUINCY ADAMS.

4. *Thomas Jefferson to his daughter Martha.*

[We give the following letter, partly because of the excellence of its style, but chiefly because of the lofty precepts it inculcates. Mr Jefferson in his letters to his daughters always mingles instructio with affection; always endeavors to inform the mind and build up the character. He directs their studies, encourages them to notice the phenomena of nature,—the time that birds appear, flowers bloom, fruits ripen, etc.; and urges to the practice of industry, economy, and all the domestic and social virtues. The italics are ours.]

Toulon, April 7, 1787.

MY DEAR PATSY,—I received yesterday, at Marseilles, your letter of March 25th, and I received it with pleasure, because it announced to me that you were well. Experience learns [teaches] us to be always anxious about the health of those whom we love. * * *

I have received letters which inform me that our dear Polly will certainly come to us this summer. When she arrives she will become a precious charge on your hands. The difference of your age, and your common loss of a mother, will put that office on you. *Teach her above all things to be good*, because without that we can neither be valued by others nor set any value on ourselves. *Teach her to be always true;* no vice is so mean as the want of truth, and at the same time so useless. *Teach her never to be angry;* anger only serves to torment ourselves, to divert others, and to alienate their esteem. *And teach her industry* and application to useful pursuits. I will venture to assure you that, if you inculcate this in her mind, you will make her a happy being in herself, a most estimable friend to you, and precious to all the world. In teaching her these dispositions of mind, you will be more fixed in them yourself, and render yourself dear to all your acquaintances. Practice them, then, my dear, without ceasing. If ever you find yourself in difficulty, and doubt how to extricate yourself, *do what is right*, and you will find it the easiest way of getting out of the difficulty. Do it for the additional incitement of increasing the happiness of him who loves you infinitely, and who is, my dear Patsy,

Yours affectionately,

TH. JEFFERSON.

5. *Martha Jefferson to her Father.*

[Not in answer to the preceding letter, but to an earlier one.]

MY DEAR PAPA,—I am very glad that the beginning of your voyage has been so pleasing, and I hope that the rest will be not less so, as it is a great consolation for me, being deprived of the pleasure of seeing you, to know that you are happy. I hope your resolution of returning in the end of April is always the same.

I do not doubt but what Mr. Short has written you word that my sister sets off with Fulwar Skipwith in the month of May, and she will be here in July. Then indeed shall I be the happiest of mortals; united to what I have the dearest in the world, nothing more will be requisite to render my happiness complete.

I am not so industrious as you or I would wish, but I hope that in taking pains I very soon shall be. I have already begun to study more. I have not heard any news of my harpsichord; it will be really very disagreeable if it is not here before your arrival. I am learning a very pretty thing now, but it is very hard. I have drawn several little flowers, all alone, that the master even has not seen; indeed he advised me to draw as much alone as possible, for that is of more use than all I could do with him. I shall take up my Livy, as you desire it. I shall begin again, as I have lost the thread of the history. As for the hysterics, you may be quiet on that head, as I am not lazy enough to fear them.

There was a gentleman, a few days ago, that killed himself

because he thought that his wife did not love him. They had been married ten years. I believe that if every husband in Paris was to do as much, there would be nothing but widows left. [A nice bit of satire on French society.] * * *

As for needlework, the only kind that I could learn here would be embroidery, indeed netting also; but I could not do much of these in America, because of the impossibility of having proper silks; however, they will not be totally useless.

You say your expectations for me are high, yet not higher than I can attain. Then be assured, my dear papa, that you shall be satisfied in that, as well as in anything else that lies in my power; for what I hold most precious is your satisfaction, indeed I should be miserable without it. You wrote me a long letter, as I asked you; however, it would have been much more so without so wide a margin. Adieu, my dear papa. Be assured of the tenderest affection of

Your loving daughter,

M. JEFFERSON.

PANTHEMONT, April 9, 1787.

6. *Lady Dufferin to Miss Berry.*

[Lady Dufferin was the granddaughter of Richard Brinsley Sheridan, and seems to have inherited his wit. We give below quotations from one of her witty, vivacious epistles, regretting that we cannot afford room for the whole of it.]

Hampton Hall, Dorchester, 1846.

Your kind little note followed me here, dear Miss Berry, which must account for my not having answered it sooner. As you guessed, I was obliged to follow my "*things*" (as the maids always call their raiment) into the very jaws of the law. I think the Old Bailey is a charming place. We were introduced to a Live Lord Mayor, and I sat between two sheriffs. The common sergeant talked to me familiarly, and I am not sure that the governor of Newgate did not call me "Nelly." As for the Rev. Mr. Carver (the ordinary), if the inherent vanity of my sex does not mislead me, I *think* I have made a deep impression there. Altogether, my Old Bailey recollec-

9

tions are of the most pleasing and gratifying nature. It is true that I have only got back three pairs and a half of stockings, one gown, and two shawls; but that is but a trifling consideration in studying the glorious institutions of our country. We were treated with the greatest respect, and—ham-sandwiches; and two magistrates handed us down to the carriage. For my part, I do not think we were in a *criminal* court, as the law was so uncommonly *civil*. * * * *

I find that the idea of *personal property* is a fascinating illusion, for our goods belong in fact to our country, and not to us; and that the petticoats and stockings I have fondly imagined *mine*, are really the petticoats of Great Britain and Ireland. I am now and then indulged with a distant glimpse of my most necessary garments in the hands of different policemen; but "in this stage of the proceedings" may do no more than wistfully recognize them. Even on such occasions, the words of Justice are, "Policeman B, 25, produce *your* gowns." "Letter A, 36, identify *your* lace." "Letter C, tie up *your* stockings." All this is harrowing to the feelings, but one cannot have everything in this life. We have obtained *justice*, and can easily wait for a change of linen.

Hopes are held out to us, that at some vague period in the lapse of time, we may be allowed to *wear* out our raiment—at least so much of it as may have resisted the wear and tear of justice; and my poor mother looks confidently forward to being restored to the bosom of her silver teapot. But I don't know! I begin to look upon all property with a philosophic eye as unstable in its nature, and liable to all sorts of pawnbrokers; moreover, the police and I have so long had my clothes in common, that I shall never feel at home in them again. To a virtuous mind the idea that "Inspector Dousett" examined into all one's hooks and eyes, tapes and buttons, etc., is inexpressibly painful. But I cannot pursue that view of the subject. Let me hope, dear Miss Berry, that you feel for us as we really deserve, and that you wish me well "thro' my clothes" on Monday next! If I were sure you are at

Richmond still, I might endeavor to return your kind visit· but at present our costumes are too *light* and our hearts too heavy for the empty forms and ceremonies of social intercourse. I hope, however, to see you ere very long, and with very kind remembrances to your sister, believe me,

Yours very truly,

SELINA DUFFERIN.

EXERCISE XII.

Write a letter to an absent friend, in accordance with the foregoing suggestions. (See foot-note, page 91.)

LETTERS OF INTRODUCTION.

Definition.—A Letter of Introduction is one by which a person introduces a friend or acquaintance to a friend who is absent.

Letters of Introduction are of two kinds,—*Social* and *Business*. We shall here confine our remarks to the former, leaving the latter to be treated of under the head of Business Letters.

Suggestions.—In the use of this kind of correspondence, the following suggestions will be found useful:—

1. *Be careful whom you introduce.* By introducing an improper person, you might do an irreparable injury to your absent friend. Never introduce socially any one with whom you would not be willing to have your mother, wife, or sister associate.

2. *Letters of introduction should be short.* They are often delivered in person, and it is embarrassing for a person to wait while a long letter is being read.

3. *Do not over-praise.* You may use the warm language of friendship, but extravagant eulogy is as much

out of place in a written as it would be in an oral introduction.

4. *Leave the letter unsealed.* To prevent the bearer from reading it by fastening the envelope would be a breach of politeness, and might excite distrust and suspicion. The bearer may, however, seal it before delivery.

Superscription.—The superscription is the same as if the letter were to be sent by mail, except that the words, "Introducing Mr. A—— B——," are written in the lower left-hand corner; thus:—

> *Hon. Charles Sumner,*
>
> *Boston,*
>
> *Introducing*
> *Mr. William Young.* *Mass.*

Stamp.—As the letter is not sent by mail, no stamp is required.

Delivery.—The proper way to deliver a letter of introduction is to send it to the person who is to receive it, together with a card bearing the name and address of the person introduced. The former should then call on the latter and extend his hospitalities. In many cases the bearer presents the letter in person; and circumstances often render it proper and necessary to do so. Care should be taken, however, not to present it when its reception will be inconvenient and embarrassing.

Specimen Letters.—We give below four specimens to illustrate the proper style to be used.

Number One.

Green Valley, Pa., May 1, 1876.

DEAR SIR,—I have the honor of introducing to your acquaintance Mr. William Worthy, whom I commend to your kind attentions.

Very truly yours,

JANE FAITHFUL.

MR. THOMAS GOOD, Vineland, N. J.

Number Two.

Chicago, Sept. 25, 1875.

MY DEAR SIR,

It gives me pleasure to introduce to you my much esteemed friend, Mr. W. Penn Johnson. Any attentions you may be able to show him will be gratefully acknowledged and cheerfully reciprocated by

Your old friend,

ARTHUR PENDENNIS.

MR. WILLIAM GRAHAM.

Number Three.

[The circumstance that occasions the introduction may be stated, as in the following:]

Philadelphia, June 30, 1876.

MY DEAR FLORENCE,—This will be handed to you by Mrs. Jerome St. Clair, who will remain in your city a few days, on her way to Richmond. It gives me much pleasure to make you known to her; for I am sure that the acquaintance of two friends who are so dear to me will enhance the happiness of both. Any attention that you may be able to pay to Mrs. St. Clair during her stay will add one more to my many reasons for being

Your loving and grateful friend,

MARY BLOOMFIELD.

MISS FLORENCE HOPE, Baltimore, Md.

Number Four.

[Here is one in the off-hand, dashing style of a young collegian A letter of introduction should be as natural and original as any other. A set phraseology makes a letter stiff and lifeless.]

Columbia College, Sept. 4, 1870.

DEAR WILL,—Open your house and heart to my dear old chum, Tom Jones, who is waiting to stick this in his pocket. He is going to make a raid on your town in search of health, and I don't want you to kill him by dragging him up those mountains, as you did me last summer. I have given him such glowing accounts of my sister's cooking as to make me as hungry as a cannibal.

Depending upon your brotherly love for my dear friend's kind reception, I am

Ever your affectionate brother,

JOHN.

WILLIAM LEE, ESQ., Bedford, Pa.

EXERCISE XIII.

Compose, fold, and superscribe a letter of introduction. (See foot-note, page 91.)

LETTERS OF CONGRATULATION.

Definition and Remarks.—A Letter of Congratulation is one written to a friend who has experienced some good fortune or great joy.

Such a letter should of course be written in a lively, cheerful style, suited to the occasion, and should be free from all admixture of envy or foreboding. It should be a rose without a thorn. If there is any unpleasant news to communicate, concerning yourself or any one else, or if you have any advice to give, leave it for a subsequent letter.

Exaggerated expressions of joy have an air of insincerity, and should therefore be avoided. To sum up all, in a word,—*feel right, and write as you feel.*

Specimen Letters.—The following letters will illustrate our remarks:—

1. *Thomas Jefferson to his Sister on her Marriage.*—(*Abridged.*)

Paris, July 12, 1788.

My dear Sister,—My last letters from Virginia inform me of your marriage with Mr. Hastings Marks. I sincerely wish you joy and happiness in the new state into which you have entered. I have seen enough of Mr. Marks to form a very good opinion of him, and to believe that he will endeavor to render you happy. I am sure you will not be wanting on your part. You have seen enough of the different conditions of life to know that it is neither wealth nor splendor, but tranquillity and occupation, which give happiness. This truth I can confirm to you from larger observation and a greater scope of experience.

I should wish to know where Mr. Marks proposes to settle and what line of life he will follow. In every situation I should wish to render him and you every service in my power, as you may be assured I shall ever feel myself warmly interested in your happiness, and preserve for you that sincere love I have always borne you. My daughters remember you with equal affection, and will one of these days tender it to you in person. They join me in wishing you all earthly felicity and a continuance of your love to them.

Accept assurances of the sincere attachment with which I am my dear sister,

Your affectionate brother,

Th. Jefferson.

2. *Sir Walter Scott to Robert Southey on his investiture as Poet Laureate.*—(*Abridged.*)

Edinburgh, November 13, 1813.

I do not delay, my dear Southey, to say my gratulator. Long may you live, as Paddy says, to rule over us, and to redeem the crown of Spenser and of Dryden to its pristine dignity. * * * *

I was greatly delighted with the circumstances of your investiture. It reminded me of the porters at Calais with Dr. Smollett's baggage, six of them seizing one small portmanteau and bearing it in triumph to his lodgings. * * *

Adieu, my dear Southey; my best wishes attend all that you do, and my best congratulations every good that attends you—yea, even this, the very least of Providence's mercies, as a poor clergyman said when pronouncing grace over a herring. * *

My best compliments attend Mrs. Southey and your family.

Ever yours,

WALTER SCOTT.

3. *To a Gentleman Elected to Congress.*

Metropolisville, Nov. 5, 1875.

Hurrah! the battle is fought and the victory won! Give me your hand, old friend, while I give it a good squeeze of congratulation on your election. The result has not surprised me in the least. I knew you would be elected, because I knew that you deserved to be, and that the people of your district had sense enough to know it too. Some say, "Principles, not men"; but I say "Principles *and* men." This honor is as much a tribute to your personal worth as to the correctness of your principles. Just such men as you are needed in Congress—never more than now; and I believe you will fulfil every expectation, and honor yourself and your constituents. That such may be the case shall ever be the prayer of—

Yours faithfully,

JAMES HOPEWELL.

CHARLES GOODMAN, Esq., Pleasant Valley, Utopia.

EXERCISE XIV.

Write a letter of congratulation to a friend on his supposed marriage, graduation, recovery from sickness, or some other occasion of joy. (See foot-note, page 91.)

Letters of Condolence.

Definition and Remarks.—A Letter of Condolence is one written to a friend who has suffered some grievous loss or bereavement.

To write a good letter of condolence, one that shall comfort and console the sufferer, requires good taste and fine feeling. Persons often, by injudicious words, probe afresh the wound they are trying to heal. In offering condolence, do not call up the harrowing details of the sad event, nor attempt to argue the sufferer out of his (or her) sorrow. Reasons that appeal to the head cannot touch the heart. Above all, do not reflect any blame, directly or indirectly. What the bleeding heart most needs, in the first gush of grief, is sympathy —that genuine, tearful sympathy that lessens another's grief by sharing it. The expression of this in a few loving words, and a pious reference to the great Source of consolation, are all that a letter of condolence requires.

Specimen Letters.—The following letters afford excellent illustrations of this kind of composition:—

1. *To a Sister on the Death of a Child.*

[The following tender and touching letter was written by a celebrated American authoress. The bereaved mother said that no other letter gave her so much comfort.]

SISTER DARLING.—I cannot write what is in my heart for you to-day; it is too full—filled with a double sorrow, for you and for myself. Tears blind me; my pen trembles in my hand. Oh, to be near you! to clasp you in my arms! to draw your head to my bosom and weep with you! Darling, God comfort you, I cannot.
S.

2. *Another on the Death of a Babe.*

[The concluding sentences are very beautiful and appropriate.]

Charleston, S. C., Dec. 4, 1875.

MY DEAR MARY,—I feel that a mother's sorrow for the loss of a beloved child cannot be assuaged by the commonplaces of condolence; yet I must write a few lines to assure you of my heartfelt sympathy in your grief. There is one thing, however, that should soften the sharpness of a mother's agony under such a bereavement. It is the reflection that little children are pure and guileless, and that "of such is the kingdom of heaven." "It is well with the child." Your precious babe is now a treasure laid up in a better world, and the gate through which it has passed to peace and joy unspeakable is left open, so that you, in due time, may follow. Let this be your consolation.

Affectionately yours,

SARAH YOUNG.

MRS. MARY BROWNING, Norfolk, Va.

3 *La Fayette to Jefferson, announcing the death of Madame de La Fayette.*

[The following sadly beautiful letter, though not strictly a letter of condolence, relates to the subject of death, and therefore belongs to this class.]

Anteuil, January 11, 1808.

MY DEAR FRIEND,—The constant mourning of your heart *will be deepened* by the grief I am doomed to impart to it.

Who better than you can sympathize for the loss of a beloved wife? The angel who for thirty-four years has blessed my life, was to you an affectionate, grateful friend. Pity me, my dear Jefferson, and believe me, for ever, with all my heart,

Yours,

LA FAYETTE.

4. *Thomas Jefferson to John Adams on the death of Mrs. Adams.*

[The following is probably one of the finest models of a letter of condolence that this kind of literature affords.]

Monticello, November 13, 1818.

The public papers, my dear friend, announce the fatal event of which your letter of October the 20th had given me ominous foreboding. Tried myself in the school of affliction, by the loss of every form of connection which can rive the human heart, I know well, and feel what you have lost, what you have suffered, are suffering, and yet have to endure. The same trials have taught me that for ills so immeasurable time and silence are the only medicine. I will not, therefore, by useless condolences, open afresh the sluices of your grief, nor, although mingling sincerely my tears with yours, will I say a word more where words are vain, but that it is of some comfort to us both that the time is not very distant at which we are to deposit in the same cerement our sorrows and suffering bodies, and to ascend in essence to an ecstatic meeting with the friends we have loved and lost, and whom we shall still love and never lose again. God bless you and support you under your heavy affliction.

TH. JEFFERSON.

EXERCISE XV.

Write a letter of condolence to some real or imaginary friend who is supposed to be in grief on account of some painful event. (See foot-note, page 91.)

SUB-SECTION II.

STYLE AND SPECIMENS OF BUSINESS LETTERS.

Requisites.—The chief requisites of a business letter are clearness, correctness, and conciseness. No more words should be used than are necessary; nor should words that are essential to the construction be omitted. The omission of pronouns and verbs, for example, is a foolish affectation and a blunder. Never write such jargon as, "Yours of 10th received, and in reply will state," etc. Say, "Your favor of the 10th inst. is received, and in reply I will state," etc. An incorrect, hurried, slip-shod letter may not unfairly be taken to indicate a slip-shod way of doing business. The best business letters are models of accurate and even elegant, though unadorned, English.*

Business only.—A business letter should be confined to business only. This rule, however, does not exclude the expression of kind wishes and other forms of courtesy. A business man should never forget to be polite. If circumstances should seem to require a departure from the rule, the personal matter should be added after the signature, as a note.

REMARK.—We hope to give in this treatise hints in regard to the mechanical execution and style of letters that will be of great value to persons of all classes, business men as well as others; but we do not attempt to teach the intricate details of mercantile and other business correspondence. These cannot be fully learned in any book:

* See the excellent collection contained in Anderson's *Practical Mercantile Letter-Writer*, published by D. Appleton & Co., New York.

they can be mastered only *in the business* to which they belong. All that we aim to do under this head is to give such instructions as will enable people of all classes to write in a business-like manner such business letters as are required in the exigencies of ordinary life. We therefore confine our particular attention to the varieties mentioned below; believing them to be most used by the greatest number of people.

Kinds here Noticed.—Of the many varieties of business letters, we shall notice only the following:—

1. Letters of Introduction (Business); 2. Letters of Credit; 3. Letters of Application; 4. Letters of Recommendation; 5. Mercantile Letters, including (1) Order for Goods, (2) Answer and Invoice: 6. Miscellaneous Letters.

Letters of Introduction.

A business Letter of Introduction is an introduction for business purposes only, and entails no social obligations. In style it should resemble other business letters; that is, it should be clear, accurate, and concise. In most other respects it resembles a social letter of introduction, and we therefore need only to refer to what is said under that head (see pages 99 and 100).

Specimen Letter.

Excelsior Business College, Sept. 30, 1875.

Mr. John D. Palmer, San Francisco, Cal.

Dear Sir,—Allow me to introduce to you the bearer, Mr. Charles Wilson, a graduate of this institution, who visits your city for the purpose of seeking employment as a bookkeeper.

It gives me pleasure to assure you that he is a young man of good education, strict integrity, and superior ability, and is entirely worthy of your confidence.

Any assistance you may find it in your power to render him I shall esteem as a personal favor.

Yours very truly,

HENRY PENNINGTON.

LETTERS OF CREDIT.

A Letter of Credit is one in which the writer loans his credit to the bearer, to a limited extent. That is, A asks C to let B have goods or other valuables to a certain amount, promising to be responsible for the same, should B fail to make payment.

It closely resembles a letter of introduction. Indeed the two are often combined; that is, a letter of introduction often contains a clause asking that credit be given if the bearer desires it.

Specimen Letter.

Pittsburg, Pa., Nov. 20, 1876.

MESSRS. D. KNICKERBOCKER & Co., New York.

DEAR SIRS,—Please allow Mr. Thomas Sanders a credit for such goods as he may select, to an amount not exceeding one thousand dollars ($1000) for four months. I will become responsible to you for the payment of the same, should Mr. Sanders fail to make payment at the proper time.

You will please inform me of the amount for which you give credit, and in default of payment notify me immediately.

Very respectfully,

Your obedient servant,

JOHN PORTER.

Mr. Sanders' signature,*—

THOMAS SANDERS.

* The signature of the bearer should be given so that he may be identified as the person named in the letter.

LETTERS OF APPLICATION.

Suggestions.—In regard to this class of letters we offer the following suggestions:—

1. *A letter of application should be very carefully written*, as the letter itself is regarded as a part—often the principal part—of the evidence of the writer's fitness or unfitness for the position applied for. Examine carefully every sentence and every word of the letter before sending it, and if a single mistake is detected, rewrite the whole. If the position is a valuable one, an hour, or even a day, spent in writing the application may prove to be time well spent.

2. *Such a letter should be modest.* The applicant may of course state briefly what opportunities of education he has enjoyed, and what preparation he has made; but his full qualifications and character should be stated by others. While the letter should be modest, it should not, however, be sycophantic. It should be not only respectful, but also *self*-respectful; for a genuine self-respect is one of the surest passports to the respect of others.

Specimen Letter.

Lancaster, Pa., October 30, 1885.

JOHN LOGAN, ESQ.,
Superintendent of Public Instruction,
Eldorado City.

SIR:—Having learned that there is a vacancy in Grammar School No. 5 of your city, I beg leave to offer myself as a candidate for the position.

I graduated at the Rugby Normal School, in 1876, and have ever since devoted myself to the work of teaching.

Enclosed you will find testimonials from B. F. Nelson, Esq., County Superintendent, and Prof. Wallace, Principal of the above-named institution; and I am also permitted to refer to Rev. R. Hunt and Hon. Thomas Brown, of this city.

Should a personal interview be desired, I shall be glad to present myself at such time and place as may be most convenient to yourself.

I am, Sir, with much respect,

Your obedient servant,

JOHN THOMPSON

LETTERS OF RECOMMENDATION.

A Recommendation is sometimes given in a letter of introduction and sometimes in a separate letter.

Great care should be exercised in giving recommendations. Never recommend an unworthy person, and never recommend too highly. It may be hard to refuse a testimonial, but it is base to give a false one.

Recommendations may be *special* or *general*. Those of the former class are addressed, like ordinary letters, to some particular person; those of the latter are not limited as to person or occasion. We give below an example of each:—

1. Special Recommendation.

[Referred to in the Letter of Application on page 111.]

Rugby Normal School, Oct. 20, 1885.

JOHN LOGAN, ESQ.,

Superintendent of Public Instruction,

Eldorado City.

SIR:—It affords me pleasure to testify to the personal worth and educational qualifications of Mr. John Thompson, who, I am informed, is an applicant for a position in one of your public schools.

He graduated at this institution, as his diploma will show, in 1876. As a student, he was distinguished for diligence, accuracy, integrity, and a conscientious discharge of every duty; and these qualities he has carried with him into the school-room and into society. Such elements of character, combined with aptness in teaching and tact in enforcing discipline, could not fail to render him what I have long known him to be, a very efficient and superior teacher. I cordially recommend him for the position to which he aspires.

Very respectfully yours,

JAMES WALLACE, Principal

2. General Recommendation.*

[Referred to in Letter of Application, page 111.]

Lancaster, Pa., Sept. 30, 1885.

Having learned that Mr. John Thompson is desirous of leaving this city and engaging in the work of teaching elsewhere, I am pleased to say, that I have known him long and intimately; that his personal character is above reproach; and that he has shown himself to be possessed of tact, learning, enthusiasm, ability to govern,—in short, all the highest elements of the successful teacher. I therefore earnestly recommend him to any who desire to employ a good instructor, feeling confident that he will satisfy all reasonable expectations.

B. F. NELSON,
County Superintendent.

HOW TO BEGIN.—Persons are often in doubt how to begin one of these open or general recommendations. "This is to certify that," is a very good way when the testimonial can be expressed in a single sentence. We give below a few examples:—

* Strictly speaking, a general recommendation is merely a certificate, not a letter. We speak of it here because of its close connection with a genuine *letter* of recommendation.

1. "Mr. John Jones being about to leave our employ, it gives us great pleasure to testify," etc.

2. "This is to certify that Mary Smith, who has been in my employ for the last six months, is a good and careful housekeeper," etc.

3. "John Williams, the bearer, who is now leaving our employ, has been," etc.

4. "To whom it may concern:

"It gives me pleasure to testify to the skill and ability of Miss Jenny Lind, who has for the past two years instructed my daughter in music," etc.

EXERCISE XVI.

1. Compose a letter of application.
2. Compose two recommendations—one special, the other general,—to accompany the application.
3. Compose a general recommendation of a house-servant, farm-laborer, or mechanic.

MERCANTILE LETTERS.

Of the great variety of letters of this class we shall speak of only two: (1) *Letters ordering Merchandise;* and (2) the *Answers* to them, with enclosed invoices.

These are business letters that almost every person, lady or gentleman, has occasion to write; and they should therefore receive special attention.

NOTE.—Letters ordering goods should state very clearly the quantity and kind of articles wanted, and how they are to be sent. In ordering books, the title and the author's and publisher's names should be stated; and if there are various editions published at different prices, the size, style of binding, and publisher's price should also be mentioned if possible. In ordering dry-goods, etc., a description of the quality should be given, by number or otherwise, or else sam ples should be sent.

Not less than a line should be given to each item; the quantity being written at the left of the page, and the price, if known, at the right.

1. Letter Ordering Merchandise (Books).

Urbana, N. Y., August 31, 187[illegible].

MESSRS. DOMBEY & SON,

No. 13 Astor Place, New York.

DEAR SIRS,—Please send to me, by Adams Express, as soon as convenient, the following:—

2 doz. Brooks's Written Arithmetic.
3 doz. Westlake's 3000 Practice Words.
2 copies Longfellow's Poems, Household ed., cloth.
1 set Little Classics, 16 volumes, green cloth.
4 copies Tennyson's Queen Mary, 12mo, cloth.

When forwarded, please notify me by letter, with enclosed invoice.

Very respectfully yours,
JOHN W. HOSMER,
Urbana, Steuben Co., N. Y.

NOTE 1. If but few items are contained in the order, as in the above example, they may be given either in the body of the letter, or at the bottom. In the latter case the letter may be written thus:—

DEAR SIRS,—Please send me by Adams Express [or otherwise, as directed] the books named below.

Yours very respectfully, etc.

NOTE 2. If the order is long, it should be made out on a separate sheet; in which case the letter may be written thus:—

DEAR SIRS,--Please send by Adams Express [or otherwise] the articles detailed in the enclosed list, addressed as below.

Yours very respectfully, etc.

NOTE 3. Always give the express or freight station, and state how goods shall be sent. The order, if separate, should be headed "Order of (stating Date)," and should be signed by the person or firm ordering.

NOTE 4. Packages of goods are sometimes marked "C.O.D." (cash on delivery). When this is the case the bill is payable to the Express Company on the delivery of the goods. When we order merchandise from a house with which we have not acquired a business standing, we should always order in this manner, unless we enclose the money or give references. We have no right to ask persons to send us goods on credit, unless we are known to them to be pecuniarily responsible.

EXERCISE XVII.

Copy, fold, and superscribe the above letter, in accordance with the directions and models in Chapter II.

DIRECTION.—Copy the letter on letter paper; and begin each item of the order as you would begin a paragraph.

2. Answer, Enclosing Invoice.

13 Astor Place, New York, Sept. 4, 1876.

MR. JOHN W. HOSMER,
Urbana, N. Y.

SIR,—We have this day sent to your address by Adams Express the books ordered in your favor of the 31st August. Enclosed you will find an invoice of the same, amounting to forty-seven $\frac{20}{100}$ dollars.

Hoping they may arrive in good condition and prove satisfactory, and soliciting further orders, we are,

Very respectfully yours,

DOMBEY & SON.
per W.

["Per W." denotes the clerk by whom the letter was written.]

The Invoice Referred to Above.*

New York, Sept. 4, 1876.

MR JOHN W. HOSMER,

Bought of DOMBEY & SON.

2	doz. Brooks's Written Arithmetic, @ 9.	18	.
3	" Westlake's 3000 Prac. Words, @ 4.20	12	60
2	Longfellow's Poems, @ 1.50	3	
1	set Little Classics, 16 vols., @ .75	12	
4	Queen Mary, @ .40	1	60
		$47	20

Received Payment.

DOMBEY & SON.

NOTE 1. When the bill is paid, it should be receipted as above. If not paid at the time it is made out, the date of payment should be given with the receipt; thus:—

Received Payment, Oct. 4, 1876.

DOMBEY & SON.

NOTE 2. Many business houses enclose the invoice without a letter; and if there is any remark to make, they write it on the same paper. This is certainly not a good method, as they themselves would doubtless admit. Indeed, there are serious objections to it, which will readily occur to any one conversant with business. The best method is to use printed blanks for this purpose, to be filled out with the amount of the invoice, and mode and date of shipment, as in the following form:—

* An *Invoice* is a statement in detail of goods sold or consigned for sale. When applied to goods sold it is frequently called a *Bill of Sales;* or, if it contains a variety of small items, a *Bill of Parcels.*

St. Louis, ..., 18 .

M. ....

SIR,—Enclosed please find invoice amounting to $.......... forwarded per ...., Bill of Lading accompanying, according to your order dated ....

The goods leave us in good condition, and we trust will prove satisfactory. Should anything, however, appear objectionable, we shall feel obliged if you will notify us promptly.

Yours very respectfully,

RICHARD ROE & CO.

EXERCISE XVIII.

Copy the above reply and the accompanying invoice, put them in an envelope, and direct to Mr. Hosmer.

DIRECTION.—The invoice should be written on a piece of cap or letter paper properly ruled. If convenient, rule with red ink.

EXERCISE XIX.

Write, in your own name, to Mozart, Bach & Co., music publishers, 922 Chestnut street, Philadelphia, for the following pieces of sheet music, to be sent by express, C. O. D.: Whispering Wind, by Wollenhaupt, 2 copies; Gouttes d'Eau, by Ascher, 4 copies; Lucrezia Borgia, by Sydney Smith, 3 copies; Rippling Waves, by Wellenspiel, 5 copies; Clochettes Galop, by D. Grau, 1 copy; German Triumphal March, by Kunkel, 6 copies.

EXERCISE XX.

Answer the above, stating that you have sent the music as ordered. Also make out a bill of the music and enclose it, charging for the first piece $1 each; for the second, 40 cts.; for the third, 60 cts.; for the fourth, 50 cts.; for the fifth, 40 cts.; for the sixth, 75 cts.

In the answer you of course personate Mozart, Bach & Co., and make out the invoice and direct the letter to yourself.

MISCELLANEOUS LETTERS.

1. Application for a Catalogue.

New Castle, Del., June 15, 1845.

Prof. D. P. PAGE,
Principal of the State Normal School,
Albany, N. Y.

SIR:—Please send me a copy of your last catalogue and circular. I design attending school next winter, and wish to obtain information concerning your terms, course of study, etc. By complying with the above request you will oblige,

Yours very respectfully,
MARY COMSTOCK.

2. Sending a Subscription to a Newspaper.

Athenia, Chester co., Pa., May 2. 1870.

TO THE PUBLISHER OF "THE LITERARY TIMES,"
Boston, Mass.

SIR,—You will find enclosed a money order for three dollars ($3), for which you will please send to my address a copy of "The Literary Times" for one year, beginning with the first number of the present volume.

Yours respectfully,
JOHN BOOKMAN.

NOTE.—In such letters be very careful to write the name and directions fully and plainly, to mention the money enclosed, and to state when you wish the subscription to begin. When no time of beginning is mentioned, the subscription will generally date from the next number, or from the beginning of the volume or quarter. If your subscription is a renewal, you should so state in your letter.

EXERCISE XXI.

1. Write for some publisher's catalogue of books.
2. Send your subscription to a periodical.
3. Send a club of five or more subscribers.

In the latter case the names may be incorporated in the letter, each on a separate line, or they may be given below. If the papers are all to be sent to the same post-office, so state; if to different post offices, write the directions after each name.

A Model Business Letter.

Philadelphia, Nov. 23, 1872.

Nathaniel Silsbee, Esq.,

Treasurer of Harvard College.

SIR:—The printed circular of the 16th inst., signed by President Eliot in behalf of the Harvard College, and describing the effect of the late fire in Boston upon the pecuniary resources of the college, has given great regret to all in this city who have read it, and to myself personally, a graduate of the college, a pain that has the sadness of sorrow. With the faithfulness, therefore, of a loving son for a nursing mother, I contribute what I can at present to the alleviation of her severe loss.

Enclosed is a draft of this date by the Philadelphia National Bank, upon the cashier of the Globe National Bank of Boston No. 673, for one thousand dollars ($1000), payable in bankable funds to my order, and by me endorsed payable to your order as Treasurer of Harvard College.

I request that this sum, when paid, may be placed at the disposal of the President and Fellows of Harvard College, for such uses of the college as upon this occasion they may think best

Please advise me of the safe arrival of my letter and its enclosure.

I remain, very respectfully,

Your obedient servant,

HORACE BINNEY,

A graduate of the Class of 1797.

CHAPTER IV.

THE LITERATURE OF LETTERS.

OUTLINE.

1. A Bird's-Eye View.
2. Gleanings.

Definition.—The Literature of Letters is the published correspondence of eminent men and women.

It constitutes, not only a large, but also an interesting and important part of our literary treasures; and the present chapter is designed to impress this truth as forcibly as possible on the mind of the reader.

Remark.—In pursuance of this design, we divide the chapter into two sections; the first giving a general view of the field, the second presenting a few golden grains of truth as specimens of its riches.

SECTION I.

A Bird's-Eye View of the Field of Letters.

OUTLINE.

1. Interest of Letters
2. Value of Letters.
3. Letter-Writers.
4. Bibliography of Letters.

Interest.—There is no other kind of writing that possesses for us such a living, human interest, as letters; for there is no other that comes so near to the private lives, "to the business and bosoms," of the writers. Though written, as all genuine letters are, for the private eye of one or two familiar friends, and without any thought of their publication, they nevertheless often form the most interesting and imperishable of an author's productions. "Such as are written from wise men," says Lord Bacon, "are of all the words of men the best: they are more natural than orations and public speeches, and more advised than conferences or private ones."

And it is this natural and unstudied character that renders their style so attractive. In other productions there is the restraint induced by the feeling that a thousand eyes are peering over the writer's shoulder and scrutinizing every word; while letters are written when the mind is as it were in dressing-gown and slippers—free, natural, active, perfectly at home, and with all the fountains of fancy, wit, and sentiment in full play.

Value.—Epistolary literature is valuable, in the first place, to the student of history and biography. "Nothing," as Horace Walpole justly observes, "gives so just an idea of an age as genuine letters; nay, history waits for its last seal for them;" and Bacon says that "letters of affairs . . . are, of all others, the best instructions of history, and to a diligent reader the best histories themselves." To a biographer, this literature is almost indispensable; for in his letters we get nearer than anywhere else to a man's inner life—to his motives, principles, and intentions. A man will often confide to the ear of friendship things that policy or pride compels him to withhold from the public. Our best biographies, indeed, are those that are most autobiographical; those that are drawn most largely from the letters and conversations of their subjects.

It is valuable, secondly, to the general reader; and for three reasons:—

1. Because of the knowledge it imparts of the persons and events described.

2. Because of its moral influence. It brings us into intimate companionship with the great and good who have lived before us; laying bare, as it were, their inmost hearts for our inspection; showing us how they thought, felt, suffered, and triumphed; and leading us to emulate their virtues and avoid their errors.

3. Because it is a means of literary culture.* Besides the general literary influence that it has in common with other good reading, it has a direct and powerful effect in the formation of a good epistolary style. Whatever may be said to the contrary, every man's style is formed, to a great extent, by unconscious imitation. The more we study Irving, for example, the more our style will resemble his; and if we study various authors, our style, though none the less our own,

---

* *Literary culture* is a term often used without any definite idea of its meaning. Perhaps it may be defined, in a general way, as *mental improvement derived from the study of literature.* On analysis it will be found to contain three elements:—

1. Literary knowledge; that is, a knowledge of books and authors.

2. Literary taste; that is, the ability to perceive and properly estimate the beauties and blemishes of literary productions.

3. Literary expression; that is, the power of expressing thought with correctness and elegance.

will be a web woven of many threads—"a coat of many colors." It is evident, therefore, that the diligent perusal of the letters of the best writers is the best possible means of improving the style of our own letters.

Letter-Writers.—The greatest authors are not always the best letter-writers; and the greatest letter-writers are not always the best authors. Excellence in letter-writing requires peculiar qualifications. It requires education, talents, information, facility of expression, and above all, *tact.* As a general rule, women are better letter-writers than men; partly, perhaps, because as a class they have more leisure, but mainly because they have more tact than men, and at the same time more vivacity and fluency.

It is unfortunate that thousands of the most sprightly and entertaining correspondents are wholly unknown to fame. Their letters are read, admired, laughed or cried over, and then laid aside or consigned to the flames. It is only after a person has distinguished himself in something else, that the world bethinks itself of his letters; and it must be confessed that the letters of great men are often neither witty nor wise.

Bibliography of Letters.—To those who desire to acquaint themselves further with this delightful department of literature, we recommend the following authors as among those whose letters have excited the admiration of the world:—*

* There are many valuable collections of letters that are not here mentioned. We notice only some of the best of those which are of interest to the general reader.

JOHN ADAMS. Letters to his Wife.

MRS. ADAMS. The familiar letters of Mr. and Mrs. Adams have recently been published in one volume, edited by their grandson, Charles Francis Adams.

JOHN QUINCY ADAMS. See Diary and Correspondence.

THOMAS JEFFERSON. See Randall's and Parton's Life of Jefferson and especially Mrs. Randolph's "Domestic Life of Thomas Jefferson." The latter is an excellent book for young or old; not only on account of the exhibition it affords of the highest private virtues; but also on account of the wise precepts expressed in its many admirable letters. Better domestic letters than Jefferson's can nowhere be found.

HORACE WALPOLE. Letters, 9 vols. They are clever, spicy, gossipy. Walpole has been called "the prince of letter-writers." He lived in the reigns of George II. and George III. (1717 to 1797.)

WILLIAM COWPER, the Poet. See Life and Works, by Southey. Cowper's letters are what may be called "*talking* letters," easy, playful, unaffected. They have been called "the finest specimens of epistolary style in the language." (*Rev. Robert Hall.*)

THOMAS GRAY (author of the Elegy). His letters are among the finest models of epistolary excellence.

ALEXANDER POPE. His letters are clever and brilliant, but somewhat affected.

LADY MARY WORTLEY MONTAGU. Letters, edited by Mrs. Hale. She was contemporary with Walpole and Pope.

MADAME DE SEVIGNE. Letters, translated from the French. Nothing can exceed their grace and naturalness of style.

MADAME SWETCHINE. Life and Letters. Full of splendid thoughts and glowing with religious fervor and consecration

MADAME RECAMIER. See "Madame Recamier and her Friends."

CHARLES and MARY LAMB. See Poems, Letters, and Remains, by Hazlitt; also the Biographies by Procter (Barry Cornwall) and Talfourd. In quaint humor, ease, and sprightliness, Lamb's letters have never been surpassed.

LORD BYRON. See Life and Letters, by Moore.

THOMAS MOORE. See Life, by Lord Russell.

Mary Russell Mitford. See James T. Fields's "Yesterdays with Authors."

Washington Irving. See Life and Letters, by Pierre M. Irving His letters, like his other writings, are delightful. The work mentioned contains, in addition to the letters of Irving, many valuable letters from Moore, Scott, and other distinguished literary men.

Charles Dickens. His letters are eminently characteristic—easy, witty, brilliant, full of life and gayety. See his Life, by Forster, also "Yesterdays with Authors," and "Anecdote Biographies of Thackeray and Dickens," Bric-à-Brac Series.

William M. Thackeray. Fresh, breezy, bubbling over with fun, like their author. See the last two works referred to above.

Mozart, Mendelssohn, and Beethoven. Their letters are full of fine feeling, finely and naturally expressed. They may be obtained in English translations.

Rev. F. W. Robertson. See Life and Letters. His letters are excellent, both in a religious and literary sense.

Henry Crabb Robinson. Diary and Correspondence, 2 vols. Very valuable.

Susan Allibone. Diary and Letters, by Bishop Lee. Full of Christian fervor and womanly tenderness and affection.

Augustus, Julius, and Maria Hare. See Records of a Quiet Life. Full of refinement, grace, and culture, with glimpses into the upper circles of English thought and influence. Models of familiar style.

Mrs. Emily C. Judson (Fanny Forrester). Life and Letters. Very beautiful and interesting, and glowing with religious devotion.

Goethe. Correspondence with Schiller, Letters to a Leipsic Friend, Correspondence with a Child (Bettine Brentano).

Rev. Alfred Cookman. See Life. It contains many fine letters, full of piety and affection.

Collections of Letters.

Library of Standard Letters, compiled by Mrs. Hale. Many of these letters are by authors mentioned above.

Literature in Letters, an interesting and valuable collection, by J. P. Holcombe.

Half-Hours with the Best Letter-Writers, by Knight, 2 vols.

SECTION II.

Gleanings in the Field of Letters.

In our rambles in the field of letters we have picked up a handful of ripe ears, filled with golden grains of truth. These we present to our readers that they may know what a goodly land it is, and be induced to go and gather for themselves—not a few ears only, but whole sheaves of this rich fruitage of wisdom.

1. Burns's Idea of a Good Wife—his Own.

The most placid good nature and sweetness of disposition; a warm heart gratefully devoted with all its powers to love me; vigorous health, and sprightly cheerfulness, set off to the best advantage by a more than commonly handsome figure; these, I think, in a woman, may make a good wife, though she should never have read a page but the Scriptures of the Old and New Testaments, nor have danced in a brighter assembly than a penny-pay wedding.—*Robert Burns to Mrs. Dunlop.*

2. Let us Love one Another.

Let me conclude by saying to you, what I have had too frequent occasions to say to my other remaining friends,—the fewer we become, the more let us love one another.—*Benj. Franklin to Mrs. Hewson.*

3. The Lot of every Public Man.

I have long been accustomed to receive more blame, as well as more praise, than I deserved. 'Tis the lot of every public man, and I have one account to balance the other.—*Franklin.*

4. Religious Comfort.

O my good friend! there is no other stable foundation for solid comfort but the Christian religion; not barely acknowledged as a truth from the conviction of external evidence (strong and important as it is), but from embracing it as a principle of hope and joy and peace, and from feeling its suitableness to the wants and necessities of our nature, as well as its power to alleviate and even sanctify our sorrows.—*Hannah More to Sir W. W. Pepys.*

5. Wordsworth's Sister.

Wordsworth and his exquisite sister are with me. She is a woman indeed! in mind, I mean, and heart; for her person is such, that if you expected to see a pretty woman, you would think her rather ordinary; if you expected to see an ordinary woman, you would think her rather pretty; but her manners are simple, ardent, impressive. In every motion her innocent soul shines out so brightly, that who saw would say,—

"Guilt is a thing impossible in her."

Her information various. Her eye watchful in minutest observation of nature; and her taste a perfect electrometer.—*S. T. Coleridge to Joseph Cottle.*

6. Leniency to the Living.

If we were only half as lenient to the living as we are to the dead, how much happiness might we render them, and from how much vain and bitter remorse might we be spared, when the grave, the all-atoning grave, has closed over them!—*Lady Blessington to Walter Savage Landor.*

7. Morning.

I know the morning; I am acquainted with it and love it, fresh and sweet as it is; a daily new creation, breaking forth and calling all that have life and breath and being to new adoration, new enjoyments, and new gratitude.—*Daniel Webster to Mrs. Page.*

8. Comfort derived from Literature.

Many, many a dreary, weary hour have I got over, many a gloomy misgiving postponed, many a mental or bodily annoyance forgotten, by help of the tragedies and comedies of our dramatists and novelists! Many a trouble has been soothed by the still small voice of the moral philosopher,—many a dragon-like care charmed to sleep by the sweet song of the poet; for all which I cry incessantly, not aloud, but in my heart, Thanks and honor to the glorious masters of the pen, and the great inventors of the press!—*Thos. Hood.*

9. "The Feast of Reason."

But "the feast of reason and the flow of soul" were still mine. Denied beef [by the doctor], I had *Bul*wer and *Cow*per; forbidden mutton, there was *Lamb;* and in lieu of pork, the great *Bacon* or *Hogg.* Then as to beverage, it was hard doubtless for a Christian to set his face like a Turk against the juice of the grape; but eschewing wine, I had still my *Butler*, and in the absence of liquor, all the *choice spirits* from Tom Browne to Tom Moore.—*Hood.*

10. Pope's Birthday.

Every year carries away something dear with it, till we outlive all tendernesses, and become wretched individuals again, as we begun. Adieu! This is my birthday, and this is my reflection upon it:—

> With added days, if life give nothing new,
> But like a sieve, let every pleasure through;
> Some joy still lost, as each vain year runs o'er,
> And all we gain, some sad reflection more!
> Is this a birthday?—'T is, alas! too clear,
> 'T is but the funeral of the former year.

—*Alexander Pope to Mr. Gay, on his recovery and the death of Congreve.*

11. An Editor's Responsibilities.

The conductor of a newspaper should, methinks, consider himself as, in some degree, the guardian of his country's reputation, and refuse to insert such writings as may hurt it. If people will print their abuses of one another, let them do it in little pamphlets, and distribute them where they think proper. It is absurd to trouble all the world with them; and unjust to subscribers in distant places, to stuff their paper with matters so unprofitable and disagreeable.—*Benj. Franklin to Francis Hopkinson.*

12. Making the Best of our Friends.

If the lady has anything difficult in her disposition, avoid what is rough. and attach her good qualities to yours. Consider what are otherwise as a bad stop in your harpsichord, and do not touch it, but make yourself happy with the good ones. Every human being, my dear, must be thus viewed, according to what he is good for; for none of us, no, not one, is perfect; and were we to love none who had imperfections, this world would be a desert for our love. All we can do is to make the best of our friends, love and cherish what is good in them, and keep out of the way of what is bad; but no more think of rejecting them for it, than of throwing away a piece of music for a flat passage or two.—*Thomas Jefferson to his Daughter.*

13. Woman's Position.

A woman's position is one of subjection, as mythically described as a curse in the Book of Genesis. Well, but I ween that all curses are blessings in disguise. Labor among thorns and thistles,—man's best health. Woman's subjection? What say you to His [Christ's]? "Obedient," a "servant"; *wherefore* God also hath highly exalted Him. Methinks a thoughtful, high-souled woman would scarcely feel degraded by a lot which assimilates her to the divinest Man. "He came not to be ministered unto, but to minister." * * * Trust me, a noble woman laying on herself the duties of her sex, while fit for higher things,—the world has nothing to show more like the Son of Man than that. * * * "There is nothing in the drudgery of domestic duties to soften,"—*you quote* that. No, but a great deal to strengthen with the sense of duty done, self-control and power. Besides, you cannot calculate how much corroding dust is *kept off*,—how much of disconsolate, dull despondency is hindered. Daily use is not the jeweller's mercurial polish; but it will keep your little silver pencil from tarnishing.—*Rev. F. W. Robertson to a Lady.*

14. The End of the World.

As to preparations for that event [the end of the world], the best way is for you always to be prepared for it. The only way to be so is, never to say or do a bad thing. If you are about to say anything amiss, or to do anything wrong, consider beforehand; you will feel something within you which will tell you it is wrong, and ought not to be said or done. This is your conscience; and be sure and obey it. Our Maker has given us all this faithful internal monitor, and if you always obey it you will always be prepared for the end of the world; or for a much more certain event, which is death. This must happen to all; it puts an end to the world as to us; and the way to be ready for it is never to do a wrong act.—*Thomas Jefferson to his daughter Martha.*

15. Never Contradict.

It was one of the rules which, above all others, made Doctor Franklin the most amiable of men in society, never to contradict any body. If he was urged to announce an opinion, he did it rather by asking questions, as if for information, or by suggesting doubts. When I hear another express an opinion which is not mine, I say to myself, He has a right to his opinion, as I to mine; why should I question it? His error does me no injury, and shall I become a Don Quixote, to bring all men by force to one opinion? If a fact be misstated, it is probable he is gratified by a belief of it, and I have no right to deprive him of the gratification. If he wants information, he will ask it, and then I will give it in measured terms; but if he still believes his own story, and shows a desire to dispute the fact with me, I hear him, and say nothing. It is his affair, not mine, if he prefers error.—*Thomas Jefferson.*

16. The Folly of War.

All wars are follies, very expensive and very mischievous ones: when will mankind become convinced of this, and agree to settle their difficulties by arbitration? Were they to do it, even by the cast of a die, it would be better than by fighting and destroying one another.—*Benj. Franklin.*

17. The Greatest of all Blessings.

I, too, your God-father, have known what the enjoyments and advantages of this life are, and what the more refined pleasures which learning and intellectual power can bestow; and with all the experience which more than three-score years can give, I now, on the eve of my departure, declare to you (and earnestly pray that you may hereafter live and act on the conviction), that health is a great blessing,—competence obtained by honorable industry is a great blessing,—and a great blessing it is to have kind, faithful, honest relatives; but that the greatest of all blessings, as it is the most ennobling of all privileges, is, to be indeed a Christian.—*S. T. Coleridge to a God-child.*

18. Indolence.

Of all the cankers of human happiness none corrodes with so silent, yet so baneful an influence as indolence.—*Thomas Jefferson.*

19. Angel's Work.

She told me the delight, the tears of gratitude, which she had witnessed in a poor girl to whom, in passing, I gave a kind look on going out of church on Sunday. What a lesson! How cheaply happiness can be given! What opportunities we miss of doing angel's work! I remember doing it, full of sad feelings, passing on and thinking no more about it; and it gave an hour's sunshine to a human life, and lightened the load of life to a human heart.—*Rev. F. W. Robertson.*

20. The Secret of Happiness.

A mind always employed is always happy. This is the true secret, the grand recipe, for felicity. The idle are the only wretched.—*Thomas Jefferson to his Daughter.*

21. Inarticulate Sorrows.

The misfortunes of genius, its false direction, its misery, I suppose rise partly from the fact of the life of genius being that which is chiefly given to the world. Many a soldier died as bravely and with as much suffering as Sir John Moore at Corunna; but every soldier had not a Wolfe to write his death-song. Many an innocent victim perished,—yes, by hundreds of thousands,—on the scaffolds of France, and in the dungeons of the robber barons, but they died silently. A few aristocrats whose shriek was loud have filled the world with pity at the tale of their suffering. Many a mediocre boy have I seen spoilt at school,—many a commonplace destiny has been marred in life. only these things are not matters of history. Peasants grow savage with domestic troubles, and washerwomen pine under brutal treatment; but the former are locked up for burying their misery in drunkenness,—the latter die of a broken-heart, with plenty of unwritten poetry lost among the soap-suds. I fancy the *inarticulate* sorrows are far more pitiable than those of an Alfieri, who has a tongue to utter them. Carlyle in this respect seems to me to hold a tone utterly diverse from that of the Gospel. The worship of the hero, that is his religion: condescension to the small and unknown, that was His.—*Rev. F. W. Robertson.*

22. To be a Poet is to be a Man.

I have a thorough aversion to his [Byron's] character, and a very moderate admiration of his genius; he is great in so little a way. To be a poet is to be a man; not a petty portion of occasional low passion worked up into a permanent form of humanity.—*Charles Lamb to Joseph Cottle.*

23. Patient Endurance.

When we see ourselves in a situation which must be endured and gone through, it is best to make up our minds to it, meet it with firmness, and accommodate everything to it in the best way practicable. This lessens the evil; while fretting and fuming only serves to increase our own torments.—*Thos. Jefferson.*

24. Grief and Gratitude over the Dead.

When I heard of his death, there mingled with my grief a feeling of gratitude that I had been preserved from saying one word, through partisan zeal or difference of opinion, which could add bitterness to his life; that I had none of the late remorse over the dead, for unkindness to the living, which is one of the saddest burdens of humanity. No words of praise are needed. They would be lost in the general eulogy. With common consent he will take his place in the Valhalla of American worthies, as one of the greatest and best.—*John G. Whittier to Dr. Chapin on the death of Horace Greeley.*

25. The Virtues of Oratory.*

The virtues of oratory are these,—truth, conciseness, perspicuity, and suitableness to the occasion. The contraries to these are its vices,—falsehood, prolixity, obscurity, and unseasonableness. For what will it avail us to be true, if we are not concise, and concise, if not clear, and clear, if not seasonable? When all these virtues meet in a composition, it is then that it is effective, and impressive, and living. It leads the hearers by the force of truth, exercises their thoughts by its brevity, captivates by its perspicuity, and is consummated by its suitableness to the occasion.—*Isidore of Pelusium, of the fourth Century, to Nilus.*

---

* "History of Letter-Writing, from the Earliest Period to the Fifth Century." By William Roberts, Esq., Barrister at Law. London: William Pickering, 1843. It contains, besides much valuable historical matter, extracts from the letters of Pythagoras, Cicero, Seneca, Pliny, and many other distinguished men of antiquity.

NOTES AND CARDS.

OUTLINE.

- I. NOTES.
  1. Of Ceremony and Compliment.
  2. Miscellaneous.
- II. CARDS.
  1. Ceremonial.
  2. Visiting.
  3. Professional and Official.
  4. Business.

REMARK.—The subject of letter-writing includes a knowledge, not only of the structure and composition of letters proper, but also of the forms and uses of Notes and Cards. These will be discussed in the present division of our work; and each part of the above title will form the subject of a distinct chapter. It will be necessary, however, to anticipate some of the uses of cards in the chapter on notes the former being often enclosed in the latter.

CHAPTER I.

NOTES.

- I. INTRODUCTION.
- II. NOTES OF CEREMONY AND COMPLIMENT.
- III. MISCELLANEOUS NOTES.
- IV. SUPERSCRIPTION AND DELIVERY.

INTRODUCTION.

Definition.—Any short letter is in one sense a note, but by the term *note*, as here used we mean those brief messages of transient and local interest by which persons in the same neighborhood, town, or city, make known to each other their wishes, compliments, or commands.

Peculiarities.—Notes (or Billets) differ from ordinary letters in the following particulars: 1. They are more formal; 2. They are written wholly or partly in the third person; 3. The date is generally at the bottom; 4. They are without signature.

These are merely general characteristics, which admit of modifications and exceptions. The latter will be pointed out in connection with the models which illustrate them.

When Used.—Notes or letters in the third person are appropriately used in the following cases:—

1. *Between equals:* (1) In all matters of ceremony, such as weddings, dinners, etc.; (2) In any brief communications between persons but slightly acquainted.

2. *Between unequals:* By a superior in addressing an inferior, and *vice versa*, in any brief and formal message.

Difficulty.—It is a difficult thing to write a note in the third person, if it extends beyond a sentence or two.

Great care must be taken not to change from the third person to the first or second. This is a mistake frequently made by inexperienced persons. The following is an example:—

Miss Smith is much obliged to Mr. Hawkins for his beautiful Christmas present. I should have thanked you sooner, but have been absent from home.

Materials.—*Quality.*—The paper and envelopes used for notes should be plain, and of the heaviest and finest quality.

Color.—For weddings only pure white is allowable; for other occasions very delicate tints may be used, but white is always in good taste.

Size—No definite size nor shape can be given, as styles are constantly varying. The sizes most in use at present are the long sheet, folding once into square envelopes or twice into oblong envelopes; and the square sheet, folding once into a very long envelope: but these styles may in a short time give place to some other.

Monogram, etc.—Both paper and envelopes may have embossed or printed on them the monogram, initial, crest, or coat-of-arms of the writer. Wedding notes formerly bore a monogram composed of the combined initials of the bride and the bridegroom; but they are now entirely plain.

Outside Envelopes.—Invitations to weddings, parties, etc., are enclosed in two envelopes; first a fine one, to match the note, then a coarser one, to protect the other. In such cases the full address is written on the outer envelope, and the name alone on the inner one. Answers to invitations do not require outside envelopes; nor do any private or personal notes, whether formal or informal.

Style.—The most fashionable notes, like the most fashionable people, are characterized by an *elegant simplicity.* The language is concise but courteous, the writing (or engraving) plain but beautiful. In notes and letters, all flourishes, whether of tongue or pen, are out of place. Here, as elsewhere, the most refined taste expresses itself in richness of material, beauty of form, harmony of parts, and perfect adaptation to circumstances, rather than in excessive ornament and ostentatious display. Indeed, it will always be found, in literature, in art, in character, and everywhere, that the severest simplicity is consistent with the truest refinement and the highest elegance.

French Phrases.—The following French words and phrases or their initials are sometimes used on notes and cards; but English phrases are usually to be preferred:—

R S. V. P. = *Repondez s'il vous plait,* answer if you please.
P. P. C. = *Pour prendre congé,* to take leave.
Costume de rigueur, full dress, in character.
Fête Champêtre, a rural entertainment.
Bal masque, masquerade ball.
En ville = *E. V.,* in the town or city.
Soirée dansante, dancing party.

Kinds.—For convenience of discussion we divide notes into two general classes: I. NOTES OF CEREMONY AND COMPLIMENT; II. MISCELLANEOUS NOTES.

NOTES OF CEREMONY AND COMPLIMENT.

OUTLINE.

- I. Invitations.
  - Weddings
    - To Ceremony.
      - At home.
      - At church.
    - To Reception.
  - Announcements of Marriage.
  - Anniversary Weddings.
  - Dinners.
  - Social Parties.
  - Balls.
  - College Anniversaries.
  - Various Occasions.
- II. Acceptances and Regrets.

I. Invitations.

Weddings.—Wedding invitations are issued ten days or more before the ceremony, by the parents or nearest friends of the bride. They may be written or printed on note paper or on cards; but the note form is generally preferred for all ceremonious invitations.

Notes and cards may be printed either from engraved plates or from type. Those printed from plates are greatly superior in style and finish to the others, and are almost exclusively used by fashionable people.

Answers.—If an answer is expected, the words, "The favor of an answer is requested," or the letters "R. S. V. P.," are written or printed at the bottom. (See "Acceptances and Regrets," page 152.)

We give below a few models of wedding notes, the first and third being complete, the others requiring one or more cards:—

Model 1.—*Ceremony and Reception.*

[This model is printed in script type, in order to exhibit the style of the best engraved billets. To economize space we print some of the other models in ordinary type.

This displayed style should not be attempted in writing, except by a skilful *penman*. For ordinary writers the style of Model 4 is best.]

This form is not so much used as those with cards.

Mr. & Mrs. John Wilson
request your presence*
at the marriage of their daughter
Elizabeth,
to
Dr. W. H. Murray,
on Wednesday Morning, January sixth,
at ten o'clock.
St. Bartholomew's Church.
Reception
from half-past ten till one,
at 314 Irving Place.

* The words "the pleasure of your *company*" seem to imply social intercourse; it is better, therefore, when persons are invited to witness a ceremony, simply, at church or elsewhere, to use the words, "your *presence*," or their equivalent. In *written* notes the *name* or *names* should be used instead of "your."

Model 2.—*Ceremony.*

Mrs. Mary H. Curran

requests the pleasure of your company at the marriage ceremony of her daughter,

Alice C. Cass,

to

Thomas W. Whitson,

on Tuesday afternoon, May twenty-fifth, 1875, at four o'clock.

Waverley Terrace. *Baltimore.*

Enclosing a reception card as follows:—

> *Reception*
>
> *On Monday, May thirty-first,*
>
> *day and evening.*

Or, "Mr. and Mrs. Thomas W. Whitson at home" at a certain time and place

Model 3.—*Ceremony and Reception.*

Ceremony,

First Congregational Church, New Gloucester, Maine, on Monday, June fourteenth, at ten o'clock.

At Home

Tuesdays and Fridays in June,
at the residence of Dr. Charles C. Porter,
415 Church Street.

FRANK R. BOYLE. ANNA H. MOORE.

Model 4.—*Reception* (with Personal Cards).

[This form is printed in script as a model for written notes. It will be observed that the first line is *indented*; that is, it begins a little further to the right than the other lines, being, in fact, the beginning of a paragraph. This indentation should be from one-half to three-fourths of an inch. If either the residence or the date is given, it should begin directly under the first letter of the note; if both are given, they should be written as in this model. If the sheet is to be folded twice, the note should be written in the middle of the page; if but once, the note, if short, should be written on the lower half of the page, to avoid creasing.

Printed invitations are partly in the second person (your), so that the same form may answer for all; or else a blank is left for the name, to be filled up with the pen. *Written* notes should be wholly in the third person, as below:—]

Mr. & Mrs. James Perkins, Jr., request the pleasure of Mr. John Hall's company at the wedding reception of their daughter, on Thursday evening, December tenth, from nine till twelve o'clock.

60 Irving Avenue,

Monday, Nov. 30th.

Besides the cards of the bride and groom, a third card is sent to those who are desired to be present at the ceremony, containing the words, "Ceremony at —— o'clock." Those who do not receive this card, of course attend the reception only.

Model 5.—*Ceremony.*

Mr. and Mrs. John B. Allen request the pleasure of your company at the marriage of their daughter, on Tuesday morning June fifteenth, at eleven o'clock.

17 Nahant Street.

Enclosing personal and reception cards; or reception card alone with the names at the bottom as in Model 3.

Miscellaneous Models.

[Of course these are models in language only, not in size or shape.]

St. Andrew's Church,
(8th above Spruce),
Tuesday, January 30, at twelve o'clock.
JAMES MORTON, MARY SUMNER.
At home after February fifth.
314 *S. Third St., Philadelphia.*
[No cards required.]

Bedding M. E. Church,
Thursday afternoon, May 20, 1875,
at two o'clock.
Mount Street, Jersey City.
[Pers. and Recep. cards enclosed.]

The Marriage of
JANE FAIRBANKS to H. W. REYNOLDS
will be solemnized at Grace Church,
Orange, New Jersey,
on Thursday afternoon, January eighth,
at five o'clock.
[Reception card enclosed.]

The Marriage Ceremony
will be solemnized at St. Paul's Church,
Milwaukee,
On Monday evening, Sept. first, 1873.
Your presence is requested.
[Reception card enclosed.]

Charles and Agnes Evans
reques the pleasure of your company at the marriage ceremony of their daughter ANNA *to* J. HOWARD HOOPES, *Fifth-day afternoon, Fifth month, fifteenth,* 1874, *at four o'clock.*
New Garden, Pa.

Her Majesty the Queen
desires the honor of your presence at the marriage of Her Royal Highness
THE PRINCESS LOUISE
to
THE MARQUIS OF LORNE,
Windsor Castle, Tuesday, March 21st,
at eight o'clock.

Announcements.—Sometimes notes are issued after the wedding, announcing the marriage and enclosing a reception card to those who are desired to call. The following form may be used:—

Mr. William B. Davidson,
Miss Laura Campbell,
Married
Wednesday, October twenty-first, 1874.

The above is written or engraved on a note sheet, in which is enclosed a reception card, in the following form:—

Mr. & Mrs. William B. Davidson
At Home
November first, day and evening,
536 N. Broad Street.

ANOTHER METHOD.—Or, the announcement may be made by sending two cards: a large one, containing the combined names, with residence and time of reception; and a smaller one, containing the bride's maiden name.

Anniversary Weddings.—Sometimes people celebrate various anniversaries of their marriage; and it is a practice much to be commended, if these celebrations are made occasions of sincere congratulations and happy reminiscences, not of cold formality and foolish ostentation. The first anniversary is called the *Paper Wedding;* the fifth, the *Wooden Wedding;* the tenth, the *Tin Wedding;* the fifteenth, the *Crystal* (glass) *Wedding;* the twenty-fifth, the *Silver Wedding;* the fiftieth, the *Golden Wedding;* and the seventy-fifth, the *Diamond Wedding.* We give below two forms of invitation.

The following have been recently added to the above list:. the twentieth anniversary, known as the *Floral Wedding;* the thirtieth, the *Pearl Wedding;* the thirty-fifth, the *China Wedding;* the fortieth, the *Coral Wedding;* the forty-fifth, the *Bronze Wedding.*

Model 1.—*Wooden Wedding.*

Mr. and Mrs. L. F. Moore

Request the pleasure of your company

on Tuesday Evening,

July 20th,

At eight o'clock.

14 Hamilton Terrace, Philadelphia.

This invitation is printed on a square note sheet folded once, and enclosing a *wooden card* inscribed as follows:—

JULY 20, 1870.

L. Fayette Moore. Lucile S. Barton

JULY 20, 1875.

Model 2.—*Golden Wedding.*

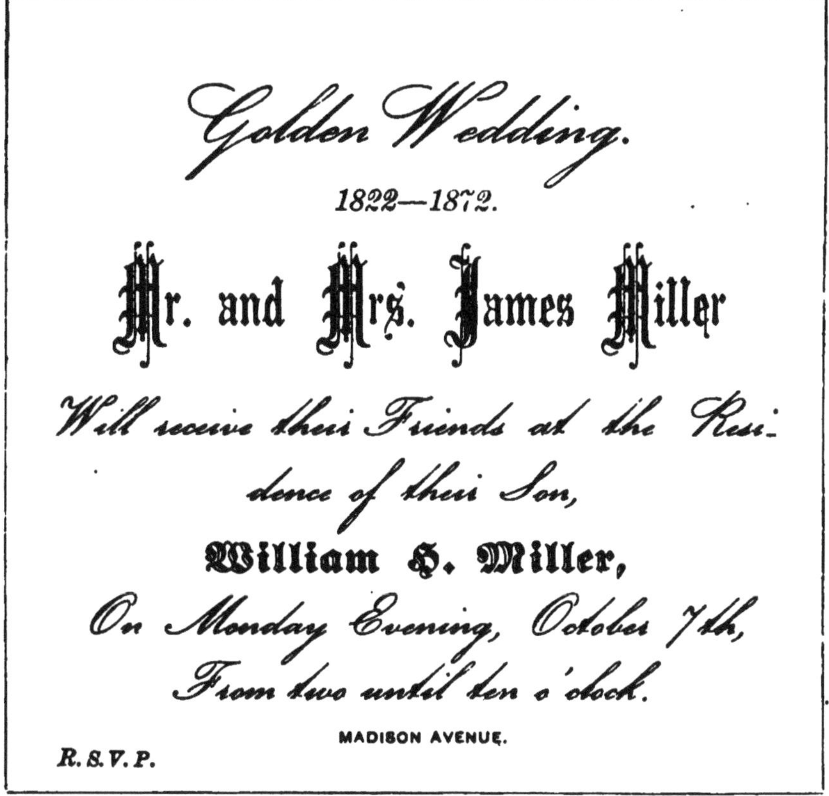
Golden Wedding.

1822—1872.

Mr. and Mrs. James Miller

Will receive their Friends at the Residence of their Son,

William H. Miller,

On Monday Evening, October 7th,

From two until ten o'clock.

MADISON AVENUE.

R. S. V. P.

Sometimes a card is enclosed containing the words, "It is preferred that no wedding gifts be offered."

Dinners.—A well-appointed dinner is one of the most delightful occasions of social life. The company is generally more select than at an ordinary party, and greater care and precision are observed in regard to all the arrangements. To avoid mistakes, the invitations should be very precise as to date and hour, and each should contain the name of the person for whom it is intended. If the party is to be small, the notes may be written; if large, printed forms may be used, with blank spaces for name, date, and hour.

ANSWERS.—A dinner invitation must always be answered, whether an answer is requested or not (see page 152).

Model 1.—*Written Invitation to Dinner.*

Mr. James M. Hawthorne requests the pleasure of Mr. Howard Watson's company at dinner, on Thursday evening, March 28th, at eight o'clock.

300 Madison Avenue.

Model 2.

Mr. and Mrs. James Russell

request the pleasure of

Dr. and Mrs. Baldwin's company at dinner, on Thursday

February 24th, at six o'clock.

1024 Walnut Street.

Parties.—The simplest forms for invitations to parties are in the best taste. The following models will suffice:—

Model 1.—*Party Invitation.*

Senator and Mrs. Sprague request the pleasure of ------ company, on Thursday evening, December seventh, from eight to twelve o'clock.*

601 E Street, Washington. *R. S. V. P.*

Model 2.—*Party Invitation.*

Mr. and Mrs. R. F. Lord request the pleasure of ------ company, on Monday evening, Nov. 22d, at eight o'clock.

Chestnut Grove. *Soirée Dansante.*

Carriages enter the west gate. *Answer to be sent to 920 Walnut St.*

Model 3.—*To Meet Visiting Friends.*

Mr. and Mrs. C. W. George request the pleasure of ------ company, on Friday evening, November 19th, from eight to eleven o'clock, to meet General and Mrs. Sherman.

Broad and Walnut Sts., Philadelphia.

Model 4.—*Presidential Reception.*

The President of the United States requests the company of ---------------------------------- at the Reception in honor of His Majesty the King of the Hawaiian Islands, on Monday evening, December 14th, at nine o'clock.

Executive Mansion.

An invitation from the President is to be regarded as a command, and must not be declined except for imperative reasons.

Model 5.—*Birthday Celebration.*

Mr. and Mrs. H. A. Matthews request the honor of ------ company to celebrate their son's majority, on Wednesday evening, January fifth, 1876.

1402 Arch St. *R. S. V. P.*

* Use the *name of the person* in written notes, "your" in printed ones.

CHILDREN'S PARTIES.—Invitations to children's parties are written or printed on smaller sheets than those used for other invitations. The following forms are appropriate, to be varied, of course, to suit circumstances:—

Model 1.

Master Harry Washington requests the pleasure of ----- company on St. Valentine's Day, from ten until four o'clock.

Woodland Terrace, February 4.

Model 2.

Miss Mary Lee requests the pleasure of ----- company on Friday evening, December 10th, from five to ten o'clock.

1624 North Broad Street.

INFORMAL RECEPTIONS.—Informal afternoon or evening entertainments or receptions are now becoming popular. The invitations to them are issued on cards instead of notes, and they will be more appropriately spoken of in the second chapter (see page 164).

Balls.—By balls we do not mean private parties at which there is dancing, but those of a more public nature, generally held under the auspices of some club or society, and directed by managers appointed for the purpose.

Model 1.—*Fête Champêtre.*

The honor of ---------------------------------- company is requested at Norwood on Tuesday, June 4th, at one o'clock.

[Signed by the Committee of Arrangements.]

R. S. V. P.

If it rain, the Fête will be postponed until Thursday.

Model 2.—(*Note or Card.*)

The pleasure of

your company is requested at a

Hop

on Wednesday evening, Feb. 17, 1865, at nine o'clock.

Continental Hotel.

College and Society Anniversaries.—These invitations are of a great variety of forms, and engravers almost exhaust their invention in making for them new and beautiful designs; but in these as in other invitations, an elegant simplicity commends itself to a refined taste. They are printed on a sheet of heavy, fine note-paper, bearing at the top the monogram of the college, often interwoven with the year of the class (for example, '76). In this is generally enclosed a card bearing the names of the orators, or of the class, and sometimes also the officers of the society or a programme of the exercises. These details may, however, be printed on one of the inside pages.

The person who sends the invitation generally encloses his visiting card, to convey his personal compliments.

We give below a few forms, without attempting, however, to imitate the elaborate designs with which some of them are ornamented:—

Model 1.—*Junior Exhibition, Rutgers College.*

[Printed on a square sheet in beautiful engraved script, as below, with Monogram of the college initials and year of class.]

[Mon.]

The honor of your presence is requested at the Junior Exhibition to be held at the Opera House, New Brunswick, N. J., on Thursday Evening, June 22d, 1875, at eight o'clock.

On an enclosed card half the size of the sheet, are printed the names of the orators.

Model 2.—*Commencement.*

[Monogram: S. C., '76; with motto, *Vis unita fortior.*]

Swarthmore College.

Junior Day

CLASS '76

Fifth Month Eighth, 1875.

EXERCISES BEGIN

Eleven o'clock, A. M.

Model 3.—*Commencement.*

[Monogram, S. N. S.]

State Normal School, Rockport, N. Y.

Compliments of

THE CLASS OF '75.

Commencement Exercises in the Normal Chapel,

Tuesday, July 6th, at ten o'clock, A. M.

Model 4.—*Commencement.*

The Class of '74 of the University of Pennsylvania request the honor of your presence at

HORTICULTURAL HALL,

Thursday, June 11th, at half-past three o'clock, P. M.

Executive Committee.

[Signed by the members of the committee.]

Miscellaneous.—We present below a few forms not embraced in the foregoing classes. The first three forms are *Formal Personal Notes;* that is, private notes written in the third person. The fourth is a funeral invitation.

EXCURSION.

Mr. Summers would be pleased to have your company on Thursday, Sept. 15th, to visit the Park.

Carriages will be in waiting at the Continental Hotel at four o'clock P.M.

Continental Hotel. R. S. V. P.

Mr. Chickering solicits the honor of attending Miss Adams to the opera on Thursday evening next.

Tuesday, Nov. 3.

The bearer will wait for the answer.

Will Miss White do Mr. Neal the honor to accompany him in a drive to Druid Hill Park this afternoon? If so, Miss White will please state what hour will be most convenient.

Barnum's Hotel,
Wednesday morning, May 4.

Yourself and family are respectfully invited to attend the funeral of

MISS SARAH PRIDEAUX,

*from the residence of the Rev. J. L. Vallandigham, on Saturday, the 29th inst., to leave the house at two o'clock P. M., and proceed to White Creek Church.**

Newark, Dec. 27th.

FAMILIAR NOTES.—If the parties are very intimate friends, the formal and ceremonious style may be dropped, and that of a familiar letter adopted, as in the following:—

Saturday Morning, May 10th.

Dear Fanny,

We are going to Irving's Cliff this afternoon for wild flowers. Will you oblige us by making one of our little party? If so, we will call for you at two o'clock. Do go.

Yours affectionately,
Charlotte.

Please answer by bearer.

My dear Sir,

If you can come next Sunday we shall be equally glad to see you, but do not trust to any of Martin's appointments in future. Leg of lamb as before, at half-past four, and the heart of Lamb for ever.

Yours truly,
C. Lamb.

30th March, 1821.

* In some places, where friends cannot be notified through the daily papers, invitations to funerals are issued. They are written or printed on note paper edged with black, and are enclosed in corresponding envelopes. Plain white is used by Friends, and sometimes by others.

Dear Allsop,
We are going to Dalston on Wednesday. Will you come see the last of us to-morrow night—you and Mrs. Allsop?
Yours truly,
C. Lamb.
Monday Evening.

Dear Sir,
We expect Wordsworth to-morrow evening. Will you look in?
Charles Lamb.
Russell House,
Thursday.

II. Acceptances and Regrets.

Definitions.—Answers to invitations are of two kinds,—Acceptances and Regrets. An acceptance is an affirmative answer; a regret is a non-acceptance.

When Necessary.—*Wedding invitations* and receptions do not require an acceptance, unless they contain the letters "R. S. V. P." or their equivalent. Indeed, the same may be said of invitations to parties, balls, and other social entertainments, except dinners. A failure to answer is understood as a tacit acceptance. A regret must invariably be sent, in case of inability to attend.

Dinners.—It is highly important that the entertainer should know exactly for how many and whom to provide. It may therefore be stated as a rule, that an invitation to dinner should be promptly accepted or declined. After having accepted such an invitation, a person should not absent himself except for the strongest reasons; and if there should be such reasons, they should by all means be stated in a regret.

"At Home" Invitations.—A distinction exists between a formal invitation in such words as "You are requested," etc., and an "At Home" reception card. The former is a positive request, but in the latter no invitation is extended; the recipient is merely notified that should he be pleased to call he will be welcome. Hence such a card does not require any answer.

How soon should an Answer be sent?—As stated above, a dinner invitation should be answered immediately. Invitations to weddings, receptions, balls, etc., should be answered, if an answer is required, not later than the third day. Should anything occur at the last moment to prevent attendance, a regret should be sent the day after the party.

To whom Addressed.—An answer should in general be addressed to the person named within it; but the answer to a joint note from a husband and wife (*Mr. and Mrs. John White*, for example), while it should contain within it a recognition of both, should be addressed, on the envelope, to the wife alone (*Mrs. John White*).

Should be Written.—Blank acceptances and regrets are sometimes used, but they are not so elegant nor respectful as written answers. No one has occasion to write many such notes; hence there can be no good reason for resorting to the use of blanks.

Style.—Answers must correspond somewhat, in style, to the invitations, each being, of course, varied to suit the circumstances of the case.

Reason of Non-attendance.—In a regret, it is more courteous and friendly to state a reason for non-attendance than to decline without an assigned cause; and if a cause is assigned, it is better, socially and morally considered, to state a real and specific reason, rather than a feigned and general one.

Forms.—The forms given below are in answer to forms of invitation given on preceding pages. But few forms are needed:—

Model 1.—*Acceptance of a Dinner Invitation.*

(See Invitation on page 146.)

Mr. Howard Watson has much pleasure in accepting Mr. Hawthorne's kind invitation for Thursday evening, March 28th.

Fifth Avenue Hotel,

Tuesday, March 19th.

Model 2.—*Regret (Answer to same, Reason Stated).*

Mr. Watson regrets that, owing to the dangerous illness of a dear friend, he is unable to accept Mr. Hawthorne's kind invitation for Thursday evening, the 28th instant.

Fifth Avenue Hotel,

Tuesday, March 19th.

Model 3.—*Regret (Reason not Stated).*

Mr. Watson regrets that he cannot accept Mr. Hawthorne's polite invitation for Thursday evening, March 28th.

Tuesday, March 19th.

Model 4.—*Regret (see Invitation on page 147)*

Mr. and Mrs. Sherwin regret that on account of the sudden illness of one of their children, they are compelled to revoke their acceptance of Senator and Mrs. Sprague's kind invitation for to-morrow evening.

1323 H St., Wednesday, Dec. 6.

Model 5.—*Acceptance (see page 147).*

Mrs. Woodward accepts the kind invitation of Mr. and Mrs. Matthews for Wednesday evening, Jan. 5th, and is happy to have the opportunity to congratulate them on the arrival of their son's twenty-first birth-day.

Tuesday, December 28th.

Model 6.—*Regret (see page 151).*

Miss Adams declines Mr. Chickering's kind invitation with thanks. She is already engaged for to-morrow evening.

Wednesday morning, Nov. 4th.

Model 7.—*Acceptance* (*Familiar Style, page 151*).

My dear Charlotte,

I shall be delighted to go with you this afternoon. It is just such an opportunity as I have been wishing for.

Fanny.

MISCELLANEOUS NOTES.

As elsewhere remarked (p. 136), notes or letters in the third person are appropriately used, not only in matters of ceremony, as exemplified on the preceding pages, but also in any brief and formal communication—(1) between persons, whether equal or unequal, who are but slightly, if at all, acquainted, and (2) between persons of unequal social or official position. These latter uses we proceed to illustrate.

Date.—It is usual, in this country, to date third-person letters or notes at the bottom; but they are sometimes dated, especially in England, at the top, as in the first and second examples given below.

Model 1.

Admiral the Earl of Hardwick to Admiral Farragut.

13th July, Sidney Lodge.

Admiral the Earl of Hardwick presents his compliments to Admiral Farragut, and begs to say that he is now resident at the above address. He is lame, and has difficulty in boarding ship, or he would wait in person on Admiral Farragut. The Earl of Hardwick hopes that he may be able in some way to gain Admiral Farragut's friendship.

Admiral Farragut, U. S. Navy.

Model 2.

Lord Rosse (owner of the great Rosse telescope) to Madame ——, thanking her for a book.

The Castle, Parsonstown, December 22, 1856.

Lord Rosse presents his compliments to Madame ——, and is much obliged for the copy of her book, which she has been so good as to send him. He has had the book but a short time in his possession, and of late he has been much engaged, so that he has been unable to read it regularly through; but he has examined it with sufficient care to be enabled to say, that it is particularly well calculated for the object she has in view. The leading facts of astronomy, up to the present time, are accurately and clearly stated; and in selection of materials, in arrangement, and in style, the work appears to him to be the best elementary work he has seen.

Model 3.

Mr. Rogers regrets that he was absent when Mr. Moore called, and hopes that Mr. Moore will mention a time when it will be convenient for him to meet Mr. Rogers.

Brighton, June 16th.

Model 4.

The Librarian of the Mercantile Library will please to send Miss Powell, by the bearer, the first volume of Irving's "Life of Washington."

1214 Arch St., June 15th.

Model 5.

Will Messrs. Hawk & Wetherbee oblige Miss Blair by giving the bearer the trunk corresponding to the accompanying check?

New York, May 25, 1875.

Model 6.—*To a Servant.*

Mrs. Dawson desires Bridget O'Neil to go to her house to-morrow morning, and put it in order to receive the family in the evening.

Orange, Friday, Sept. 1st.

Such a note may be appropriately written partly in the third and partly in the second person. In such cases, the superior, or the one assumed to be such, is always mentioned in the third person, whether writing or written to. Of course an equal, or even a superior, may through politeness or modesty assume inferiority, as is often done when a person subscribes himself, "Your obedient servant." In accordance with this principle, the above note (Model 6) might be properly expressed thus:—

Model 7.—(*Second and Third Persons.*)

Bridget,

Mrs. Dawson desires you to go to her house to-morrow morning and put it in order to receive the family in the evening

Orange, Friday, Sept. 1st.

The following note is another application of the same principle This form of note is perfectly correct, but is rarely used, probably owing to the skill required in writing it. It is the only kind of formal note that admits of a signature.

Model 8.—(*First and Third Persons.*)

Will Mr. Winthrop be so good as to favor me with a line stating in what manner and with what success I discharged my duties while serving as tutor in his family? Such a certificate, if as favorable as I have reason to expect, may be of great use to me in procuring a desirable situation.

Hoping that Mr. Winthrop will comply with my request as soon as convenient, I remain,

His obedient and humble servant,

James Marshall.

Boston, Jan. 10, 1876.

In closing a note written in this manner, it would not do to say "*Your* obedient," etc., as that would be changing from the third to the second person. (See "Difficulty," page 136.)

SUPERSCRIPTION AND DELIVERY.

I. Superscription.

Ceremonial Notes.—Notes of invitation should bear upon the envelope (the inner one, if two are used) only the name and title of the person invited. Thus, the note on page 141 would be addressed, *Mr. John Hall.* This superscription should be written, as on ordinary letters, a little below the centre of the envelope. The word *Present*, or *Addressed*, formerly written under the name, is no longer so used.

In notes intended for a married couple, a distinction may be observed, in regard to the superscription, between those that are *printed* and those that are *written*. In the former, *your* is used instead of the names; hence the envelope must be addressed to both; as, *Mr.* and *Mrs. John Hall.* In the latter, the names are mentioned in the note; hence it is allowable, and generally preferable, to address the envelope to the wife only.

If an outside envelope is used, it may have upon it the full address of the person to be invited. (See page 57, *et seq.*)

Acceptances and regrets are addressed like other ceremonial notes. It is not required that they be enclosed in extra envelopes, though there is no impropriety in so enclosing them.

Miscellaneous Notes.—Personal and familiar notes, like most of those on pages 151, 152, 155, 156, 157, are enveloped and superscribed in the same manner as ordinary letters.

II. Delivery.

Notes addressed to persons living in another town or city are of course sent by mail, like ordinary letters, and it is becoming customary to send them in the same manner to persons living in a distant part of the same city. Usually, however, they are delivered by private messenger.

EXERCISES IN NOTES.

Write, fold, and superscribe notes in accordance with the data and directions given below.

Wedding Invitation and Answers.

1. Miss Lamb's parents invite Mr. and Mrs. Sower to the marriage of Sarah Lamb to William Wolff, at home. Write the invitation in four forms: (*a*) Without cards; (*b*) with reception card; (*c*) with reception and personal cards; (*d*) with personal cards (the reception invitation being contained in the note).
2. An acceptance of the above invitation.
3. A non-acceptance or regret.

Invitation to Dinner, and Answers to the same.

1. Mr. and Mrs. John Clark invite Mr. Charles Brooks to dinner at a certain time, requesting an answer.

2. Mr. Brooks's acceptance of the invitation.

3. Mr. Brooks's non-acceptance.

Invitation to a Party, and Answers.

1. Mr. and Mrs. James Baldwin invite Mr. and Mrs. Clark Bell to an evening party.

2. An acceptance of the invitation.

3. A non-acceptance.

Invitation to a Ball.

An invitation to Mr. Harry Lightfoot to attend a ball at the Assembly Rooms, in honor of Washington's Birthday. Signed by the managers. (Supply names.)

Invitation to a School or College Anniversary.

An invitation to attend the next commencement exercises of your institution, or the anniversary of a literary society; enclosing a card containing the (supposed) names of the participants, or the order of exercises.

Invitation to a Lady to attend a Lecture, with Answer.

1. An invitation to a lady to attend a lecture by Mr. Gough at a certain time and place.

2. An acceptance.

3. A non-acceptance.

Order for a Carriage.

A note in the third person (or second and third) to James Roberts, requesting him to send a carriage to your house at a certain time, to take two passengers and one trunk to the railroad depot.

CHAPTER II.

CARDS.

- I. INTRODUCTION.
- II. KINDS.
  - Ceremonial.
  - Visiting.
  - Professional and Official.
  - Business.

INTRODUCTION.

Importance.—A card, which, in its simplest form, is merely "a bit of pasteboard with a name upon it," may at a superficial glance seem to be a very trifling affair; and yet it plays an important part in social intercourse. This importance arises from its representative capacity. As a bank-note, worthless in itself, represents so much gold or other valuable commodity; so a card is accepted in many cases as a substitute for the person whose name it bears, and carries with it whatever influence attaches to that name.

REMARK.—It is not possible to give in this work a complete explanation of the various uses of cards; nor is such an explanation desirable, as it belongs to etiquette rather than to letter-writing. Indeed there are some things connected with the subject which cannot be learned in books: they belong to those "graces beyond the reach of art," which are learned only in society, among those "to the manner born." The leading points, however, are capable of being expressed in writing and reduced to something like a social code. And such a code is greatly needed, not only to inform those who have enjoyed but limited opportunities of social culture; but also to reconcile conflicting opinions, even among those who move in the highest circles. We do not aim to do all that may be done in this direction: our principal business is to treat of the *forms* of the various kinds of cards; but we shall also endeavor to give, under appropriate heads, such *information concerning their* use as the scope of our work will allow.

Kinds.—Cards may be divided into four classes: I. Ceremonial; II. Visiting; III. Professional and Official; IV. Business.

CEREMONIAL CARDS.

Use.—Cards may be used to convey invitations to weddings, receptions, parties, etc.; and, indeed, for most of the purposes for which billets are employed. Notes, however, are generally preferred if the occasions are formal and important; also for acceptances and regrets.

Materials.—*Quality.*—The material used is the finest English card board, unglazed.

Color.—For weddings, only pure white is allowable. For other occasions, delicate tints are allowable, but are not much used.

Size.—Cards of ceremony are generally large—about 3 by 5 inches—nearly the size of a postal card.

Envelopes.—Cards are enveloped, superscribed, and delivered in the same manner as notes. (See pages 137 and 157.)

Forms.—But few forms are necessary, as most of those given for notes (especially the shorter ones) are equally suitable for cards. The following will suffice:—

Invitation Card.

[About two-thirds the original size.]

BURD ORPHAN ASYLUM

OF ST. STEPHEN'S CHURCH.

The Rector, Wardens, and Vestrymen invite you to be present at the Asylum on "Founder's Day," *Thursday, June 5th, 1873, at three o'clock.*

65th & Market Streets.

Invitation Cards.—*Miscellaneous.*

[These models are a little less than one-third the original size.]

Mr. & Mrs. T. B. Patterson's

Compliments, requesting the pleasure of your company on Tuesday evening, February thirteenth,* 1866.

R. S. V. P. 1520 *Girard Av.*

SATURDAY EVENING CLUB.

---------------------- *requests the pleasure of* ------------- *company, on Saturday evening next, at eight o'clock.*

The favor of an answer is requested.

Mr. & Mrs. Cary

At Home

Wednesday, September twenty-ninth, from two until four o'clock.

19 *East 34th Street.*

Mr. George W. Childs requests the pleasure of ------------- *company, on Saturday, March 9th,* 1872, *to meet the President of the United States.*

Walnut and 22d Sts.,

Philadelphia.

Wedding Cards.—Wedding invitations are generally printed on note-paper. Most of the forms given in the preceding chapter—especially the shorter ones—may, however, be printed upon cards. Of the cards generally enclosed in a wedding invitation, we have already spoken. The size of these is a matter of taste. The reception card is generally larger than the personal cards, and the gentleman's card is a little larger than that of the lady. The personal cards contain, respectively, the names of the parties, and nothing more.

Betrothal Cards.—Among the Hebrews it is customary to announce betrothals. For this purpose notes or cards may be used. The following is a good form :—

Mr. Benjamin Hollander,

Miss Rebecca Baum,

Betrothed,

January sixteenth, 1876.

* The use of the word *compliments* in invitations is not now considered in good form.

Or, three cards may be used: a small one bearing the word *Betrothed*, a larger one bearing, near the lower right hand corner, the lady's name, and a still larger one bearing, in a similar position, the gentleman's name; the three to be tied together at the upper edge with a white satin ribbon.

Presentation Cards.—A card is a very neat and convenient substitute for a note, to accompany a book or any other gift; or for a Christmas or New Year's greeting. For example:—

> *Mrs. Bouligny sends her Christmas greetings to Mr. Leslie, and begs his acceptance of the accompanying trifle, as a token of her regard.*
>
> *Christmas, 1875.*

Memorial Cards.—It is customary in England, and partially so in this country, to send Memorial Cards to the friends of the deceased. Such cards have a black border,—narrow for the young, wide for the aged. The following is a good example:—

> In Memory of
>
> *Abraham Lincoln,*
>
> *President of the United States of America.*
>
> *Born February 12, 1809;*
>
> *Died April 15, 1865.*
>
> WITH MALICE TOWARD NONE; WITH CHARITY FOR ALL.
>
> *"After life's fitful fever he sleeps well."*

Memorial Cards should be sent out about a week after the funeral.

Informal Reception Cards.—Informal Afternoon or Evening Receptions are now frequent in our large cities. The invitations are on cards inscribed somewhat as follows:—

Mr. & Mrs. John L. Woods. *Thursday, January sixth.* *From three till six o'clock.* *250 N. Charles St.*	*Mr. & Mrs. Henry Moore.* *Thursday Evenings.* *1672 Chestnut Street.*

Answers.—To these informal invitations no reply is expected. In general, the custom with respect to answers is the same, whether invitations are given by note or card. (See *Acceptances and Regrets*, page 152.)

VISITING CARDS.

Introductory Remark.—Visiting cards are so familiar as not to need description. Their uses, however, are not so well understood. To say that they are used in visiting, as their name indicates, is not enough; the question arises, *How* are they used in visiting? This is a difficult question to answer, as it involves many fine points of social etiquette, concerning some of which the leaders of society in different cities hold different opinions. Without stopping to discuss disputed points, we give as briefly as possible those uses which seem to have the sanction of the best social authority, as derived, not from books, but from society itself.

Uses.—The chief uses of visiting cards are the following:—

1. *To announce a visitor's name.*

On making a call, a card is handed to the person who opens the door, and the caller inquires for the person or persons for whom the visit is intended.

If the person called on is "not at home," the caller leaves a card, turning over one end or side, to denote a call in person. If there is a visitor with the family, two cards should be left, one for the family and the other for the visitor; or, *one* card may be left, with the right end bent or creased.* A young lady calling on a family where there are elderly as well as young ladies leaves two cards. A married lady ordinarily leaves but one card, but when the lady visited has a daughter who had just gone into society, she leaves two cards.

2. *To announce a guest's name at a reception.*

When a person attends a reception or party, he should always hand his card to the usher at the door. A card should also be left in the card receiver.

---

* In some cities the former method prevails; in some, the latter; in others, both. A person must conform to the custom of the society in which he lives.

3. *To represent the owner in making calls.*

Society exacts *formal visits* on certain occasions, as, for example, after an invitation to a dinner, or other ceremonious entertainment; on any occasion deemed worthy of personal congratulation or condolence; on the return of a visiting acquaintance to his residence; and on the arrival and stay of a visitor at the house of a friend: and such visits should be paid within a few days—not longer than a week—after the event. But for ordinary calls a card is by common consent accepted as a substitute for the person.

4. *To announce a departure from home.*

A person living in a city, on leaving for any considerable stay, sends to his friends a card having *P. P. C.* (*pour prendre congé*, to take leave) on one of the lower corners.

5. *To announce a return home.*

It is customary and proper to announce a return to the city by sending cards to visiting friends, with the address, if need be, and the reception days.

6. *To express congratulation and condolence.*

As above stated, a personal visit is required when there is occasion for congratulation or condolence, but if the person visited is not at home, a card is left, on one corner of which is written the word *Congratulation* or *Condolence*, as the case may require. (The object of the visit was formerly denoted by the turning down of a certain corner; but this stiff mechanical practice is happily discontinued.)

7. *As a substitute for a note of non-acceptance.*

A visiting card with the word *Regret* written upon it is sometimes, though improperly, sent to denote the non-acceptance of an invitation.

8. *To accompany a letter of introduction.*

A gentleman in a strange city with a letter of introduction, should always send his card, bearing *his temporary address*, with the letter, both enclosed in an envelope.

9. *To make known one's name to a stranger.*

A person who wishes to make himself known to another, whether for friendly or unfriendly purposes, hands him a card.

10. *To serve as a credential, or certificate of authority.*

A person sometimes hands another his card, with a written endorsement or introduction on it, to give him credit, in a certain matter, with those to whom the bearer is unknown.

These are the principal and essential uses of cards, and they are sufficient to show that these "bits of pasteboard" are almost indispensable in modern social life. The other uses are such as a person's good sense will suggest as the occasions arise.

The Inscription.—The inscription consists of the name alone, or the name and the residence. When the latter is given, it is put in very small letters in the lower right-hand corner. If a lady receives on a certain day, she indicates it in the lower left-hand corner; thus, "*Thursdays*," or "*Tuesdays and Fridays*," as the case may be.

TITLES.*—A title may or may not be used, according to the taste of the person. The social titles used are *Mr.*, *Mrs.*, and *Miss*. A man and his wife sometimes use a joint card, inscribed *Mr. and Mrs. Blank*, *Chief Justice and Mrs. Drake*, as the case may be. A married lady, if her husband be living, uses her husband's name instead of her own; as, *Mrs. Dr. John Williams*. If a lady visits in company with her daughter, a card may be used containing both names,—the daughter's being placed about half an inch lower than the mother's. When there are two or more daughters in society, the card of the eldest is inscribed, for example, *Miss Fairchild;* those of the others, *Miss Jane Fairchild*, *Miss Mary Fairchild*, etc. Sisters visiting together often use a common card, inscribed, *e. g.*, *The Misses Fairchild*.

Clergymen, physicians, and dentists use their professional title, instead of *Mr.* (see models). and their cards may be used both for social and professional purposes.

Persons occupying high positions in the civil, military, or naval service, annex or subscribe their official rank or title (see models). The cards of such persons, like those of professional gentlemen, serve a double purpose. Persons never assume the title of *Honorable* on their cards; nor do they use scholastic titles, except those that are at the same time professional.

Style.—Visiting cards vary in size to suit the caprices of fashion, or individual taste. Ladies' cards are generally a little larger than gentlemen's. They must be perfectly plain, both as to material and inscription. A refined taste discards all ornaments, whether embossed, printed, or written. The most elegant cards are engraved or written; those printed from type are not used by the most fashionable people. The letter-

* See the article on Appellative Titles in Part III.

ing generally used is the "English round-hand," or the "angular script." Old English also is frequently used for the name and title. Persons in mourning use a card with a black border.

Models.—We give below a number of models copied from actual cards, to illustrate the various peculiarities above-mentioned:—

Models of Visiting Cards.—(*Diminished Size.*)

Miss Thomson.	The Misses Delafield, *Edgemont.*
Dr. & Mrs. Robert Pearson. *3214 Green St.* *Tuesday.*	*Mrs. Edward T. Beale.* *The Misses Beale.* *Tuesdays.* *Lafayette Square.*
Eliza Jackson, M. D. *211 West 39th St.*	William Bennett. *Keen & Bennett,* *New Orleans.*
Gen Albert J. Myer. *Chief Signal Officer, U. S. A.*	William Strong, *Associate Justice Supreme Court U. S.*

PROFESSIONAL AND OFFICIAL CARDS.

These are cards used by professional men and officers, mainly for professional and official purposes. In many cases, however, the same cards may be used for social purposes also (see page 166). Such cards contain, in addition to the person's name, his professional or official title or designation.* Three of the forms given above are examples of professional and official cards. We give in addition the two following:—

M .... *has* *an appointment with* C. A. KINGSLEY, M. D., D. D. S., *on* .... *at* ..... *o'clock.* *1199 Walnut St.,* *Philadelphia.*	JOHN G. NICOLAY, *Marshal of the Supreme Court* *of the United States.*

BUSINESS CARDS.

These are cards used by business men, to show their kind and place of business. Some are handsomely engraved, but they are generally printed from ordinary job type. No examples are needed; nor is it necessary to make any remarks in regard to them, except to suggest that they should be neat and tasteful. This suggestion may indeed be made in regard to anything that is intended for the public eye. It should be remembered that people have an æsthetic nature, as well as an intellectual; and that they are therefore influenced, not only by what is useful, but often, in an equal degree, by what is ornamental and agreeable. Business men, therefore, if they would consult their own interests, should take advantage of this fact, and appeal in their cards, as well as in other respects, to the taste, no less than the judgment, of the public.

---

* See *Titles*, page 166; also the article on Titles, in Part III.

PART II.

ORTHOGRAPHY AND PUNCTUATION

ORTHOGRAPHY.*

OUTLINE.

1. Rules for Forming Derivatives.
2. Special Rules.
3. Rules for the Use of Capitals.

Remark.—No person can become a good speller by rule. Most rules are subject to so many exceptions; that it is generally easier to learn to spell words by direct study, than to learn all the rules and exceptions that apply to them. The following, however, being of wide application and subject to but few exceptions, have been found to be exceedingly valuable: and we therefore recommend that they be thoroughly learned, and carefully applied in practice. (See our remarks on spelling, pages 73, 74, 75.)

RULES FOR FORMING DERIVATIVES.

RULE I.—Silent E Final.

Part I. *E* final is *rejected* when a suffix beginning with a *vowel* is added; as, *blame* + *able* = *blamable.*

---

* The rules are taken, in substance, from the author's book entitled *Three Thousand Practice Words*, published by Eldredge & Brother Philadelphia.

Exceptions.—*E is retained:* **1.** After *c* or *g* when followed by *a* or *o*, as in *changeable, peaceable;* **2.** After *o*, as in *shoeing;* **3.** When it is necessary to preserve the identity of the word, as in *swingeing, singeing, dyeing, tingeing.*

Part II. *E* final is *retained* when a suffix beginning with a *consonant* is added; as *move* + *ment* = *movement.*

Exceptions.—*Duly, truly, wholly, awful, nursling, wisdom, abridgment, argument, acknowledgment, judgment, lodgment* (sometimes spelled *lodgement*).

RULE II.—Y Final.

Part I. If *y* final is preceded by a *consonant*, it is *changed* to *i* when a suffix is added; as, *merry* + *ly* = *merrily.*

Exceptions.—1. *Y* is changed to *e* in *beauteous, bounteous, duteous, piteous, plenteous.* **2.** *Y* is not changed in derivatives of *dry* (except *drier, driest*), *shy, sky, sly, spry, wry.* **3.** *Y* is not changed when the suffix begins with *i*, as in *trying.*

Part II. If *y* final is preceded by a *vowel*, it is *not changed* when a suffix is added; as, *boy* + *hood* = *boyhood.*

Exceptions.—*Day, daily; lay, laid, lain; pay, paid; say, saith, said; slay, slain; stay, staid;* with their compounds.

RULE III—Final Consonant.

Part I. A single final consonant *is doubled* on adding a suffix, when it is preceded by a single vowel, and the suffix begins with a vowel, and the accent is on the last syllable; as, *fop* + *ish* = *foppish; begin'* + *ing* = *beginning.*

Examples.—1. Add *ed* to *prefer'.* Here *r* is preceded by a single vowel (*e*), the suffix (*ed*) begins with a vowel, and the accent is on the last syllable (*fer*); hence *r* must be doubled; thus: *prefer* + *ed* = *preferred.*

2. Add *ing* to *bet*. Here *t* is preceded by a single vowel (*e*), and the suffix (*ing*) begins with a vowel; hence *t* must be doubled; thus: *bet* + *ing* = *betting*.

Exceptions.—**1.** The letters *x, k, v* are never doubled. **2.** *S* in derivatives of *gas* is not doubled: as, *gas* + *es* = *gases*.

Part II.—The final consonant is *not doubled* on adding a suffix, if it is not preceded by a single vowel, or if the suffix does not begin with a vowel, or if the word is not accented on the last syllable; as, *cheat* + *ed* = *cheated*; *prefer'* + *ment* = *preferment*; *ben'efit* + *ed* = *benefited*.

Examples.—1. Add *ed* to *cheat*. Here *t* is preceded by a double vowel (diphthong); hence it is not doubled on adding *ed*, and *cheat* + *ed* = *cheated*.

2. Add *ment* to *prefer*. Here the suffix does not begin with a vowel; hence *r* is not doubled, and *prefer* + *ment* = *preferment*.

3. Add *ing* to *profit*. Here the accent is not on the last syllable; hence *t* is not doubled, and *profit* + *ing* = *profiting*.

Exceptions.—**1.** From *tranquil*, contrary to rule, we have *tranquillity*; from *crystal*, *crystalline*; from *filial*, *filially*. **2.** Many writers also double the final consonant on adding a suffix beginning with a vowel to *travel, level, bevel, cancel, marvel, worship, kidnap*, and several similar words; as, *travelling, levelling, bevelled, cancelling, marvellous, worshipper*, etc. This is the only spelling of these words authorized by Worcester. Webster *allows* this spelling, but prefers *traveling, leveling*, etc., in accordance with the rule.

SPECIAL RULES.

I. Words Containing **ei** or **ie** (sound of ē).

Ei is used after the sound of *s*, as in *ceiling*, *seize*; except in *siege*, and a few words ending in *cier*. *Inveigle*, *neither*, *leisure*, and *weird*, also have *ei*.

In other cases *ie* is used, as in *believe*, *achieve*.

Note.—In German words, *ei* always represents the sound of *i*, as in *Steinman;* and *ie* represents the sound of *e*, as in *Siegel*.

II. Words Ending in **ceous** or **cious**.

Words relating to matter, end in *ceous*, as *herbaceous*; all others in *cious*, as *loquacious*. (*Silicious*, an apparent exception, is sometimes written *siliceous*.)

EXERCISE I.

Form the derivatives indicated below, and explain each operation; also fill the blanks.

Love + ing, move + able, shame + ful, excel + ing, benefit + ed, debate + able, peace + able, play + ful, apply + ed, apply + ing, beauty + ous, hoe + ing, refer + ing, true + ly, waste + ful, waste + ing, fit + ing, perform + ing, commit + ing, commit + ment, stop + ed, strive + ing, charge + able, outrage + ous, hot + est.

Under Special Rules: gr . . ve, s . . ze, retr . . ve, conc . . ve, ch . . ftain, s . . zing; argillac . ous, grac . ous, spac . ous, farinac . ous, mendac . ous, meretric . ous, carbonac . ous.

Models.—1. Form a derivative of *love* by adding *ing*. *Love* ends in silent *e* and the suffix begins with a vowel; hence *e* is rejected according to Rule I. Part I. (repeat the rule), and the derivative is spelled, *l-o-v-i-n-g*.

2. Form a derivative of *excel* by adding *ing*. The final consonant of *excel* is preceded by a single vowel, the suffix begins with a vowel and the word is accented on the last syllable; hence *l* is doubled according to Rule III. Part I. (repeat the rule), etc.

RULES FOR THE USE OF CAPITALS.

[For the method of capitalizing the heading, introduction, conclusion, and superscription of letters, see the sections treating of these parts, and the accompanying models. See also the remarks on capitals, page 76.]

Rule I. Every sentence should begin with a capital.

Rule II. Every line of poetry should begin with a capital.

Rule III. Every quotation that forms a sentence should begin with a capital; as, Pope says, "*Whatever is, is right.*"

Rule IV. Words denoting the Deity should begin with a capital; as, "Trust in *Providence.*"

Most writers of the present day capitalize also personal pronouns referring to the Deity; as, "Trust in *Him* who has power to save."

Rule V. Proper nouns and titles should begin with capitals; as, "The work is by *Prof. John Ruskin, A. M.*, of *Oxford, England.*"

In geographical names composed of a proper and a common noun, such as *Ohio river, New York city*, we should capitalize only the first part, because the first part may be used alone; but in such names as *Jersey City, Rocky Mountains*, etc., both parts must begin with capitals, because both are necessary to describe the place.

Rule VI. Proper adjectives should begin with capitals; as, "the *French* people"; "the *Republican* party"; "the *Methodist* church"; "the *Greek* language".

Rule VII. Names of things spoken of as persons should begin with capitals; as, "Jocund *Day* stands tip-toe on the misty mountain top."

Rule VIII. The important words in a heading should begin with capitals; as, The book is entitled, "A Dictionary of the Noted Names of Fiction".

The "important words" are generally the nouns, adjectives, and verbs. Other words are capitalized when they are emphatic.

Rule IX. The names of the months and of the days of the week should begin with capitals.

Names of the seasons do not begin with capitals unless they are personified.

Rule X. The pronoun *I* and the interjection *O* should be capitals.

EXERCISE II.

Copy the following sentences and supply the capitals where they are required by the foregoing rules:—

1. the following lines are from an ode by collins:—

   "there honor comes, a pilgrim gray,
   to bless the turf that wraps their clay;
   and freedom shall awhile repair,
   to dwell, a weeping hermit, there."

2. the dying lawrence exclaimed, "don't give up the ship."

3. the great shepherd will protect the lambs of his flock; so his word assures us.

4. he read the following selections: gray's "elegy in a country churchyard"; goldsmith's "deserted village"; and browning's "how they brought the good news from ghent to aix."

5. they were married on monday, march 20th, in the episcopal church, by the rev. mr. brown.

PUNCTUATION.

INTRODUCTION.

Definition.—Punctuation (from the Latin *punctum*, a point) is the art of dividing written composition by means of points.

NOTE.—Punctuation is a comparatively modern art. A few points were introduced by Aristophanes, a Greek grammarian of Alexandria, about 250 B. C.; but punctuation as now practised was not generally known until about 1600 A. D., after the invention of the art of printing.

Use.—The chief use of punctuation is to divide written discourse into sentences, and show the relation and dependence of their several parts.

A *point* is to some extent the expression or representation of a *pause*, as a letter is of a sound; but it is not true, as we were taught in the old books, that the chief use of punctuation is to show where and how long the voice is to be suspended in reading.

A pause is often required where it would be wrong to place a point; as in the following line:—

"*My words* fly up; my *thoughts* remain below."

Here we must pause as long after *words* and *thoughts* as we do after *up;* but it would be absurd to represent these pauses by semicolons, or even by commas.

And, on the contrary, *a point is often required where it would be wrong to make a perceptible pause;* as in the expressions, "Come, John;" "Yes, sir;" "Oh, yes."

Basis.—Punctuation is based upon grammatical analysis. A good analyzer will have little difficulty in learning to punctuate well; and the study of punctuation is to some extent a study of analysis.

The Use of Rules.—Rules cannot exhaust the subject: they can render important aid; but much must be left, after all, to the exercise of an intelligent judgment. The best rule, after having learned the relative value of the points, is *the rule of common sense.* Punctuation cannot be made a mere mechanical process; nor can a person ever learn to punctuate well by *ear;* i. e., by observing the pauses in reading.

Importance.—As we have shown elsewhere (see page 81), a knowledge of punctuation is indispensable to the clear expression of thought in writing. Sometimes serious, and often ludicrous mistakes occur, on account of the omission or misuse of a point. Of the numberless illustrations of this truth that might be given, we select the following (see also the illustration on page 81):—

ILLUSTRATIONS. 1. John Quincy Adams, when practising law, once gained a suit involving $50,000, the decision of which turned on the position of a comma.

2. A tariff act was passed by the XLIId Congress, providing that fruit-plants and certain other commodities should be admitted free of duty; but it happened that in engrossing or printing the act, a comma was either accidentally or fraudulently inserted between "fruit" and "plants." Accordingly all fruits and all plants were put upon the

free list; and this mistake (if mistake it was) cost the United States about two million dollars! It required a special act of Congress to get rid of that mischievous and stubborn comma.

[Sometimes ludicrous mistakes are made by bad punctuation; as in the following:]

3. Among the toasts drunk at a public dinner was this: "Woman without her, man would be a savage." It was printed, the next day thus: "Woman, without her man, would be a savage."

4. The following notice was once read in church: "John Brown having gone to sea [see] his wife, desires the prayers of the congregation in his behalf." The comma should have been placed after *sea*.

5. In the report of a clergyman's remarks on the increase of intemperance, appears the following announcement: "A young woman in my neighborhood died very suddenly last Sabbath, while I was preaching the gospel in a state of beastly intoxication." A comma should of course be inserted after *gospel*.

6. Punctuate the following lines so as to make them express a fact:—

Every lady in the land
Has twenty nails upon each hand
Five and twenty on hands and feet
This is true without deceit.

Points Used.—The principal Points used are the following:—

The Period	.	The Comma	,
The Interrogation	?	The Dash	—
The Exclamation	!	The Curves	( )
The Colon	:	The Brackets	[ ]
The Semicolon	;	Quotation Marks	" "

Note.—These points are sometimes classified as *terminal* (those used at the end of a sentence), *interclausal* (those used between clauses or members), and *interstitial* (those used between parts of clauses); but as this classification is of no practical importance, it is not here adopted.

RULES AND EXERCISES.

THE PERIOD (.).

Rule I. A Period should be placed after every declarative and every imperative sentence; as, "Truth is the basis of every virtue." "Dare to do right."

NOTE.—The word *period* means *circuit*. It was first used to denote the sentence, and is still so used in rhetoric. The dot used to denote the completion of the period, afterwards, by metonymy, was itself called a period, the sign being put for the thing signified.

Rule II. A Period should be used after every abbreviation; as, Prof., for Professor; C.O.D., for Cash on Delivery.

Exception.—An abbreviation pronounced as written is not followed by a period; as, *Ben* Butler, *Will* Shakspeare. These are not really abbreviations, but nicknames. Benj. is the abbreviation of Benjamin; Wm., of William.

NOTE 1. Letters used to represent numbers are followed by a period; as, Book I., Chap. IV., p. 22.

NOTE 2. The Arabic figures (1, 2, 3, etc.) are followed by periods when used to number sections, paragraphs, etc.; as, "Three questions are to be considered: 1. What is it? 2. Where is it? 3. What is it for? (Notice the colon after "considered.")

EXERCISE I.

Copy the following, dividing it into sentences and, if necessary, into paragraphs, and using capitals where they are required:—

Death is the king of terrors religion breathes a spirit of gentleness and affability a man cannot live pleasantly, unless he uses wisely and honestly honor, glory, and immortality are promised to virtue the happiness allotted to man in his present state is indeed faint and low, compared with his immortal prospects Wm C Bryant was born in 1794.he began to write verses when but nine years of age,he was educated at Williams college, and afterwards studied law," thanatopsis" was written in his nineteenth year;this poem alone would establish the author's claim to the honors of a genius.dare to do right.an honest man is the noblest work of God. Henry W. Longfellow, was born feb 27, 1807 he lives on brattle st, cambridge, mass, the room above his study was at one time occupied by gen Washington as his bed chamber

[The teacher may give several such exercises, if need be, writing them on the board, or dictating from a book,—taking care, however, in all cases, not to indicate, by voice or otherwise, where periods are required.]

EXERCISE II.

Copy, punctuate, and capitalize the following:—

Chas I was beheaded A D 1649 hon j p Wickersham, LL D, state Supt, is the author of two valuable works: 1 School economy; 2 methods of Instruction the quotation may be found in Vol I, Chap VI, p 24 the work was written by Tayler Lewis, dd, lld, prof of Greek in Union college " O rare ben Jonson!"

THE INTERROGATION (?).

Rule.—An Interrogation must be placed after every question; as, Who wrote "Snow-Bound"?

NOTE.—An interrogation point generally, not always, marks the end of a sentence; hence the following word generally, not always, begins with a capital; as, "The question, What do we live for? is a solemn one." Sometimes, by the omission of a common part, several questions are thrown together, so as to form one sentence; in which case an interrogation must be placed after each question, because each requires a separate answer; as, "Whence did he come? with whom?

for what purpose?" When, however, the common part is reserved for the final question, but one interrogation is required; as, "Whence with whom, for what purpose, did he come?" This note is also applicable to the exclamation point.

THE EXCLAMATION (!).

Rule.—The Exclamation is used after every expression or sentence that denotes strong emotion; as, "How are the mighty fallen!" "Alas! I am undone."

NOTE 1. *Interjections.*—An interjection is generally followed by an exclamation. But when the interjection is unemphatic, it may be followed by a comma, or by no point at all; as, "Oh, yes."

NOTE 2. *O* and *Oh.*—A distinction is to be observed in the use of *O* and *oh.* The former we will call the "vocative O"; and the latter, the "emotional oh."

Vocative O.—Vocative *O* is used before a noun in excited address, and is not followed by any point; as, "O Liberty!" "O my Country!"

Emotional Oh.—Emotional *oh* is chiefly used to denote wishing, suffering, surprise, or admiration, and is followed by an exclamation point or a comma; as, (wishing) "Oh, that he were here!" (suffering) "Oh! I am ruined;" (surprise) "Oh! look there!" (admiration) "Oh, how lovely!"

REFERENCE.—See the note under the interrogation point, page 181 which applies also to the exclamation.

EXERCISE III.

Copy the following, using interrogations, exclamations, periods, and capital letters, where necessary:—

Where are you going I am going to lancaster will you stay for dinner I think so oh, how warm it is Alas my hopes are dead O my people O my brothers let us choose the righteous side O grave where is thy victory O death where is thy sting How lovely are the flowers can anything be more perfect

EXERCISE IV.

Copy the following poetical extract, supplying points and capitals where they are required.

[Do not change it in any other respect. The printed points in this and all subsequent exercises are correct. Only those points are to be supplied for which rules have been given.]

Titinius These tidings will comfort cassius
Messala Where did you leave him
Tit All disconsolate
With Pindarus, his bondman, on the hill
Mes is it not he that lies upon the ground
Tit he is not like the living O my heart
Mes is that not he
Tit No: this was he, Messala;
But cassius is no more O setting sun
As in thy red rays thou dost set to-night,
so in his red blood Cassius' day is set;
the sun of rome is set—*Julius Cæsar*

QUOTATION MARKS (" ").

[These points are introduced out of their usual order, because they will be much needed in the examples and exercises that are to follow.]

Rule.—Quoted, or borrowed, expressions must be enclosed in Quotation Marks; as, Socrates said, "*I believe that the soul is immortal.*"

REMARK.—It matters not whether the quoted expression was spoken or written. A writer may use the marks even when he quotes words previously used by himself.

NOTE 1. A quotation included in another is distinguished by single marks; a second quotation included in this one, by double marks, and so on alternately; as,—

1. What a lesson is contained in the word "diligence"!

2. Trench says, "What a lesson is contained in the word 'diligence'!" (Notice the position of the points at the end.)

3. I find in Hart's Rhetoric the following sentence: "Trench says, 'What a lesson is contained in the word "diligence"!'"

4. The teacher said, "I find in Hart's Rhetoric the following sentence: 'Trench says, "What a lesson is contained in the word 'diligence'!"'"

REMARK.—It thus appears that several sets of closing marks may come together at the end of a sentence. When this is the case a little space must be preserved between them. The closing marks must of course be placed at the end of the quotation to which they belong, whether at the end of the sentence or elsewhere.

NOTE 2. A quotation may be divided by other words, in which case each part must be enclosed in quotation marks; as,—

"Let me make the ballads of a nation," said Fletcher of Saltoun, "and I care not who makes the laws."

NOTE 3. When successive paragraphs are quoted, marks are put at the beginning of each, but the closing marks are put only at the end of the last.

RULE FOR CAPITALS.—See Rule III., page 175.

EXERCISE V.

Supply the omitted points and capitals in the following sentences:—

1. The command, Thou shalt not kill, forbids many crimes besides murder.

2. It has been said, the command, thou shalt not kill, forbids many crimes besides murder.

3. If, says Sir James Mackintosh, you display the delights

of liberality to a miser, he may always shut your mouth by answering, the spendthrift may prefer such pleasures: I love money more.

4. I ventured to congratulate him upon his coming back to his home. Ah, sir, he answered, but to a home how altered—my family broken up, my kindred gone—These feelings about home are deep, I murmured forth. Very deep, sir, he rejoined, and walked away.

5. Some one has said what an argument for prayer is contained in the words, our father who art in heaven

6. He wrote upon the blackboard this sentence: some one has said, what an argument for prayer is contained in the words, our father who art in heaven.

THE COLON (:).

Rule I. A Colon is used between parts that are subdivided by semicolons.

REMARK.—This rule is the statement of a general principle, but its application is seldom required—never, except in long sentences. It may be illustrated by the following figures:—

(1) ————————; ————————: ————————.
(2) ————————; ————————: ————————; ————.

In analyzing such sentences, the parts separated by the colon are called members.

Rule II. A Colon is used before a quotation, enumeration, or observation, that is introduced by "as follows," "the following," or any equivalent expression.

REMARK.—Such an introduction is called *formal*. An informal introduction requires a comma, if the quotation is short. If the quotation consists of several sentences—a speech, for example—a colon must precede it, no matter how it is introduced; as, Mr. Sumner obtained the floor, and said: (here follows the speech.)

16*

EXAMPLES.

Formal Introduction:—

1. He spoke as follows: "Mr. President, I rise," etc.

2. The following persons were elected: Pres., John Williams, Vice Pres., James Carr.

3. Be our plain answer this: The throne we honor is the people's choice

Informal Introduction:—

1. Lawrence said, "Don't give up the ship."

2. The line, "The child is father of the man," was written by Wordsworth.

SPECIAL RULE.—An easy and sure rule for determining whether an introduction is formal or informal is the following:—

If, in reading, the introduction takes, on the last word, the falling inflection, it is formal, and requires a colon; if it takes the rising inflection, it is informal, and requires a comma.

EXERCISE VI.

Tell which of the quotations in the following sentences are introduced *formally*, and which *informally*, and supply quotation marks, colons, and commas, where needed:—

1 Remember the maxim Know thyself.

2. Parse the following sentence To see the sun is pleasant.

3. Webster, when dying, uttered these words I still live.

4. This was the motto of the celebrated Dr. Nott Perseverance conquers all things.

5. O Heaven he cried my bleeding country save.

6. Patrick Henry exclaimed Give me liberty or give me death.

7. The tomb bore this inscription I am Cyrus, he who subdued the Persian Empire.

8. The apostle thus gives expression to the intensity of his emotions! Oh, wretched man that I am! who shall deliver me from the body of this death?

Rule III. A Colon is used after a clause or member which is complete in itself, but is followed, without a conjunction, by some remark, inference, or explanation.*

EXAMPLES.

1. Let me offer you my earnest friendship: you would laugh if I were to offer you more.

2. I went to the glen betimes next morning: the book was gone, and so was my patience.

3. Of these he should make himself master: he should "leave no enemies in the rear."

4. To reason with him was vain: he was infatuated.

[When the conjunction is expressed, a semicolon is used; as,—]

5. To reason with him was vain; for he was infatuated.

REMARK.—The colon, as used in the above examples, performs an office that can be performed by no other point, and yet an unskilful punctuator would have used a semicolon or a period in every instance. This use of the colon is one of the refinements of modern punctuation, and can best be learned by careful observation of the practice of our best authors. Instances of it abound in all our correctly printed books and magazines.

NOTE 1. When the time of day is denoted by figures, a colon is put between hours and minutes; as, The train leaves at 9:28 A. M. Sometimes a period is used instead of a colon

REMARK.—A colon is sometimes, though rarely, used between the numbers denoting chapter and verse in Bible references; as, 2 Cor. 15:54. (So used in Hart's Rhetoric.) A period is generally used.

* This rule is taken from Wilson's Treatise on Punctuation, the best work on the subject in the language.

There are thus three ways of writing Bible references: 1 Kings xviii. 27; 1 Kings 18.27; 1 Kings 18:27.

Note 2. *Yes* or *No*, in answer to a question, is generally followed by a colon, if the following words are a repetition of the answer; as, "Can you do this?"—"Yes: I have often done it." Some writers, however, prefer the semicolon.

Remark.—If a noun follows *yes* or *no*, the colon must come after the noun; as, "Yes, sir: I will." "Yes, my lords: I am ready."

Reference.—See Remark 2, page 190.

EXERCISE VII.

Separate the following into sentences; and use periods, colons, quotation marks, and capitals, where needed; also commas, where needed before quotations:—

All our conduct toward men should be influenced by this precept do unto others as ye would that others should do unto you Do not flatter yourself with the idea of perfect happiness there is no such thing in the world the discourse consisted of two parts* in the first was shown the necessity of exercise; in the second, the advantages that would result from it All admire the sublime passage God said let there be light; and there was light Have you ever been to Washington yes sir I once lived there.

THE SEMICOLON (;).

Rule I. A Semicolon is put between parts that are subdivided by commas; as,—

It is the first point of wisdom to ward off evil; and, since you are not sure of a minute, throw not away an hour.

* See Note 1, *b*, p. 189.

Remark.—This is a very common use of the semicolon. It may be illustrated by the following figures:—

(1) ———, ———; ———, ———, ———.
(2) —————; —————, —————.

Rule II. The Semicolon is used between clauses or members that are loosely connected in sense, and between the terms of any disconnected series of expressions.

EXAMPLES.

1. Everything has its time to flourish; everything grows old; everything passes away.

2. President, John Hall; Vice Pres., F. A. Lyon; Sec., Anna Laurie.

Note 1. *a.* A Semicolon may be used before an enumeration, when the items are separated by commas; as, "I bought three books; Aftermath, The Circuit Rider, and Little Women." Most writers, however, prefer a comma and a dash before such an enumeration; as, "I have four studies,—Arithmetic, Grammar, Latin, and Literature."

b. When the terms of an enumeration are separated by semicolons, a colon must be used before it; as, "I bought three books: Aftermath, by Longfellow; The Circuit Rider, by Eggleston; and Little Women, by Miss Alcott."

Note 2. When *as*, *namely*, or *that is*, is used to introduce an example or enumeration, a semicolon is put before it, and a comma after it.

EXAMPLES.

1. A noun is a name: as, Cincinnati, Gen. Sherman. (The above rules and notes afford numerous examples of this use of *as*.)

2. There are three cardinal virtues; namely, faith, hope, and charity.

3. Some animals are amphibious; that is, they can live on the land or in the water.

[illegible]

[illegible] words, with the [illegible] ... a comma preceding [illegible]. Of [illegible] ... and marry the [illegible] ... denotes a stretchi[illegible]

[illegible] means the same as namely, [illegible] always preceded by a c[illegible] ... individuals are clas[illegible] ... friendship; b[illegible]

EXERCISE VIII.

Supply the omitted points and capitals in [illegible]

[illegible] ... the people r[illegible] ... the people mourn, [illegible] ... and the third he tha[illegible] ... he that perverteth his [illegible] ... was debated resc[illegible] ... the following [illegible] ... collections of a bu[illegible] ... schoolmasters, by hug[illegible] ... it is too expensi[illegible] ... much time.

THE COMMA (,).

Rule I. Co-ordinate clauses, and subordina[illegible] restrictive, are generally set off* by comm[illegible]

I believe him, because I have always found him tru[illegible]
The good shall be rewarded, but the wicked shall pe[illegible]

*Set off means, separated from what precedes or foll[illegible]

3. The good which you do will not be lost, though it may be forgotten.

Note 1. If clauses are short and closely connected, no point is required between them; as, "Learning is better *than riches (are).*" "*John is playing* and *his sister is studying.*" "The wicked flee *when no man pursueth.*"

Note 2. No point is allowable between a restrictive phrase or clause and the word which it limits, unless there are intervening words; as, "Death is the season *which tests our principles.*"

Explanation.—A clause is said to be *restrictive*, when it limits a particular word to a particular sense. Thus, in the sentence, "The boy who studies will improve," the meaning is not "*The boy* will improve," but "*The boy who studies* (*i. e.*, the *studious boy*) will improve." Hence the clause "who studies" is restrictive. Clauses that are not restrictive are called *circumstantial*. Thus, in the sentence, "John, *who is a diligent student*, knows his lesson," the clause, "who is a diligent student," is *circumstantial*, not restrictive.

EXERCISE IX.

[This may be used either as an oral or a written exercise.]

Tell which of the clauses in the following sentences are restrictive, and which circumstantial, and insert commas where needed:—

The flowers which bloom in spring are most regarded. My favorite bird is the robin which appears about the first of April. No man who is a real friend would speak so. The man who hath done this thing shall surely die. The time when compromise was possible has passed. This man who is my friend assures me of the fact. Every teacher must love a pupil who is docile. The child was much attached to his teacher who loved him dearly. Urbanity often lends a grace to actions that are of themselves ungracious. Study nature whose laws and phenomena are all deeply interesting. Adopt a life founded on religion and virtue.

Rule II. The comma is used to set off transposed phrases and clauses; as,—

1. When the wicked entice thee, consent thou not.
2. Before giving way to rage, try to find a reason for being angry.

REMARK.—If the inversion seems easy and natural, no point is required; as, "In this way he obtained the prize."

Rule III. A comma is used to set off interposed words, phrases, or clauses; as,—

1. This, however, was not my purpose.
2. Every passion, however base or unworthy, is eloquent.
3. Let us send light and joy, if we can, to every one around us.

EXPLANATION.—"Interposed" means, placed between. An expression is said to be interposed, when it is introduced somewhat abruptly between parts that are closely related.

EXERCISE X.

Punctuate the following sentences according to Rules II. and III.:—

1. Of all our senses sight is the most important.
2. Christianity is in a most important sense the religion of sorrow.
3. Charity on whatever side we contemplate it is one of the highest Christian graces.
4. Charity like the sun brightens every object on which it shines.
5. Happiness therefore depends on yourself.
6. Of all bad habits that of idleness is the most incorrigible.
7. Till we can go alone we must lean on the hand of a guide.
8. He had no doubt great aptitude for learning languages.
9. It is mind after all that does the work of the world.
10. To most religion is a mere tradition.

Rule IV. The comma is used between similar or repeated words or phrases; as,—

1. *Earth, air*, and *water* teem with life. (Similar words.)

2. *Live or die, sink or swim, survive or perish*, I give my heart and my hand to this vote. (Similar pairs.)

3. He lived *in seclusion, in poverty*, and *in disgrace*. (Similar phrases.)

4. *Come, come, come;* I fear we shall be late. (Repeated words.)

EXPLANATION.—"Similar," as used here, means, "in the same construction."

NOTE 1. In a series of similar expressions, three cases may arise:—

1. *Where all the conjunctions are expressed.*
2. *Where all are omitted except between the last two.*
3. *Where all are omitted.*

In the *first* of these cases no point is required; in the *second*, all the terms are separated by commas; in the *third*, all are separated by commas, and a comma is placed after the last to separate it from what follows.* These cases are illustrated in the following examples:—

1. *First Case.*—We should live soberly and righteously and piously in the present world.

2. *Second Case.*—We should live soberly, righteously,† and piously in the present world.

3. *Third Case.*—We should live soberly, righteously, piously, in the present world.

---

* If the terms are adjectives, a comma must not be put between the last one and the noun it limits; as, "He is an honest, industrious man."

† Many persons improperly reject the comma between the last two terms when the conjunction is expressed. The method of punctuating here given is in accordance with nearly all recognized authorities on the subject, as well as with the usage of the best authors and publishers. The reasons for it may be found in Wilson's excellent treatise, to which reference has already been made.

NOTE 2. Two or more similar terms under Case 1st (Note 1) must be separated by commas, if either of them has an adjunct or modifier that does not apply to the others; as, "Joseph woke, and thought upon his dream."

In this example, "upon his dream" belongs to "thought," but not to "woke." Without the comma, the sentence would mean, "Joseph woke upon his dream and thought upon his dream"—an absurdity.

EXERCISE XI.

Use commas where they are required by Rule IV. and the notes under it:—

1. The principal metals are gold silver mercury copper tin and lead.
2. A man that is temperate generous reliant faithful and honest, may at the same time have wit humor mirth and good breeding.
3. Power riches prosperity are sometimes conferred on the worst of men.
4. Death levels the rich and the poor the proud and the humble the strong and the feeble the young and the old.
5. Undue susceptibility and the preponderance of mere feeling over thoughtfulness, may mislead us.
6. Can flattery soothe the dull cold ear of death? (See first foot-note on p. 193.)

Rule V. The comma is used to set off independent elements; as, "*John*, come here, *sir*."

REMARK.—This rule applies to—

1. The nominative case independent; as, "I rise, *Mr. President*, to a point of order."
2. The nominative case absolute; as, "*The morning being clear*, we proceeded."
3. An unemphatic interjection: as, "*Oh*, how pretty!"
4. An independent adverb; as, "*Well*, how are you succeeding?"

Rule VI. The comma is used to set off an appositive element; as, James McCosh, *D. D.*, is a distinguished metaphysician.

REMARK.—If the appositive is quite short,—only a word or two,—no commas are required; as, "Paul the apostle was a man of energy."

EXERCISE XII.

Punctuate the following sentences according to Rules V. and VI.:—

1. Socrates the Greek philosopher never gave way to anger.
2. Sir Isaac Newton the eminent astronomer was remarkable for his modesty.
3. Charles V. King of Spain and Emperor of Germany died in a convent.
4. Boy bring me my boots.
5. The book was written by Francis Wayland D. D. LL.D.
6. Shame lost all virtue is lost.
7. Show pity Lord! O Lord forgive.
8. Accept my dear young friends this expression of my regard.
9. The question What is beauty? is hard to answer.
10. Why how well you look!

Rule VII. A comma is placed at the end of a long compound or complex subject; as,—

1. Love for study, a desire to do right, and carefulness in the choice of friends, are important traits of character.
2. He that places himself neither higher nor lower than he ought to do, exercises the truest humility.

REMARK.—If the subject is *very* long, especially if it is subdivided by points, a dash should be put after the comma.

Rule VIII. A comma is generally used to mark the ellipsis of a verb or other important words; as,—

"Hurry is the mark of a weak mind; despatch, of a strong one."

Rule IX. The comma is used to set off a short quotation informally introduced;* as,—

Agassiz once said, "I have not time to make money."

REMARK 1. This rule applies to any remark or observation resembling a quotation; as, "An important lesson in education is Learn to distrust your own opinions." "*Resolved*, That women shall be allowed to vote."

REMARK 2. An informal introduction generally ends with *say*, *exclaim*, *remark*, or some similar verb. Sometimes the quotation is in apposition; as, The maxim, "Know thyself," should not be forgotten.

REMARK 3. A divided quotation† requires two commas; as, "Virtue," says Dryden, "is its own reward."

Rule X. The comma is used to prevent ambiguity, and to give prominence to emphatic and contrasted parts; as,—

1. He who teaches, often learns himself. (If the comma were omitted, the sentence would be ambiguous.)
2. Strong proofs, not a loud voice, produce conviction.
3. I remain, yours respectfully, John Smith.

NOTE.—Phrases and clauses that are placed at a distance from the word on which they depend, or that have a common dependence on several words, are preceded by a comma; as,—

1. No *man* can be a thorough proficient in navigation, *who* has never been at sea.
2. I *prepare* those lessons which require the closest thinking, *early in the morning*.
3. Law is a *rule* of civil conduct, *prescribed* by the supreme power in the state, *commanding* what is right, *prohibiting* what is wrong.

---

* See Rule II. and Remark, page 185.

† See Note 2, page 184.

4. He questioned me of the battles, sieges, fortunes, that I have passed. (*That* refers equally to *battles*, *sieges*, and *fortunes*.)

5. We ought not to betray, but to defend, our country. (*Betray* and *defend* are in contrast, and *our country* is equally related to both.)

EXERCISE XIII.

Supply the omitted commas and capitals in the following sentences:—

1. "A faithful friend" it has been beautifully said "is the medicine of life."

2. A new feeling of what is due to the ignorant the poor and the depraved has sprung up in society.

3. We live in deeds not years; in thoughts not breaths; in feelings not in figures on a dial.

4. Homer was the greater genius; Virgil the better artist.

5. It is as great a breach of propriety to send an awkward careless badly written letter as it is to appear in a company of refined people with swaggering gait soiled linen and unkempt hair.

6. The books the pictures the statuary that were bought in Europe were all lost. [*All* the articles were bought in Europe.]

EXERCISE XIV.—MISCELLANEOUS.

Supply the omitted points and capitals, and give the rule for each:—

1. The essence of poetry may be said to consist in three things invention expression and inspiration.

2. View the path you are entering on with an enlightened mind.

3. Paul the apostle of the gentiles was a man of energy.

4. I inquired how did you like the sermon john—Pretty well he replied but it was too long.

5. Break break break on thy cold gray stones O sea.

6. Stones grow plants grow and live animals grow live and feel.

7. Wordsworth's great work is the excursion but it is not so much admired as tintern abbey ode to duty we are seven lucy and other short poems.

8. He who masters his passions conquers his greatest enemy

9. Most of those who have nothing to do commonly do nothing.

10. A paper contains the following Advertisement wanted a room for a single Gentleman twelve feet long and six feet wide

11. The following officers were elected for the ensuing year president William Wallace of salem vice president John Wentworth of boston secretary john greenleaf of Amesbury treasurer henry wilson of natick executive committee john smith charles Williams and henry winslow all of boston.

12. Flowers seem intended for the solace of ordinary humanity children love them quiet contented ordinary people love them as they grow luxurious and disorderly people rejoice in them gathered they are the cottager's treasure and in the crowded town [they] mark as with a little broken fragment of rainbow the windows of the workers in whose hearts rests the covenant of peace.—*Ruskin.*

THE DASH (—).

Rule I. Dashes may be used to set off a parenthetical expression; as,—

"There was a pond—no, rather a bowl—of water in the centre."

REMARK.—The dash—probably owing to its greater neatness and convenience—has to a great extent displaced the curves, or parenthesis; and the comma (see Rule III., p. 192) has a similar use. It may be stated that the commas in this use denote the least, the dashes the medium, and the curves the greatest degree of separation. *Both the dashes and the curves are correctly used in this Remark.*

Rule II. The dash may be used to denote an interruption or a sudden change of thought; as,—

1. "I knew I should find you at"—She cut me short by rising.

2. Is it possible that my friend—but I will not suspect him of the deed.

REMARK.—The dash sometimes denotes merely a significant pause; as, "The best way to punish him is to—let him alone."

Rule III. The dash may be used to denote a summing up of particulars; as,—

He has lost wealth, home, friends—everything but honor.

Rule IV. The dash may be used to add effect to other points.

REMARK.—Two instances under this rule—namely, the use of the dash before an enumeration (page 189, Note 1, *a*), and its use after a long subject (page 195, Rule VII., Remark)—have already been given. Among other uses may be mentioned the following:—

1. After a side head. (See head of this Remark.)

2. Between two quotations brought together in the same line; as, "Are you ready?"—"Yes."

3. At the end of an extract, before the name of the author or work; as,—

"The groves were God's first temples."—*Bryant.*

4. After *as*, *namely*, *as follows*, or other introductory word or words, when the example, quotation, or enumeration forms a separate paragraph. (Many illustrations of this use may be found on this and the preceding pages.)

EXERCISE XV.

Supply dashes where required in the following:—

1. But there lies the source so at least I believe of my sorrow.

2. But not one of them [the women] betrayed the mysterious something or other really, I can't explain precisely what it was! which I was looking for. *Atlantic Monthly.*

There are thus three ways of writing Bible references: 1 Kings XVIII. 27; 1 Kings 18.27; 1 Kings 18:27.

NOTE 2. *Yes* or *No*, in answer to a question, is generally followed by a colon, if the following words are a repetition of the answer; as, "Can you do this?"—"Yes: I have often done it." Some writers, however, prefer the semicolon.

REMARK.—If a noun follows *yes* or *no*, the colon must come after the noun; as, "Yes, sir: I will." "Yes, my lords: I am ready."

REFERENCE.—See Remark 2, page 190.

EXERCISE VII.

Separate the following into sentences; and use periods, colons, quotation marks, and capitals, where needed; also commas, where needed before quotations:—

All our conduct toward men should be influenced by this precept do unto others as ye would that others should do unto you Do not flatter yourself with the idea of perfect happiness there is no such thing in the world the discourse consisted of two parts* in the first was shown the necessity of exercise; in the second, the advantages that would result from it All admire the sublime passage God said let there be light; and there was light Have you ever been to Washington yes sir I once lived there.

THE SEMICOLON (;).

Rule I. A Semicolon is put between parts that are subdivided by commas; as,—

It is the first point of wisdom to ward off evil; and, since you are not sure of a minute, throw not away an hour.

---

* See Note 1, *b*, p. 189.

REMARK.—This is a very common use of the semicolon. It may be illustrated by the following figures:—

(1) ———, ———; ———, ———, ———.
(2) —————; —————, —————.

Rule II. The Semicolon is used between clauses or members that are loosely connected in sense, and between the terms of any disconnected series of expressions.

EXAMPLES.

1. Everything has its time to flourish; everything grows old; everything passes away.

2. President, John Hall; Vice Pres., F. A. Lyon; Sec., Anna Laurie.

Note 1. *a.* A Semicolon may be used before an enumeration, when the items are separated by commas; as, "I bought three books; Aftermath, The Circuit Rider, and Little Women." Most writers, however, prefer a comma and a dash before such an enumeration; as, "I have four studies,—Arithmetic, Grammar, Latin, and Literature."

b. When the terms of an enumeration are separated by semicolons, a colon must be used before it; as, "I bought three books: Aftermath, by Longfellow; The Circuit Rider, by Eggleston; and Little Women, by Miss Alcott."

NOTE 2. When *as*, *namely*, or *that is*, is used to introduce an example or enumeration, a semicolon is put before it, and a comma after it.

EXAMPLES.

1. A noun is a name; as, Cincinnati, Gen. Sherman. (The above rules and notes afford numerous examples of this use of *as*.)

2. There are three cardinal virtues; namely, faith, hope, and charity.

3. Some animals are amphibious; that is, they can live on the land or in the water.

REMARK 1. When such introductory words, with the terms after them, are used parenthetically, a comma precedes; as, "Of the three cardinal virtues, namely, faith, hope, and charity, the greatest is charity" "The word *reck*, that is, *care*, denotes a stretching of the mind.'

REMARK 2. *Viz.*, though it means the same as *namely*, requires different punctuation. It is now always preceded by a comma and followed by a colon; as, "Our duties to individuals are classed under four heads, *viz.:* as arising from affinity; friendship; benefits received; contract."

EXERCISE VIII.

Supply the omitted points and capitals in the following:—

When the righteous are in authority, the people rejoice but when the wicked beareth rule, the people mourn there are three persons the first, the second, and the third he that walketh uprightly walketh surely but he that perverteth his ways shall be known the following resolution was debated resolved that the death penalty should be abolished the following books are recommended for young men recollections of a busy life, by horace greeley my schools and schoolmasters, by hugh Miller I have two objections to the plan first it is too expensive second, it would require too much time.

THE COMMA (,).

Rule I. Co-ordinate clauses, and subordinate clauses not restrictive, are generally set off* by commas; as,—

1. I believe him, because I have always found him truthful.
2. The good shall be rewarded, but the wicked shall perish.

---

* "Set off" means, separated from what precedes or follows, or both.

3. The good which you do will not be lost, though it may be forgotten.

NOTE 1. If clauses are short and closely connected, no point is required between them; as, "Learning is better *than riches (are)*." "*John is playing* and *his sister is studying*." "The wicked flee *when no man pursueth*."

NOTE 2. No point is allowable between a restrictive phrase or clause and the word which it limits, unless there are intervening words; as, "Death is the season *which tests our principles*."

EXPLANATION.—A clause is said to be *restrictive*, when it limits a particular word to a particular sense. Thus, in the sentence, "The boy who studies will improve," the meaning is not "*The boy* will improve," but "*The boy who studies* (*i. e.*, the *studious boy*) will improve." Hence the clause "who studies" is restrictive. Clauses that are not restrictive are called *circumstantial*. Thus, in the sentence, "John, *who is a diligent student*, knows his lesson," the clause, "who is a diligent student," is *circumstantial*, not restrictive.

EXERCISE IX.

[This may be used either as an oral or a written exercise.]

Tell which of the clauses in the following sentences are restrictive, and which circumstantial, and insert commas where needed :—

The flowers which bloom in spring are most regarded. My favorite bird is the robin which appears about the first of April. No man who is a real friend would speak so. The man who hath done this thing shall surely die. The time when compromise was possible has passed. This man who is my friend assures me of the fact. Every teacher must love a pupil who is docile. The child was much attached to his teacher who loved him dearly. Urbanity often lends a grace to actions that are of themselves ungracious. Study nature whose laws and phenomena are all deeply interesting. Adopt a life founded on religion and virtue.

Rule II. The comma is used to set off transposed phrases and clauses; as,—

1. When the wicked entice thee, consent thou not.
2. Before giving way to rage, try to find a reason for being angry.

REMARK.—If the inversion seems easy and natural, no point is required; as, "In this way he obtained the prize."

Rule III. A comma is used to set off interposed words, phrases, or clauses; as,—

1. This, however, was not my purpose.
2. Every passion, however base or unworthy, is eloquent.
3. Let us send light and joy, if we can, to every one around us.

EXPLANATION.—"Interposed" means, placed between. An expression is said to be interposed, when it is introduced somewhat abruptly between parts that are closely related.

EXERCISE X.

Punctuate the following sentences according to Rules II. and III.:—

1. Of all our senses sight is the most important.
2. Christianity is in a most important sense the religion of sorrow.
3. Charity on whatever side we contemplate it is one of the highest Christian graces.
4. Charity like the sun brightens every object on which it shines.
5. Happiness therefore depends on yourself.
6. Of all bad habits that of idleness is the most incorrigible.
7. Till we can go alone we must lean on the hand of a guide.
8. He had no doubt great aptitude for learning languages.
9. It is mind after all that does the work of the world.
10. To most religion is a mere tradition.

Rule IV. The comma is used between similar or repeated words or phrases; as,—

1. *Earth, air,* and *water* teem with life. (Similar words.)

2. *Live or die, sink or swim, survive or perish,* I give my heart and my hand to this vote. (Similar pairs.)

3. He lived *in seclusion, in poverty,* and *in disgrace.* (Similar phrases.)

4. *Come, come, come;* I fear we shall be late. (Repeated words.)

EXPLANATION.—"Similar," as used here, means, "in the same construction."

NOTE 1. In a series of similar expressions, three cases may arise:—

1. *Where all the conjunctions are expressed.*
2. *Where all are omitted except between the last two.*
3. *Where all are omitted.*

In the *first* of these cases no point is required; in the *second,* all the terms are separated by commas; in the *third,* all are separated by commas, and a comma is placed after the last to separate it from what follows.* These cases are illustrated in the following examples:—

1. *First Case.*—We should live soberly and righteously and piously in the present world.

2. *Second Case.*—We should live soberly, righteously,† and piously in the present world.

3. *Third Case.*—We should live soberly, righteously, piously, in the present world.

---

* If the terms are adjectives, a comma must not be put between the last one and the noun it limits; as, "He is an honest, industrious man."

† Many persons improperly reject the comma between the last two terms when the conjunction is expressed. The method of punctuating here given is in accordance with nearly all recognized authorities on the subject, as well as with the usage of the best authors and publishers. The reasons for it may be found in Wilson's excellent treatise, to which reference has already been made.

NOTE 2. Two or more similar terms under Case 1st (Note 1) must be separated by commas, if either of them has an adjunct or modifier that does not apply to the others; as, "Joseph woke, and thought upon his dream."

In this example, "upon his dream" belongs to "thought," but not to "woke." Without the comma, the sentence would mean, "Joseph woke upon his dream and thought upon his dream"—an absurdity.

EXERCISE XI.

Use commas where they are required by Rule IV and the notes under it:—

1. The principal metals are gold silver mercury copper tin and lead.
2. A man that is temperate generous reliant faithful and honest, may at the same time have wit humor mirth and good breeding.
3. Power riches prosperity are sometimes conferred on the worst of men.
4. Death levels the rich and the poor the proud and the humble the strong and the feeble the young and the old.
5. Undue susceptibility and the preponderance of mere feeling over thoughtfulness, may mislead us.
6. Can flattery soothe the dull cold ear of death? (See first foot-note on p. 193.)

Rule V. The comma is used to set off independent elements; as, "*John*, come here, *sir*."

REMARK.—This rule applies to—

1. The nominative case independent; as, "I rise, *Mr. President*, to a point of order."
2. The nominative case absolute; as, "*The morning being clear*, we proceeded."
3. An unemphatic interjection: as, "*Oh*, how pretty!"
4. An independent adverb; as, "*Well*, how are you succeeding?"

Rule VI. The comma is used to set off an appositive element; as, James McCosh, *D. D.*, is a distinguished metaphysician.

REMARK.—If the appositive is quite short,—only a word or two,—no commas are required; as, "Paul the apostle was a man of energy."

EXERCISE XII.

Punctuate the following sentences according to Rules V. and VI.:—

1. Socrates the Greek philosopher never gave way to anger.
2. Sir Isaac Newton the eminent astronomer was remarkable for his modesty.
3. Charles V. King of Spain and Emperor of Germany died in a convent.
4. Boy bring me my boots.
5. The book was written by Francis Wayland D. D. LL.D.
6. Shame lost all virtue is lost.
7. Show pity Lord! O Lord forgive.
8. Accept my dear young friends this expression of my regard.
9. The question What is beauty? is hard to answer.
10. Why how well you look!

Rule VII. A comma is placed at the end of a long compound or complex subject; as,—

1. Love for study, a desire to do right, and carefulness in the choice of friends, are important traits of character.
2. He that places himself neither higher nor lower than he ought to do, exercises the truest humility.

REMARK.—If the subject is *very* long, especially if it is subdivided by points, a dash should be put after the comma.

Rule VIII. A comma is generally used to mark the ellipsis of a verb or other important words; as,—

"Hurry is the mark of a weak mind; despatch, of a strong one."

Rule IX. The comma is used to set off a short quotation informally introduced;* as,—

Agassiz once said, "I have not time to make money."

REMARK 1. This rule applies to any remark or observation resembling a quotation; as, "An important lesson in education is Learn to distrust your own opinions." "*Resolved*, That women shall be allowed to vote."

REMARK 2. An informal introduction generally ends with *say*, *exclaim*, *remark*, or some similar verb. Sometimes the quotation is in apposition; as, The maxim, "Know thyself," should not be forgotten.

REMARK 3. A divided quotation† requires two commas; as, "Virtue," says Dryden, "is its own reward."

Rule X. The comma is used to prevent ambiguity, and to give prominence to emphatic and contrasted parts; as,—

1. He who teaches, often learns himself. (If the comma were omitted, the sentence would be ambiguous.)

2. Strong proofs, not a loud voice, produce conviction.

3. I remain, yours respectfully, John Smith.

NOTE.—Phrases and clauses that are placed at a distance from the word on which they depend, or that have a common dependence on several words, are preceded by a comma; as,—

1. No *man* can be a thorough proficient in navigation, *who* has never been at sea.

2. I *prepare* those lessons which require the closest thinking, *early in the morning*.

3. Law is a *rule* of civil conduct, *prescribed* by the supreme power in the state, *commanding* what is right, *prohibiting* what is wrong.

---

* See Rule II. and Remark, page 185.

† See Note 2, page 184.

4. He questioned me of the battles, sieges, fortunes, that I have passed. (*That* refers equally to *battles*, *sieges*, and *fortunes*.)

5. We ought not to betray, but to defend, our country. (*Betray* and *defend* are in contrast, and *our country* is equally related to both.)

EXERCISE XIII.

Supply the omitted commas and capitals in the following sentences:—

1. "A faithful friend" it has been beautifully said "is the medicine of life."
2. A new feeling of what is due to the ignorant the poor and the depraved has sprung up in society.
3. We live in deeds not years; in thoughts not breaths; in feelings not in figures on a dial.
4. Homer was the greater genius; Virgil the better artist.
5. It is as great a breach of propriety to send an awkward careless badly written letter as it is to appear in a company of refined people with swaggering gait soiled linen and unkempt hair.
6. The books the pictures the statuary that were bought in Europe were all lost. [*All* the articles were bought in Europe.]

EXERCISE XIV.—MISCELLANEOUS.

Supply the omitted points and capitals, and give the rule for each:—

1. The essence of poetry may be said to consist in three things invention expression and inspiration.
2. View the path you are entering on with an enlightened mind.
3. Paul the apostle of the gentiles was a man of energy.
4. I inquired how did you like the sermon john—Pretty well he replied but it was too long.
5. Break break break on thy cold gray stones O sea.

6. Stones grow plants grow and live animals grow live and feel.

7. Wordsworth's great work is the excursion but it is not so much admired as tintern abbey ode to duty we are seven lucy and other short poems.

8. He who masters his passions conquers his greatest enemy

9. Most of those who have nothing to do commonly do nothing.

10. A paper contains the following Advertisement wanted a room for a single Gentleman twelve feet long and six feet wide

11. The following officers were elected for the ensuing year president William Wallace of salem vice president John Wentworth of boston secretary john greenleaf of Amesbury treasurer henry wilson of natick executive committee john smith charles Williams and henry winslow all of boston.

12. Flowers seem intended for the solace of ordinary humanity children love them quiet contented ordinary people love them as they grow luxurious and disorderly people rejoice in them gathered they are the cottager's treasure and in the crowded town [they] mark as with a little broken fragment of rainbow the windows of the workers in whose hearts rests the covenant of peace.—*Ruskin.*

THE DASH (—).

Rule I. Dashes may be used to set off a parenthetical expression; as,—

"There was a pond—no, rather a bowl—of water in the centre."

REMARK.—The dash—probably owing to its greater neatness and convenience—has to a great extent displaced the curves, or parenthesis; and the comma (see Rule III., p. 192) has a similar use. It may be stated that the commas in this use denote the least, the dashes the medium, and the curves the greatest degree of separation. *Both the dashes* and the curves are correctly used in this Remark.

Rule II. The dash may be used to denote an interruption or a sudden change of thought; as,—

1. "I knew I should find you at "—She cut me short by rising.

2. Is it possible that my friend—but I will not suspect him of the deed.

REMARK.—The dash sometimes denotes merely a significant pause; as, "The best way to punish him is to—let him alone."

Rule III. The dash may be used to denote a summing up of particulars; as,—

He has lost wealth, home, friends—everything but honor.

Rule IV. The dash may be used to add effect to other points.

REMARK.—Two instances under this rule—namely, the use of the dash before an enumeration (page 189, Note 1, *a*), and its use after a long subject (page 195, Rule VII., Remark)—have already been given. Among other uses may be mentioned the following:—

1. After a side head. (See head of this Remark.)

2. Between two quotations brought together in the same line; as, "Are you ready?"—"Yes."

3. At the end of an extract, before the name of the author or work; as,—

"The groves were God's first temples."—*Bryant.*

4. After *as*, *namely*, *as follows*, or other introductory word or words, when the example, quotation, or enumeration forms a separate paragraph. (Many illustrations of this use may be found on this and the preceding pages.)

EXERCISE XV.

Supply dashes where required in the following:—

1. But there lies the source so at least I believe of my sorrow.

2. But not one of them [the women] betrayed the mysterious something or other really, I can't explain precisely what it was! which I was looking for. *Atlantic Monthly.*

3. There he sits before his table and lets his coffee cool and God knows I was ready to drink it warm two hours ago and never looks at me.

4. And since there was no rehearsal delicious thought how it occurred to me again and again! since I was free, I walked.

5. He was witty learned industrious plausible *everything* but honest.

6. Was there ever a braver captain? Was there ever but I scorn to boast.

7. The three greatest names in English poetry are among the first we come to Chaucer Shakspeare Milton.

8. "I have" "Nothing in the world," said the other.

THE CURVES ( ).

Rule.—The curves are used to enclose a remark, reference, or explanation, that has little if any connection with the rest of the sentence; as,—

"I was eager to discover the fair unknown, (she was again fair, to my fancy!) and I determined to go down to the party."—*Atlantic Monthly.*

Exp.—The enclosed expression is called a *parenthesis*. The same name is sometimes applied to the enclosing marks, but the term *curves* is shorter and more appropriate.

Reference.—See remark under Rule I. for the dash, p. 198.

Rem. 1. *Inside Points.*—The parenthesis is punctuated as if it were not enclosed, with this exception no point is used at the end (inside the curve). unless it be an interrogation, or exclamation, or period denoting an abbreviation. Other points seem to be superseded by the curve.*

---

* Sometimes an entire sentence is enclosed in curves; that is, it is a parenthesis with reference to the paragraph. In that case the *closing point* is placed inside the last curve.

Example 1. "He says (I don't believe it) that my friend told him so." Here the parenthesis is a full sentence, but no period is used at the end. *Example* 2. "He tells me (is it so?) that you are going home." Here the parenthesis is interrogative, and requires a question mark.

REM. 2. *Outside Points.*—To ascertain whether any point is required outside the curves, ask yourself the question, Would any point be required in this place, if the parenthesis were removed, and the parts before and after it brought together? If so, the same point must still be used; but *where shall it be?*—before the first, or after the last, curve? *Answer:* It must be placed *after the last curve*,* unless there is a point *inside* that curve: if there is a point inside, then the outside point must be placed *before the first curve.*

EXAMPLES.

1. Know, then, this truth (enough for man to know): Virtue alone is happiness below. [Here the parenthesis is, as it were, pushed in between *truth* and the colon required after it.]

2. Know, then, this truth: (oh, that all could be brought to realize it!) virtue alone is happiness below. [Here an exclamation is inside the last curve, hence the colon is put before the first. See also the example under the above rule.]

EXERCISE XVI.

Supply curves and other points where needed in the following sentences:—

1. There had been no want of "chivalrous" she used the word! respect and attention.

2. Many have wondered perhaps you among the rest at my success.

3. While the Christian desires the approbation of his fellow-men and why should he not desire it he disdains to receive their good-will by dishonorable means.

---

* Some writers place the point before the curve, and repeat the point inside the last curve. This method is now nearly obsolete.

4. The rocks hard hearted varlets! melted not into tears.

5. I gave said he and who would not have given? my last dollar to the miserable beggar.

6. She had managed the matter so well oh how artful a woman she was as to ensnare my father's heart.

THE BRACKETS [ ].

Rule.—The brackets are used to enclose some interpolation or correction made by an editor, reporter, or transcriber; as,—

1. "The number of our days are [is] with thee." (Correction.)
2. "My colleague [Mr. Scott] is mistaken."

REM.—The words enclosed in curves are part of the original composition; those enclosed in brackets generally are not. But a writer sometimes uses the brackets to enclose something that seems somewhat foreign to the context—a remark, for instance, under the head of "Examples," as on page 201 of this work, and elsewhere.

REFERENCE.—See the Remarks under Curves (pp. 200, 201) They apply to the brackets also.

EXERCISE XVII.

Punctuate the following extract from a report of one of Chatham's speeches; bearing in mind the rules and remarks on dashes, curves, and brackets:—

They should have beheld him when addressing himself to Mr. Granville's successors he said As to the present gentlemen those at least whom I have in my eye looking at the bench on which Conway sat I have no objection I have never been made a sacrifice by any of them. Some of them have done me the honor to ask my poor opinion before they would engage to repeal the act: they will do me the justice to own I did advise them to engage to do it but notwithstanding for I love to be explicit I cannot give them my confidence sensation Pardon me gentlemen bowing to them *confidence* is a plant of slow growth.

EXERCISE XVIII.—GENERAL.

1. While the world lasts some will lead others be led
2. Is it possible that he is but why borrow trouble
3. He began his speech as follows Mr. Chairman we have met for the freest discussion of this subject
4. A lady should be as to her dress modest pretty sensible as to her behavior dignified graceful self-forgetful as to her motives pure benevolent aspiring
5. A fool always wants to shorten space and time a wise man wants to lengthen both A fool wants to kill space and time a wise man first to gain them then to animate them —*Ruskin*
6. His closing words were these Gentlemen I have detained you too long already and will not further trespass cries of go on go on upon your patience No gentlemen I cannot go on now and I close by bidding you good night loud and prolonged cheers during which the speaker withdrew
7. Wherever we may fix there is still some one whom we may find superior or inferior and these relations are mutually convertible as we ascend or descend the shrub is taller than the flower which grows in its shade the tree than the shrub the rock than the tree the mountain than the single rock and above all are the sun and the heavens it is the same in the world of life

EXERCISE XIX.—CONTINUED DISCOURSE.

WIT AND HUMOR.

Falstaff has both wit and humor but more wit I think than humor between wit and humor there is an evident distinction but to subject the distinction to minute criticism would require more time than we can spare and after all it is more easy to feel than to explain it if I should say alexander pope has great wit charles dickens has great humor all would give me their assent but if reversing the positions I should say charles dickens has great wit alexander pope great humor the assertion would be met by an instinctive denial wit implies thought humor sensibility wit deals with ideas humor with actions and with manners wit may be a thing of pure imagination humor involves sentiment and character wit is an essence humor an incarnation wit and humor however have some elements in common both develop unexpected analogies both include the principles of contrast and assimilation both detect inward resemblances amidst external differences and the result of both is pleasurable surprise [but] the surprise from wit excites admiration the surprise from humor stimulates merriment and produces laughter humor is a genial quality laughter is indeed akin to weeping and true humor is as closely allied to pity as it is abhorrent of derision.—*Henry Giles.*

[*Further exercises* may be had in abundance, and of the best kind, from any well-printed book or magazine.]

CONCLUDING SUGGESTIONS.—1. If you desire to improve in punctuation, notice the points used in whatever you are reading, and try to discover why they are used. You should also punctuate carefully whatever you write.

2. Do not use too many points. Do not insert a point where it simply *may* be inserted, but only where it *must* be; or, at least, where it adds to the clearness or force of the sentence.

PART III.

MISCELLANEOUS:

APPELLATIVE TITLES.

FORMS OF ADDRESS AND SALUTATION

ABBREVIATIONS.

FOREIGN WORDS AND PHRASES.

POSTAL INFORMATION.

BUSINESS FORMS.

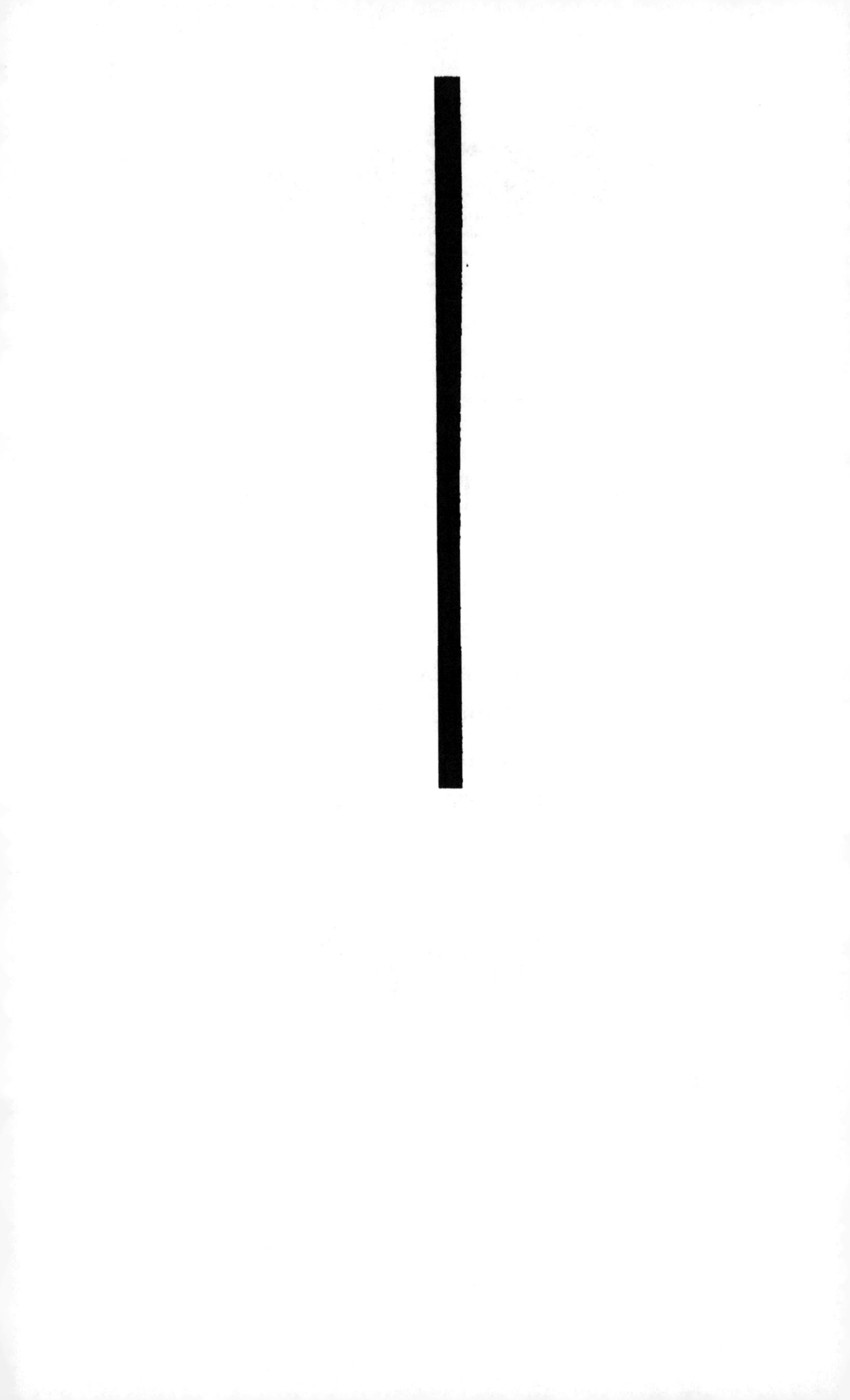

Appellative Titles.

OUTLINE.

1. Use and Abuse of Titles.
2. List of Titles and their Abbreviations.

Introductory Remark.—An attempt is here made to reduce to something like a system the "unwritten law" recognized by the highest authorities in social, professional, and official circles, relating to the use of the various appellative titles employed in the United States. This is done mainly for the purpose of assisting those who have occasion to employ these titles in correspondence; but beyond this, we hope to do something for the diffusion of correct ideas on the subject, to the end that the public at large may learn to bestow these titular honors with intelligent and just discrimination.

Parts.—This article will consist of two parts: in the *first* will be discussed the significance and use of the various kinds of titles; and in the *second* will be presented a full classified list of them, with their authorized abbreviations.

I. USE AND ABUSE OF TITLES.

Classification.—American titles may be classified as follows:—

1. Titles of Respect and Courtesy.
2. Titles of Attainment in Course.
3. Titles of Service ex-officio.

For brevity, these may be respectively designated as *Social*, *Scholastic*, and *Official* titles.

Social Titles.—Titles of respect and courtesy are of universal application; and are usually employed in polite intercourse, unless superseded by some professional or official title To omit them in addressing others (except members of the Society of Friends, or those with whom we are on terms of the closest intimacy) betrays in any case a want of delicacy and refinement, and in some cases amounts to actual rudeness.

The social titles usually employed are *Mister* (formerly *Master*), *Sir*, *Esquire*, *Gentlemen* (plural only), *Master* (applied to boys), *Mistress* (pronounced *Missis*), *Madam*, *Miss*, and *Ladies* (plural only).

Mr., *Master*, *Mrs.*, and *Miss* are always prefixed to the name. *Esquire* is always suffixed. *Sir*, *Gentlemen*, *Madam*, and *Ladies* are always used without the name, as in the salutation of a letter. *Sir*, *Esq.*, *Master*, and *Miss* are used in both the singular and the plural; *Gentlemen* and *Ladies* (as titles), in the plural only; *Mrs.* and *Madam*, in the singular only. *Mr.* has no English plural, but its place is supplied by *Messrs.*, a contraction of the French *Messieurs*. The want of a plural of *Madam* is in like manner supplied by the word *Ladies*. But we have no word to serve as the plural of *Mrs.*, unless it be the French *Mesdames* (plural of *Madame*). The objection to this is, that it is not yet Anglioized, and its use therefore savors of pedantry. The want of a good native plural of *Mrs.* is a serious defect in the language. We address a firm composed of Mr. Smith and Mr. Jones, as "Messrs. Smith & Jones;" but how shall we address a firm composed of *Mrs.* Smith and *Mrs.* Jones? Evidently we must either address them individually, as "Mrs. Smith and Mrs. Jones;" or else collectively (using the obnoxious French term *Mesdames*), as "Mmes. Smith and Jones."

MRS. AND LADY.—Besides being vulgar, it is a shocking ambiguity to use "lady" instead of "wife" or "Mrs;" but *Mr. and Mrs. Jones* is understood by every one. It is true that the other style, *Mr. Jones and Lady*, was once, in Dr. Johnson's time, for instance, in good usage in England; but this affords no valid reason for its use at the present day.

In invitations to prominent officials, *Lady* is sometimes employed to denote the wife of the officer, as "The Secretary of the Navy and *Lady*;" but in general invitations to gentlemen, the plural form should be used, as "Mr. Charles Wilson and *Ladies*."

The use of *Mrs.* or *Miss*, without the name, in address, is no more to be tolerated than the use of *Mr.* alone.

MR. AND ESQ.—In this country these terms are generally interchangeable, but the former has a somewhat wider application than the latter. *Mr.* may be applied to men of all classes, whether high or low; but *Esq.* is properly applied only to persons of some prominence in society. It would be a misuse of language to address an ignorant man, for example, as Joseph Murray, *Esq.*; but he might without impropriety be addressed as *Mr.* Joseph Murray. In aristocratic countries, this choice of title would be determined by a man's occupation alone, some kinds of labor being regarded as essentially menial and degrading; but in this country, in accordance with the spirit of free institutions, it should be determined, not by a person's vocation or station, but by his acquirements, training, character, refinement, and public services. Honest worth, refined character, and valuable services to the country, are the foundations of true republican nobility, and have a right to command respect.

Members of the legal profession are always addressed in writing as *Esq.*

SPECIAL USES OF MR., MRS., AND MISS.—There are some interesting facts in regard to the use of these titles, which, though not directly relating to correspondence, are not out of place here:—

1. *To denote pre-eminence.*—As persons rise to distinction, other titles seem to drop off as unmeaning and superfluous; and the plain title of *Mr.*, borrowing a lustre from their own characters and from the citizenship which they have done so much to ennoble, becomes to them

a mark of true nobility. Thus we say *Mr.* Adams, *Mr.* Lincoln, *Mr* Sumner, *Mr.* Chase; and no other titles, such as Excellency, Honorable, or Senator, would be so expressive of the respect and esteem with which they are regarded. *Mrs.* and *Miss* are similarly used to denote distinction; as, Mrs. Stowe, Miss Dix. Indeed, in speaking of persons of the very highest distinction, we reject all titles. Such men, for example, as Shakspeare, Milton, Martin Luther, Edmund Burke, Patrick Henry, and Daniel Webster, are most honored in their own illustrious names alone.

The common American vulgarism of contracting and mutilating the Christian name in referring to prominent or elderly persons, as Dan Webster, Joe Johnston, Ben Wade, and Andy Johnson, is disrespectful, presumptuous, and altogether indefensible.

2. *To denote seniority.*—If a person has an unusual name, or if he is the only person of the name in a particular place, the title may be prefixed to the family name alone; as, "Mr. Eastlake, Mrs. Lefevre." If there are two or more persons of the same name, the oldest or most prominent may be addressed as *Mr.* Smith, the others of the name being addressed and spoken of as "*Mr. Wm* Smith, *Mr. James* Smith," etc., joining the title to the full name. As elsewhere stated, it is better, in addressing a married woman, if her husband is living, to prefix the title *Mrs.* to her husband's name; as, "Mrs. John Smith." When the woman is married to the eldest male member of the family, or is the only one of the name, she receives merely the title of "Mrs. Smith," while each of the others is distinguished by her husband's name; as, "Mrs. *Peter* Smith," "Mrs. *Thomas* Smith," etc. Whenever the eldest dies, the wife of the eldest son or brother, or whoever may be next in the order of succession, succeeds to the honor of "Mrs Smith." In the case of two or more unmarried daughters, the eldest alone is "Miss Brown," while the others are "Miss *Jane* Brown," "Miss *Susan* Brown," etc. The same usage is sanctioned with respect to two or more sons. When all are addressed or spoken of together, we may say, "the *Misses* Brown," or "the *Miss* Browns;" "the *Messrs.* Brown," or "the *Mr.* Browns." If, however, the family name ends in *s*, the title must be made plural, for the sake of euphony; as, "the *Misses* Jones," "the *Messrs.* Rogers."

3. *To avoid invidious distinctions.*—*Mr.* is used among gentle-

men meeting as such, for social, literary, scientific, or other purposes of mutual interest. when professional or official titles which attach to a part only of the company might seem to imply an invidious comparison; as, Mr. Benjamin Rush, Mr. Agassiz, Mr. Edward Everett, Mr. Bryant, etc. Great delicacy of feeling is implied in this use of *Mr*. It arises from that instinct of genuine politeness which carefully avoids everything which could wound the sensibilities of any one present by reminding him of his inferiority.

4. *Before other Titles.*—*Mr*. is sometimes used before the official or professional titles of prominent personages; as, "Mr. President." "Mr. Chief Justice." "Mr. Senator." *Rev*. is similarly used, always with *the* prefixed; as, "The Rev. Dr. Tyng," "The Rev. Prof. Hodge." "The Rev. Father Brown." The title *Rev*. should never be used immediately before the surname. Either the Christian name should be given, as "The Rev. Albert Barnes," or some other title should intervene, as in the above examples. If no scholastic title is applicable, *Mr*. may be used; as, "The Rev. Mr. Elliott."

Mrs. may in like manner be used, in speaking of or addressing married women, before the names and titles of their husbands; as, "Mrs. Admiral Porter," "Mrs. Senator Sherman," "Mrs. General Sheridan." Objections may be urged against this style of address; but it has the sanction of good usage at the National Capital; and use gives law to etiquette as well as to language.

Scholastic Titles.—These are degrees and other honors conferred by universities, colleges, scientific schools, and other institutions of learning, or acquired in the lawful exercise of a learned profession.

Collegiate degrees, and those of scientific, art, and other learned associations, are conferred in two ways: regularly, or in course; and *honoris causâ*. Regular degrees are conferred upon those who have completed a prescribed course and passed a formal examination; honorary degrees, on persons who have become distinguished in public life, or in liberal and scientific studies. Being bestowed as rewards of personal achievement, they belong for life to the recipients, unaffected by any positions and honors that may be subsequently obtained.

Reverend, President, etc.—The title of *Reverend*, though it is not regularly conferred, is always given, by common consent, to those who have passed the necessary examination and been regularly ordained: and it may therefore without impropriety be said to be conferred in course.

President, *Provost*, *Chancellor*, *Rector*, *Dean*, *Registrar*, *Professor*, and *Master*, as titles of service, attach primarily to the offices, rather than the officers; and when the duties of these offices are discontinued, the titles themselves generally fall into disuse. After long and distinguished service, however, the title may be retained, as in the case of Emeritus Professors, Emeritus Rectors, etc.

Professor.—The title of *Professor* may be possessed *of right* or *by courtesy*. It belongs *of right* to any one elected by the proper authorities to a regular chair or professorship in any educational institution organized with full departments and faculties, and conferring degrees under a legal charter. One cannot become a professor of his own choice—*i. e.*, be self-elected; he must be elected by others who are vested with proper authority.*

The title is given *by courtesy* to scholars and scientists who have become noted as specialists in any department of knowledge, and to those who have distinguished themselves as educators.

Abuse of the Title.—It is not uncommon at the present day for teachers of the Squeers sort, dancing-masters, horse-tamers, barbers, and pretenders of all kinds, to assume the

* *Professor* is now, in academic language, applied to a salaried graduate, either actually employed in teaching, or at least whose duty it is to teach.—*Encyclopædia Britannica.* This duty is not always recognized. The course of time has generated sinecure professorships.—*Malden, Origin of Universities*, p. 111.

title of *Professor*, in order to give them, in the eyes of the ignorant, an importance that they could never hope to attain by honest means. This abuse should be frowned upon by all intelligent people, as it tends to bring an honorable and useful title into contempt. All titles, and especially that of *Professor*, should be used sparingly and with wise discrimination.

MASTER.*—The term *Master* is used in England, and also in some parts of this country, instead of Principal or Teacher; as "Head-Master of Rugby," "Master of Adams Grammar School." Formerly all male instructors were designated as "Master," or "Schoolmaster," but the more democratic term "Teacher" has now pretty generally supplanted it.

DOCTOR OF MEDICINE (M. D.).—No one has a right to this title who is not a regular graduate of a college in good standing. It may now be obtained by a person of either sex. A woman who is entitled to the degree may be addressed as "Florence Howard, M. D.," or as "Dr. Florence Howard."

Abuse of the Title.—The unwarranted appropriation of titles, and especially of this title, is in any case a gross violation of taste; and when, as is too often the case, it is done to deceive the public for the sake of personal gain, it is a base and dangerous fraud. The professions—and society still more—need some authoritative and effective protection from such impostors; persons who, usurping professional titles, inflict upon the public unprofessional practice, and fill their pockets with money obtained by false pretences from over-credulous patients. Such announcements as, "*Doctor* Buncome's Elixir of Life," "*Dr.* Gullaway, Medical Adviser and Electrician," "*Dr.* Jalap, *M. D.*, cures all fatal diseases," etc.,

* *Master* and *Doctor* were formerly synonymous terms; but in process of time the name *Master* was restricted to teachers of the liberal arts, and the title of *Doctor* was assumed by teachers of theology, law, and medicine.

ought at least to suggest doubt and investigation to invalids Life and health are too precious to be entrusted to the care of ignorant and unprincipled quacks.

Official Titles.—These include all the titles applicable to officers in the civil, military, and naval services of the United States and of the several States. Civil titles belong to the office and not to the incumbent. Though the officer, on retiring from public service, again becomes a private citizen, it is customary, as a form of compliment, to continue the official title during life, unless superseded by one more honorable. Indeed, it is not unusual to retain it even when different or inferior public service is afterward accepted.

This anomaly in the use of titles in a country whose institutions forbid titled classes, made it possible to have as advocates in a recent celebrated trial, two "Judges," two "Generals," and several "Honorables." Observing this in the published reports, an English gentleman wrote to a friend residing in this country, asking how and by what commission the cause was being tried. "You have," said he, "a judge on the bench; but then you have two judges, two generals, and as many honorables at the bar. Is the defendant being tried by a court of law, a court-martial, or a court ecclesiastic?"

The retention of titles after retirement from service seems to be at variance with the spirit of our institutions, and it may therefore be questioned whether it would not be more patriotic, as well as in better taste, to discontinue the title with the office.

HIS EXCELLENCY.—The title given to the President in Washington's time was *His Excellency*. *Highness* was proposed, but coming as it did from the Princes and Princesses Royal of England, it was rejected as unrepublican. The title of *Excellency* has gradually fallen into disuse in addressing the Chief Magistrate; but it is still given to Governors and Foreign Ministers. It is the legal title of the Governors of *Massachusetts* and South Carolina; but so repugnant were titled forms to the founders of our National and State constitutions and laws, that with perhaps these two exceptions, no civil titles other than those naming the officers have legal recognition.

HON. AND ESQ.—The *general* official titles in the civil service are *Honorable* and *Esquire*. The first is applicable to judges, mayors, senators and representatives in Congress, the heads of government departments, and others of similar rank, below that of Governor or President; and the title is generally retained through life.* All civil officers not having a right to the title of *Honorable*, are addressed as *Esquire* or *Sir*.

Abuse of Hon.—The abuse of *Honorable* has brought it into such disrepute, that without a knowledge of the character and services of those to whom it is given, it has come to have little significance. Only those whose abilities, character, and services have caused them to be elected or appointed to the most important and responsible trusts of the nation, or of a State or city, are entitled to be enrolled as *Honorable*.

MILITARY AND NAVAL TITLES.—Military and Naval, like professional titles, are properly retained after long or distinguished service. The title which properly belongs to an officer and by which he is addressed is that named in his commission. Those who rank under Captain in the Army, and Commander in the Navy, are addressed by their title, or simply as *Mr.*, *Sir*, or *Dr.*, as the case may be. *U. S. A.* and *U. S. N.* are given after their names by the officers of the United States Army and Navy respectively.

Selection and Order of Titles.—When titles or degrees applicable to the same person are the same in kind, only the most honorable is used. When they differ in kind, and but one is given, the most honorable is used; if all are given,

* For a more specific statement of the officers to whom this title may be applied see page 219. For the uses of *Esquire* and *Honorable* in England, see page 240.

they are placed in the order of their honor or precedence, which is presumed to be the order in which they were conferred or acquired.

Titles and degrees are not assumed by the writer in private correspondence; but in an official communication of any kind the signature should be followed by the writer's office or rank, or its abbreviation; as, "George W. Sharswood, *Associate Justice of the Supreme Court of Pennsylvania;*" "W. T. Sherman, *General.*" A scholastic title is not appended to a signature, unless it is at the same time professional. Thus, "John Jones, *LL.D.*," as an official signature, would be in bad taste; but "John Smith, *M. D.*," or "Wm. Brown, *D. D. S.*," would be entirely proper, because M. D. and D. D. S. are not only scholastic or collegiate, but also professional titles. (See page 48.)

II. CLASSIFIED LIST OF APPELLATIVE TITLES,

WITH THEIR ABBREVIATIONS.

CLASSIFICATION.

I. Titles of Respect and Courtesy. (Social.)

II. Titles of Attainment. (Scholastic.)
1. Divinity.
2. Law.
3. Medicine.
4. Phil. and Science.
5. Arts and Letters.
6. Music.
7. Technics.
8. Didactics.
9. Fellowships, etc.

III. Titles of Service. (Official.)
1. Clerical.
2. Civil.
3. Professional.
4. Military and Naval.
5. Diplomatic.

Note.—Scholastic Degrees (A. M., D. D., etc.) are always abbreviated. No abbreviations are allowable in addressing an officer of high rank; a President, Governor, or Archbishop, for example. A list of general abbreviations may be found on page 242, *et seq.*

Remark.—Many abbreviations of titles may be used in catalogues, on the title-pages of books, and elsewhere, that are inadmissible in addressing letters. In addresses, no degree is used lower than Master or Doctor. Thus, we may write "John Smith, A. M., or M. D.," but not "John Smith, A. B., or B. S." If a person has no higher title than a bachelor's degree, we should use simply *Mr.* or *Esq.* In formal letters any of the higher titles, such as S. T. D., L. H. D.. A. A. S., may be used. If a person has a number of honorable distinctions, one or more may be used, followed by *etc.;* as, "John Tyndall, LL.D., F. R. S., etc." In the following list, the more usual abbreviations are preceded by a section-mark (§); as, §LL.D.

I. Titles of Respect and Courtesy.

[*Fr.* denotes French; *pl.*, plural; *pron.*, pronounced; *italics*, foreign.]

Mister (formerly Master)	§**Mr.**	Mistress (pron. Missis)	§**Mrs.**
Messieurs (Fr. pl.)	§**Messrs.**	*Mesdames* (Fr. pl.)	**Mmes.**
Gentlemen	——	Madam	**Mad.**
Sir, Sirs	——	*Madame* (Fr.)	**Mme.**
Esquire, Esquires	§**Esq., Esqs.**	Ladies	——
Master (a boy)	——	Miss, Misses	——

II. Titles of Attainment in Course.

All of the following degrees, and many more, are authorized; but many of them are rarely if ever given. B. C. L., D. C. L., and a few others are conferred only by foreign universities. Harvard College confers only the following degrees: *regular*—A. B., A. M., Ph. D., B. D., LL.B., S. B., S. D., C. E., M. D., D. M. D.: *honorary*—LL.D., D. D. Yale confers nearly the same, with the addition of Ph. B., D. E., and Mus. D.

[The Latin terms are given only when they are necessary to explain the abbreviation.]

1. Divinity.

Bachelor of Divinity	**B. D.**
Doctor of Divinity	§**D. D.**
Doctor of Divinity, *Sanctæ Theologiæ Doctor*	**S. T. D.**
Doctor of Divinity, *Doctor Theologiæ*	**D. T.**
Professor of Divinity, *Sanctæ Theologiæ Professor*	**S. T. P.**

2. Law.

Bachelor of Laws	**LL.B.**
Master of Laws	**M. L.**
Doctor of Laws	§**LL.D.**

Dr. of Laws, *Jurum Doctor*, J. D.
Doctor of Civil Law, *Juris Civilis Doctor* . . . . . J. C. D.
Bachelor of Civil Law . B. C. L.
Doctor of Civil Law . . D. C. L.
Dr of both Laws, Canon and Civil, *Juris utriusque Doctor* J. U. D.

3. Medicine.

Doctor . . . . § Dr.
Bachelor of Medicine . M. B.
Doctor of Medicine . . § M. D.
Master in Surgery, *Chirurgiæ Magister* . . . . . . C. M.
Graduate in Pharmacy Phar. G.
Master in Pharmacy . Phar. M.
Doctor in Pharmacy . Phar. D.
Dr. of Dental Surgery § D. D. S.
Dr. Dental Medicine § D. M. D.

4. Philosophy and Science.

Bachelor of Philosophy . Ph. B.
Doctor of Philosophy . § Ph. D.
Bachelor of Science . . . B. S.
Master of Science . . . M. S.
Doctor of Science . . . S. D.

5. Arts and Letters.

Bachelor of Arts § B. A. or A. B.
Master of Arts M. A. or A. M.
Bachelor of Letters, *Baccalaureus Literarum*. . . . . B. Lit.
Doctor of Letters, *Literarum Doctor* . . . . . . Lit. D.
Doctor of Polite Literature, *Literarum Humaniorum Doctor* . . . . . . L. H. D.
Poet Laureate (Eng.) . . P. L.

6. Music.

Bach. of Music M.B. or B.Mus.
Dr. of Music D.M. or § Mus.D.

7. Didactics.

(Pa. State Normal Schools.)

Bachelor of the Elements . B. E.
Master of the Elements . M. E.
Bachelor of Science . . B. S
Master of Science . . M. S
Bachelor of the Classics . B. C.
Master of the Classics . . M. C.

8. Technics.

Civil Engineer . . . § C. E.
Topographic Engineer . . T. E.
Dynamic Engineer . . . D. E.
Military or Mechanical Engineer . . . . M. E.

The degrees of Bachelor and Master in each of the departments of engineering, and in chemistry and architecture, are authorized, bu rarely conferred.

9. Fellowships, etc.

(American.)

Fellow of the Am. Academy *Academiæ Americanæ Socius* A. A. S.
Member of Am. Antiquarian Society *Americanæ Antiquarianæ Societatis Socius* A. A. S. S.
Member of the Am. Oriental Soc., *Americanæ Orientalis Societatis Socius* . . . . A. O. S. S.
Member of Am. Phil. Soc., *Societatis Philosophicæ Americanæ Socius* . . . . S. P. A. S.
Fellow of the Mass. Med. Soc., *Massachusettensis Medicinæ Societatis Socius* M. M. S. S

Fellow of the Hist. Society, *Societatis Historiæ Socius* **S. H. S.**

Fellow of Connecticut Academy, *Conn. Academiæ Socius* **C.A.S.**

These are the only American societies that confer memberships or fellowships that are recognized as titles.

III. Titles of Service Ex-Officio.

1. The Clerical Service.*

A Bishop (Epis., Cath., *et al.*) :—
Right Reverend . ‡ **Rt. Rev.**

A Bishop (Methodist) :—
Reverend . . . . . ‡ **Rev.**

A Presiding Elder (Meth.) :—
Reverend . . . . . **Rev.**

A Rector, Minister, Priest, Rabbi, or Reader . . . . . **Rev.**

2. The Civil Service.

1. National Government.

The Chief Executive :—
1. Civil : The President ‡ **Pres.**
2. Military : Commander-in-Chief of the Army and Navy.

The Vice-President, Ex-Officio President of the Senate :—
Honorable . . . . ‡ **Hon.**

Chief-Justice of Supreme Court :—
The Chief-Justice . . . **C. J.**
His Honor . . . . . . ——

Associate Justices :—
Justice . . . . **Jus.**
His Honor . . . . . . ——

Foreign Ministers :—
His Excellency . . **H. Exc.**
Honorable . . . . . . **Hon.**

Members of the Cabinet and Members of Congress . . . **Hon.**

Heads of Bureaus, Asst. Secretaries, Comptrollers and Auditors of the Treasury, Clerks of the Senate and House of Representatives . . . . ‡ **Esq.**
By courtesy . **Hon.**

All other United States Officers, **Esq.** or **Mr.**

2. State Governments.

The Governor . . . . ‡ **Gov.**
Civil : His Excellency **H. Exc.**
Military : Commander-in-Chief.

Sen. Judge of Supreme Court :—
Chief-Justice . . . . **C. J.**
His Honor . . . . . ——

Associate Justices :—
Justice . . . . . **Jus**
Judge . . . . ——
His Honor . . . . . ——

Lieutenant-Governor, Heads of Departments, State Senators,† Law Judges . . . . **Hon.**

* For Roman Catholic clerical titles see page 228, *et seq.*

† Authorities are divided on the question whether the title *Hon.* should be applied to members of the upper and lower houses of the legislature. It is the prac-

Mayors of Cities:—

Honorable	**Hon.**
His Honor	—

Members of the House of Representatives* . . . . . . **Esq.**
By courtesy . . **Hon.**

Aldermen, Magistrates, and all Officers not specified . . **Esq.**

3. Professional Services.

Officers of Universities and Colleges:—

Chancellor	**Chanc.**
Vice-Chancellor	**V. Chanc.**
President	§ **Pres.**
Vice-President	§ **V. Pres.**
Provost	**Prov.**
Dean§	—
Rector	**Rect**
Registrar	§ **Reg**
Librarian	§ **Lib.**

Faculty and Instructors:—

Professor	§ **Prof.**
Lecturer	—
Tutor	—

4. The Military and Naval Service.

The command pertaining to the rank of general and line officers is printed under the title in finer type. Commands are however subject to change by assignment, and "the laws governing the army organization have left it in an anomalous state, and the rank of commands in an unsettled condition." The titles of the general and line officers, placed opposite in the two columns, indicate relative rank in the two departments of service.

Military Service (U. S. A.). GEN'L AND LINE OFFICERS.		**Naval Service** (U. S. N.). LINE OFFICERS.	
General The Armies of the U. S.	**Gen.**	Admiral The Fleets of the U. S.	**Adm.** or **Adml.**
Lieutenant General An Ar. Corps and territorial Div.	**Lt. Gen.**	Vice Admiral A Fleet or Fleets.	**V. Adml.**
Major General A Division, and territorial Div.	**Maj. Gen.**	Rear Admiral A Fleet or Squadron.	**R. Adml.**
Brigadier General A Brigade, and territorial Dept.	**Brig. Gen.**	Commodore Squadron. Ships of First Class.	**Commo.**
Colonel A Regiment.	**Col.**	Captain Vessels of Second Class.	**Capt.**

tice of the State Department at Washington to apply the title Esq. to members of both: but the custom of most States is different. Probably the greater weight of opinion is in favor of the usage here indicated; *i. e.*, the application of Hon. to members of the upper house, and Esq. to those of the lower. In some States the title of Hon. is applied also to the Speaker of the lower house.

* See the preceding foot-note, beginning on page 219.

LINE OFFICERS (*Continued*).

Lieutenant Colonel . **Lt. Col.**
A Battalion. 2d in com'd, Reg't.

Major . . . . **Maj.**
A Battalion. 3d in com'd, Reg't.

Captain . . . . **Capt.**
A Company.

First Lieutenant . **1st Lieut.**
A Platoon. 2d in com'd, Comp.

Second Lieutenant . **2d Lieut.**
A Platoon. 3d in com'd, Comp.

Cadet . . . . —
Student at West Point Mil. Acad.

STAFF OFFICERS.

Adjutant General . **Adj. Gen.**
Rank of Brigadier General.

Assistant Adj. Gen. . **A. A. G.**
Rank of Colonel to Major.

Inspector General **Insp. Gen.**
Rank of Colonel.

Assistant Insp. Gen. . **A. I. G.**
Rank of Colonel.

Quartermaster General **Q. M. G.**
Rank of Brigadier General.

Assistant Q. M. Gen. **A. Q. M. G.**
Rank of Colonel.

Deputy Q. M. G. . **Dep. Q. M. G.**
Rank of Lt. Colonel.

Quartermaster . . . . **Q. M.**
Rank of Major.

Assistant Quartermaster **A.Q.M.**
Rank of Captain.

Commissary Gen. of Subsistence.
Rank of Brig. Gen. **C. G. S.**

Assistant C. G. S. . **A. C. G. S.**
Rank of Colonel to Lt. Colonel.

Commissary of Subsistence **C. S.**
Rank of Major to Capt.

LINE OFFICERS (*Continued*).

Commander . . . . . . **Com.**
Vessels of Third Class.

Lieutenant Com. . . **Lt. Com.**
Vessels of Fourth Class.

Lieutenant . . . . . . **Lieut.**
Executive Officer of Fourth Class.

Master . . . . **Mas.**
Assistant Navigator.

Ensign . . . . **Ens.**

Midshipman . . . . . **Mid**
Student at Annapolis Nav. Acad.

STAFF OFFICERS.

Surgeon General . **Surg. Gen.**
Rank of Commodore.

Medical Director . . **Med. Dir.**
Rank of Captain.

Medical Inspector . **Med. Insp.**
Rank of Commander.

Surgeon . . . . **Surg.**
Rank of Lieutenant Commander.

Passed Assist. Surg. **P. A. Surg.**
Rank of Lieutenant.

Assistant Surgeon **Asst. Surg.**
Rank of Master to Ensign.

Paymaster General . . **P. M. G.**
Rank of Commodore.

Pay Director . . . **Pay Dir.**
Rank of Captain.

Pay Inspector . . **Pay Insp.**
Rank of Commander.

Paymaster . . . . . . **P. M.**
Rank of Lieutenant Commander.

Passed Asst. P. M. **P. A. P. M.**
Rank of Lieutenant.

Assistant Paymaster . **A. P. M.**
Rank of Master.

STAFF OFFICERS (*Continued*).

Surgeon-General . **Surg. Gen.**
Rank of Brigadier General.

Chief Medical Purveyor,
Rank of Col. **Chf. Med. Pur.**

Surgeon . . . . . . **Surg.**
Rank of Major.

Assistant Surgeon **Asst. Surg.**
Rank of Captain to 1st Lieut.

Paymaster-General . **P. M. G.**
Rank of Colonel.

Assistant P. M. G. **Asst.P.M.G.**
Rank of Colonel.

Paymaster . . . . . **Pay M.**
Rank of Major.

Chief of Engineers . . **Chf. E.**
Rank of Brigadier General.

Chief of Ordnance . **Chf. Ord.**
Rank of Brigadier General.

Judge-Adv.-Gen. . . . **J. A. G.**
Rank of Brig. Gen.

Judge-Advocate . . . **J. A.**
Rank of Major.

Chief Signal Officer . **C. S. O.**
Rank of Colonel.

STAFF OFFICERS (*Continued*).

Engineer-in-Chief **Eng.-in-Chf.**
Rank of Commodore.

Chief Engineers . . . **Chf. E.**
Rank of Captain to Lieutenant.

Passed Asst. Eng. . **P. A. Eng.**
Rank of Lieut. to Master.

Assistant Engineer . . **A. Eng.**
Rank of Master to Ensign.

Cadet Engineer : **Cadet Eng.**
Graduates of Naval Academy.

Chaplain . . . . . . **Chap.**
Rank of Capt. to Lt. Com.

Chief of Construction **Chf. Con.**
Rank of Commodore.

Naval Constructor **Nav. Con.**
Rank of Captain to Lieutenant.

Commandant . . . . **Comdt.**
Navy Yards and Stations.

Navigator . . . . . . **Nav.**
Master of a Vessel.

Captain (by courtesy) . . **Capt.**
Master of a Merchant Vessel.

5. The Diplomatic and Consular Service.

Envoy Extraordinary and Minister Plenipotentiary, **E. E. and M. P.**

Minister Plenipotentiary, **Min. Plen.**

Minister Resident . **Min. Res.**

Minister Resident and Consul-General . . **M. R. and C. G.**

Secretary of Legation **Sec. Leg.**

Interpreter . . . . . . **Int.**

Consul-General . . . . **C. G.**

Vice-Consul-General . **V. C. G.**

Consul . . . . **C.**

Vice-Consul . . . . . **V.-C.**

Deputy Consul . . . . **D. C.**

Consular Agent . . **Con. Agt.**

Commercial Agent . . **C. A.**

Agent . . . . **Agt.**

Marshal . . . . . . **Mar.**

Consular Clerk . . . . **C. C.**

Forms of Address and Salutation

I. American.

[The form of *Address* is printed in plain Roman type, the *Salutation* in italic. *A*—— denotes the Christian name; *B*——, the surname. See Part I., p. 25 *et seq.*]

1. Persons in Private Life.

The forms and directions under this head are fully given in Part I., Chap. II., Sec. II., rendering any further forms unnecessary.

2. Persons in the Learned Professions.

The Clergy.*

A Bishop (other than a Methodist).†

To ‡ the Right Reverend Alonzo Potter, D. D., Bishop of Pennsylvania *Right Reverend Sir:*— or *Right Rev. and dear Sir.*

A Rector, Minister, Priest, Rabbi, § or *Reader.* §

To the Rev. A—— B——. To the Rev. Dr. A—— B——. The Rev. George Brown, D. D., Rector (or Pastor, as the case may be) of—— Church, Philadelphia. *Sir:*— *Reverend Sir:*— *Rev. and dear Sir:*—

The Bench and the Bar.

The Chief-Justice of the Supreme Court of the United States.

To the Hon. Salmon P. Chase, Chief-Justice of— etc. To the Chief Justice of the Supreme Court, etc. *Sir:*— *Mr. Chief-Justice:*— *Your*

---

* For the addresses and salutations to be used in addressing the clergy of the Roman Catholic Church, see page 228.

† Methodist bishops disclaim the title of *Rt. Rev.*, and are addressed simply as *Rev.*

‡ *To* may be omitted; but it is better to retain it in writing to distinguished personages or corporate bodies.

§ In the Jewish Church all ordained ministers are styled *Rabbi*, and in this country are addressed as *Rev.* The Hebrew title is *Moreh Tsedek* (teacher of righteousness), or *Moranu* (our teacher), or *Moreh Moranu* (the teacher of our teachers). The *Reader* is also addressed as *Rev.* His Hebrew title is *Hazan* (conductor of services).

Honor:— May it Please Your Honor:— May it Please the Honorable Court:—

Note.—Your Honor, May it Please, etc., are the terms that are used in court, not in private letters.

An Associate Justice.

To the Honorable A—— B——, Justice, etc. Or, Honorable Justice B——. *Sir:— Your Honor:—etc.*

Other Judges.

The Hon. A—— B——, Judge of the Court of Quarter Sessions (or as the case may be). Or simply, The Honorable A—— B——. *Sir:— Dear Sir:— Your Honor:—etc.*

Lawyers, Justices of the Peace, etc.

John H. Jones, Esq. *Sir:— Dear Sir:—*

The Medical Profession.

A Physician or Surgeon.

Dr. O. W. Holmes. Or, O. W. Holmes, Esq., M. D. *Sir:—*

A Dentist.

Dr. John Alexander. Or, John Alexander, Esq., D. D. S. (or D. M. D.). *Sir:— Dear Sir:—*

Literary and Scientific Men.

The President of a College.

The Rev. Eliphalet Nott, D. D., LL.D., President of Union College. Or, The Rev. Dr. Nott (with or without the official designation) *Sir:— Dear Sir:— Rev. and dear Sir:—*

A Professor.

John Lewis, D. D., LL.D., Professor of Greek in —— College. Or, Prof. John Lewis, D. D., LL.D. Or, Dr. John Lewis, Prof. of——, etc. *Sir:— Dear Sir:—*

3. Officers in the Civil Service.

The President of the United States.

To the President, Executive Mansion, Washington, D. C. *Sir:—* or *Mr. President:—*

Note.—The term "His Excellency" was formerly applied to the President, thus To His Excellency, George Washington, Pres. of the U. S.; but is now nearly if not quite discontinued. (See page 214.)

The Vice-President.

To the Honorable Henry Wilson, Vice-President of the United States. Or (unofficial), Hon. Henry Wilson. *Sir*:—

Cabinet Ministers.

To the Honorable E. M. Stanton, Secretary of War. Or, To the Honorable the Secretary of War. Or, Hon. E. M. Stanton. *Sir*:—

All others not specified who are entitled to "Honorable" (see pages 215 and 219) are addressed in a similar manner.

Foreign Ministers.

To His Excellency Edward Everett, Envoy Ex., etc., at the Court of St. James. *Your Excellency*:— *Sir*:—

Assistant Secretaries, Heads of Bureaus, etc.

To John Smith, Esq., Assistant Secretary of State. *Sir*:— (Sometimes, by courtesy, addressed as *Hon.*)

The Governor of a State.

To His Excellency John A. Dix, Governor of the State of New York. Or, His Excellency Governor John A. Dix. Or, To His Excellency the Governor. *Sir*:— *Your Excellency*:—

Heads of State Departments, Members of the State Senate, etc.

Hon. Samuel E. Dimmick, Attorney-General of Pa. *Sir*:—

4. Officers in the Military or Naval Service.

Army Officers.

The General of the Army.

To General W. T. Sherman, Commanding the Armies of the United States. Or, General W. T. Sherman, Commanding U. S. A. Or, To the General of the Army.* *General*:— (or *Sir*:— See Note).

Note.—The general practice in the army is to use the military title (*General*, *Col.*, *Captain*, etc.) in the "salutation," in addressing all officers above the grade of Lieutenant. A Lieut. has the salutation of *Sir*. In the superscription, his rank is generally mentioned. In army correspondence "the address" is generally, not always, written at the top of the letter. (See page 30.)

A Colonel.

Col. Henry May, commanding 1st Cavalry. Or, Col. Henry May, U. S. A. *Colonel*:—

* It is a rule of the War Department at Washington, to address all officers in this manner; that is, by their *office*, not by name.

The Quartermaster-General. See form on page 36.

Other officers of the Army are addressed in a similar manner.

NAVY OFFICERS.

The Admiral of the Navy.

To Admiral D. G. Farragut, Commanding the Fleets of the United States. Or, Admiral D. G. Farragut, Commanding U. S. N. Or, To the Admiral of the Navy. *Sir :—*

NOTE.—In the Navy, *Sir* is invariably used as the salutation; and the address, consisting of the name, title, and command, is written at the bottom. We make the following extract, from the Navy Regulations:—

"Line officers in the Navy, down to and including Commander, will be addressed by their proper title; below the rank of Commander, either by the title of their grade, or *Mr.* Officers of the Marine Corps above the rank of 1st Lieut. will be addressed by their military title, brevet or lineal; of and below that rank, by their title of *Mr.* Officers not of the line will be addressed by their titles, or as *Mr.* or *Dr.*, as the case may be."

A Commodore.

Commodore A—— B——, commanding South Atlantic Squadron (or as the case may be). Or, Commodore A—— B——, U. S. N. *Sir :—*

Other officers of the Navy are addressed in a similar manner.

5. Legislative and Other Organized Bodies.

REMARK.—Communications to an organized body are generally addressed to the President of that body, as its chief representative. A communication may, however, be addressed to the body itself; but in this case, as in the other, it goes to the President, and is by him formally presented. Communications—especially petitions—are often addressed "To the President and Members of ——," etc., meaning, of course, the President and *other* members

The Senate of the United States.

To the Honorable the Senate of the United States in Congress Assembled. *Honorable Sirs :—* Or, *May it Please your Honorable Body* (or, *the Honorable Senate*) *:—*

The President of the Senate.

To the Honorable the President of the Senate of the United States. Or, To the Honorable Henry Wilson, President of the Senate of the United States. *Sir :—* Or, *Honorable Sir :—*

The House of Representatives.

Address and salutation similar to those of the Senate.

The Speaker of the House.

To the Honorable the Speaker of the House of Representatives. *Sir*, or *Mr. Speaker.*

State Legislatures.

They are addressed in the same form as the Houses of Congress; except, of course, the name, and the formula "in Congress assembled."

NOTE.—The title *Honorable* is generally applied to legislative bodies when addressed collectively, even though the individual members are not entitled to it. Thus, in addressing the House of Representatives of a State, for example, we would use the title *Honorable*, but in addressing any member of the House, we would use the title *Esq.*, with the salutation *Sir.* The same remark applies to city governments. In some States the Speaker of the House is addressed as *Hon.*

A Court.

To the Honorable Judges of the ——— Court. *Your Honors:—* Or. *May it Please Your Honors:—*

A Board of Education.

To the President and Members of the Board of Education (or whatever the corporate name may be). *Sirs:—* Or (if in a large city), *May it Please Your Honorable Body:—*

As stated above, communications (except petitions) are generally addressed to the President of such bodies, as follows:—

The Pres. of a Board of Education, Directors, or Commissioners.

To John T. Morris, Esq., President of the Board of School Commissioners of Baltimore City. *Sir:—*

To a Company.

To Thos. A. Scott, Esq., President of the Pa. R. R. Co. Or, To A——— B———, Esq., President of the ——— Insurance Co., New York. *Sir:—*

A PETITION.

To a Legislature.

To the Honorable the Senate and House of Representatives of the Commonwealth of Pennsylvania:

The undersigned respectfully represent, etc. Or,

The petition of A. B. (or the undersigned) *humbly showeth*, etc.

(Close, when there are several signers.)

And your petitioners, as in duty bound, will ever pray, etc.

(Signatures.) | (Signatures.)

In a petition to Congress, or to either House, add the words "in Congress assembled," as on page 226. A petition to a Court or other body is in the same general form.

Roman Catholic Titles and Forms.

*With Directions for Addressing the Pope and other Dignitaries of the Church, and a List of the Abbreviations allowed and used by Roman Catholics.**

Explanation.—*A*—— denotes *Christian* name; *B*——, *family* name; (*a*), the *address* of the letter; (*b*), the *salutation*; (*c*), the *complimentary close*.

The Pope.

(*a*) 1. To our Most Holy Father, Pope Pius the Ninth (or Pope Pius IX.).

2. To His Holiness Pope Pius the Ninth (or Pope Pius IX.).

(*b*) 1. Most Holy Father. 2. Your Holiness.

(*c*) Prostrate at the feet of your Holiness,
And begging the Apostolic Benediction,
I protest myself now and at all times to be,
Of your Holiness, the most obedient son,
A—— B——.

Note.—The first forms of address and salutation would be used by Catholics. The second forms might also be used by them, but would not sound so affectionate and loyal as the others. They would be used chiefly by those who, having to communicate with the Pope, but not acknowledging him as the head of their Church, would still wish to treat him with respect. The concluding form is of course for Catholics only. Non-Catholics would have to trust to their good taste or common sense to conclude suitably. If several join in the concluding form, it must be put in the plural. If the writer is a female, she writes "child," instead of "daughter;" if a boy or youth, he writes "child" instead of "son;" if the writers are of both sexes, they write "children."

A Cardinal.

(*a*) 1. To His Eminence Cardinal B——. (If he is also a bishop, an archbishop, or a patriarch, add) Bishop (or as the case may be) of ———.

2. To His Eminence the Most Reverend Cardinal B——.

(*b*) 1. Most Eminent Sir. 2. Most Eminent and Most Reverend Sir.

(*c*) 1. Of Your Eminence,
The most obedient and most humble servant,
A—— B——.

* For the interesting and valuable information contained in this article we are indebted to Monsignor Seton, D. D., to whom we were kindly referred by the *Most Reverend* Archbishop Wood, of Philadelphia.

2. I have the honor to remain,
Most Eminent Sir,
With profound respect,
Your obed't and humble serv't,
A—— B——

NOTES.—1. If the writer is a Catholic and belongs to the cardinal's diocese (supposing him to have one), he adds, if he is an ecclesiastic, after the words "humble servant," the words "and subject;" but if he is a layman, he adds the words, "and son."

2. The Christian name is not generally used in addressing prelates, if the family name is a distinguished one, and if there is no danger of its being mistaken for the name of another person. To such common names as Smith and Jones, however, the Christian name should generally be added, to avoid confusion. If the official title follows the name, the Christian name must always be used; as,

"His Eminence A—— B——, Archbishop of New York."

3. The title D. D. or S. T. D. (Doctor of Divinity) may be written after the name of a cardinal, archbishop, or bishop; but the best authorities condemn its use in these cases, for the reason that such persons are doctors ex-officio, and the title is therefore redundant. It is never used when the official title precedes the name. Thus, we may write "Right Reverend A—— B——, D. D., but not "Right Reverend *Bishop* B——, D. D."

A Patriarch.

The forms used are the same as those given in the next paragraph, except that *Patriarch* is substituted for *Archbishop*.

An Archbishop.

(*a*) 1. Most Reverend Archbishop B——. Or,
2. Most Reverend A—— B——, Archbishop of ——.

(*b*) 1. Most Reverend and Respected Sir. Or,
2. Most Reverend and Dear Sir.

(*c*) 1. I have the honor to be,
{ Most Reverend Sir, or
Most Reverend Archbishop, or
Most Reverend and Dear Sir,
Your obedient servant,
A—— B——.

NOTE.—The second form of salutation (*b* 2) is to be used only by a clergyman or a friend.

A Bishop.

(*a*) 1. Right Reverend Bishop B——. Or,
2. Right Reverend A—— B——, Bishop of ——

(*b*) 1. Right Reverend Sir. 2. Right Reverend and Dear Sir.
3. Right Reverend and Dear Bishop.

(*c*) I have the honor to remain,
Right Reverend Sir (or any of the formulas *b*, 1, 2, 3)
Your obedient servant,
A—— B——.

Mitred Abbots.

(*a*) 1. Right Reverend Abbot B—— (name of abbey, post-office, county, State). Or,
2. Right Reverend A—— B—— (initials of Order), Abbot of ——.

(*b*) 1. Right Reverend Abbot. 2. Right Reverend Father Abbot.
3. Right Reverend Father. 4. Right Reverend and Dear Sir.

(*c*) 1. I remain,
Right Reverend Sir,
Your obedient servant,
A—— B——. Or,

2. Begging your blessing,
Right Reverend and dear Father,
I remain, as ever,
Your dutiful son
(or your affectionate child),
A—— B——.

NOTES.—1. By courtesy all abbots, whether mitred or not, have the same style and address. However, in addressing an abbot merely residing in an abbey, without being its abbot, of course "Abbot of ——" would be omitted, for the reason that, although an abbot, he has no abbey.

2. The form (*c* 2) would perhaps be used only by a monk subject to the abbot or belonging to his order; or by a boy or girl educated by monks or nuns of his order, or in some way connected with the order or the abbot.

(Roman) Prelates.

I. *Apostolic Prothonotaries.*
II. *Domestic Prelates* (viz., of the Pope).

(Both are styled, like bishops and abbots, Right Reverend, and are generally called Monsignores, a title, however, which is given, in Italy, to all prelates above them, except to cardinals and abbots; and to some dignitaries below them. *Among English*-speaking Catholics it is not use. of archbishops and bishops.)

(a) 1. Right Reverend Monsignor* B——. (I., II.) Or,
2. Right Reverend A—— B——. (I., II.) Or,
3. Right Reverend Monsignor B——. Prothonotary Apostolic (I. only.)
4. Right Rev. Monsignor A —— B——, Prothonotary Apostolic, etc. (I. only.) (*Etc.* is added when, as is usually the case, he has other dignities.)
5. Right Reverend A—— B——,
Domestic Prelate of His Holiness (or of the Pope). (II. only.)

It will be noticed that the 1st and 2d of the above forms apply equally to I. and II.; the 3d and 4th to I. only; the 5th to II. only.

(b) 1. Right Reverend Sir.
2. Right Reverend Monsignore. Or,
3. My dear Monsignor (if well acquainted). Or, simply
4. Monsignor.

The above forms (b) apply both to I. and II. The 4th is stiff, such as might be used by a total stranger or not very friendly correspondent. To begin, "Monsignor B——," would be rude, and forebode that the writer meant to say something disagreeable.

(c) 1. Right Reverend Sir.
2. Right Reverend and Dear Sir. Or,
3. My Dear Monsignor,

Your friend and servant,

A—— B——.

Inferior Dignitaries.—All dignitaries inferior to the above-mentioned (viz.: to patriarchs, archbishops. bishops, abbots, and prelates) are addressed "Very Reverend," except archdeacons,† who are styled venerable. Dignitaries are Roman Monsignores other than the two sorts of Prelates mentioned above. Administrators of vacant

* *Monsignor* has become more or less anglicized; consequently, *Monseigneur*, which is French, should not be used except when writing in that language. *Monsignor* and *Monsignore* (Italian) are used indifferently, but in English the former is preferable.

† There are no archdeacons in the U. S., but there was one for many years—the late Archdeacon McCarron. of New York.

dioceses, Vicars General, Provosts, Archpriests, Canons, Deans Heads and Provincials of Religious Orders, and Priors of Priories (which are separate establishments). These, and by *courtesy* some others, such as Priors of Monasteries over which abbots preside, Rectors and local Superiors of Religious Houses, Presidents or heads of seminaries, colleges, and larger religious institutions, are properly addressed as "Very Reverend."

Doctors of Divinity or of Laws (1), Vicars Forane (2), Rural Deans (3), Vice-Presidents of colleges, or other assistant superiors of religious institutions (4), Members of the Episcopal Council (5), Examiners of the Clergy (6), Chancellors of a diocese (7), the Secretary of a bishop or of a diocese (8), and others, along with simple Priests, have no claim to be styled "Very Reverend," although a somewhat abusive custom seems to allow it to classes 2, 3, and 4. These and all others in Priests' or Deacons' orders should be styled simply "Reverend."

Administrators of Vacant Sees.

(*a*) 1. Very Reverend A—— B—— (with initials of office). Or
2. Very Reverend Father A—— B——,
Administrator of ——.

(*b*) Very Reverend Sir.

NOTE.—Such expressions as "My dear Vicar-General, or Dean, or Provost, or Canon," etc., are used; but never the expression, "My dear Administrator."

A Vicar General.

(*a*) 1. Very Reverend A—— B—— (with initials of office). Or,
2. Very Reverend Vicar General B——. Or,
3. Very Reverend A—— B——,
Vicar General of —— (name of diocese).

(*b*) 1. Very Reverend and Dear Sir.
2. Very Reverend Sir. Or,
3. My dear Vicar General (only if the writer belong to the diocese). Or simply, 4. Dear Sir.

Monsignores of the Inferior Degrees.

(*a*) 1. Very Reverend A—— B—— (followed by the name of office, for instance, "Private Chamberlain to the Pope")
2. Very Reverend Monsignore A—— B—— (or B——).

(*b*) 1. Very Reverend and Dear Monsignore. Or,
2. Very Reverend Doctor (should he have this degree).

The Rector of a Religious House, Provincial of an Order, or a Prior.

(*a*) 1. Very Reverend Father A—— B—— (initials of order) Rector (or Prior) of —— (name of House). Or, Provincial of —— (name of Order, or, better, of the members of the Order taken collectively).

Doctors of Divinity (*D. D.*) *or of Laws* (*LL.D.*).

(*a*) 1. Reverend A—— B——, D. D. (or LL.D.). Or,
2. Reverend Dr. A—— B——.

If such an one be the pastor of a church, or a professor in a seminary or other institution, add, "Pastor of ——," or "Professor of ——."

Archdeacon.

(*a*) Venerable A—— B——,
Archdeacon of —— (church or diocese),

(*b*) 1. Venerable Father. Or, 2. Venerable and Dear Sir.

Priest (simply).

(*a*) 1. Reverend A—— B——. Or, 2. Reverend Father A—— B——. Or, 3. Reverend Father B——.

(*b*) 1. Reverend Sir. Or, 2. Reverend and Dear Sir. Or, 3. Reverend Doctor.

NOTE.—"Your Reverence" is courteous and correct, but is local in its use; being confined mainly to Irish Catholics.

Female Superiors of Religious Orders.

(It is quite customary, but abusively so, to call every female superior of a religious order, or house, "Reverend Mother." The proper style is as follows:—)

(*a*) 1. Mother —— (name in religion, *e. g.*, Elizabeth). Or,
2. Mother —— (name in religion, unless she preserves, as in some orders, her family name),
Superior of —— (*e. g.*, Sisters of Charity).

NOTE.—Members of one religious order in the United States, the "Ladies of the Sacred Heart," are always addressed and spoken of as "Madame." In England, an abbess is styled "The Right Reverend Lady Abbess of ——" (name of abbey), or "The Right Reverend Lady Abbess ——" (Christian and family names, or family name only). It is customary, even in the United States, to style religious women who are at the head of some religious order (as, for instance, the Sisters of Charity),—not merely superiors of houses of that order,—or who are the superiors of houses belonging to *ancient* orders (as, for instance, the Benedictines, the Dominicans, etc.), "Reverend"; as, "The Reverend Abbess" or "Prioress," or "The Reverend Mother Abbess" or "Prioress," or "The Reverend Mother Superior."

My Lord, Your Lordship, Your Grace.—In Great Britain these terms are always used in addressing cardinals, archbishops, bishops, and sometimes in addressing abbots (see forms on page 240). An American, therefore, in communicating with such dignitaries, would do well, in the spirit of courtesy, to give to them the titles that belong to them in their own country; but neither custom nor the wishes of the corresponding dignitaries in the United States sanctions the adoption of a style which, from being so peculiarly English and associated with a state of society utterly un-American, grates harshly on the ears of their fellow-citizens. Archbishop Bayley, of Baltimore, who is chief of the Hierarchy in this country, is much opposed to this form of address, as needlessly shocking to other citizens; Bishop Becker, of Wilmington, Delaware, and Bishop Lynch, of Charleston, S. C., hold the same opinion.

The same objection applies to the use of "Your Grace," etc., in connection with archbishops (see page 229). This style has been employed here, to a limited extent, among Catholics; but it has always been received with disfavor, and seems to be dying out as a form of address,—except, of course, when applied to the archbishops of England and her dependencies.

Letters and Petitions to the Pope and Others.

Letters.—In letters to the Pope, the salutation must stand alone upon one line at the top of the page; the body of the letter occupies the middle portion of the page, and the place of writing and date are put at the bottom, near the left edge. A certain vacant space should be left between the salutation and the beginning of the letter, an equal space between the complimentary close and the signature, and a less space between the end of the letter and the complimentary close. By reason of these requirements, note paper or any small form of letter-paper should never be used for this purpose. The same requirements must be observed in writing to Cardinals and other high ecclesiastics in all parts of Italy,—at least when writing in anything like a formal or official manner,—except that the spaces diminish with the rank of the dignitaries.

Petitions.—The form of a petition is somewhat different; and the language should be Latin or Italian. French, however, is tolerated if the Pope understand it, which may not always be the case.

A sheet of official letter-paper is folded lengthwise into two equal parts, by turning the left or folded edge over to the right (thus bringing half of the fourth page uppermost). Near the top of this fold is written the address of the Pope ("To His Holiness, Pope Pius IX.," *e.g.*); half-way down, the word "for" (in the proper language); and near the bottom, the name and residence of the petitioner. Then the sheet is unfolded, bringing it to its original position. On the left-hand column of the first page, near the top, the petitioner writes the salutation ("Most Holy Father," *e.g.*), then,—leaving the customary space,—his petition; and at the bottom, without his signature, a formula corresponding to our closing form, "And your petitioner, as in duty bound, will ever pray," etc. On the right-hand fold or column the Pope's answer is written, either in his own hand-writing or that of the person who has been charged with that duty.

The object of folding the page, and of writing the petition on one fold of it, is that the answer to it may be written on the other column or fold, and thus the two parts of the document be put, for convenience, in juxtaposition.

One Side Only.—A petition, and, in fact, a letter, address, or any other communication to the Pope, should generally occupy only one side (the face) of the leaf; but if the matter cannot be contained on one page only, it should be continued on the third page of the sheet, and not on the second page.

Place of Address.—In a letter to a Cardinal, the place and date should be written in the upper right-hand corner (the usual position), and the Cardinal's address in the lower left-hand corner. Indeed it is better in all cases to put a clergyman's address (as is customary in Rome) at the bottom rather than at the top, to distinguish the letter in form from ordinary business and other secular letters.

Abbreviations Used by Roman Catholics.

Remark.—In writing to the Pope, a Cardinal, or any high dignitary, abbreviations relating to the dignitary may be used in the outside address, but not in the inside address or the body of the letter. Abbreviations that do not relate to the dignitary himself may, however, be tolerated in the letter. (See a similar remark on page 217)

Explanation.—The words and letters in italics are always printed so.

Holy Father . . . . . **H. F.**	Abbott, Abbess . . . . **Abb**
His Holiness . . . . . **H. H.**	Prior, Prioress . . . . . **Pr.**
Cardinal . . . . . **Card.**	Monsignor . . . **Monsig.***
His Eminence **H. E.** or **His Em.**	Prothonotary Apostolic, **Prot. Ap.**
Archbishop . . . . . **Abp.**	Domestic Prelate . **Dom. Prel.**
Bishop . . . . **Bp.**	

* Mgr. is frequently, but ignorantly, used for the abbreviation of *Monsignor.* It is the abbreviation of the French *Monseigneur.*

Private Chamberlain, **Priv. Chamb.**
Provincial . . . . **Prov.** or **P.**
Superior . . . . . . **Sup.**
Administrator . . . **Adm.**
Vicar Gen'l **V. G.** or **Vic. Gen.**
Vicar Forane **V. F.** or **Vic. For.**
Rural Dean . **R. D.** or **Rur. Dn.**
Chancellor . . . . . **Chanc.**
Canon . . . . **Can.**
Provost . . . . . . **Prov.**
Secretary . . . . . . **Sec.**
Brother . . . . **Br.** or **Bro.**
Sister . . . . . **Sr.** or **Sist.**
Rector . . . . **Rect.**
Father, Friar . . . . . **Fr.**
Most Reverend { **Most Rev.** or **Mt. Rev.**
Right Reverend . . **Rt. Rev.**
Very Rev. **V. R.** or **Very Rev.**
Dr. of Civil or Canon Law **LL.D.**
Doctor of Divinity . . . **D. D.***
Vicar Apostolic, **V. A.** or **Vic. Ap.**
Diocese . . . . **Dioc.**
Pastor . . . . **Past**
Saint . . . . **St.**
Coadjutor, Coadjutor Bishop, *Coad.*,† **Coad. Bp**
In partibus infidelium, *in part.*,‡ or ***i. p. i.***
Parish Priest . . . . . **P. P**
Monastery . **Mon.** or **Monast.**
Convent . . . **Con.** or **Conv.**
Community . . . . . . **Com.**
Congregation§ . . . . **Cong.**
Novitiate . . . . **Nov.**
Primate . . . . **Prim.**
Metropolitan **Metr.** or **Metrop.**
Diocesan Seminary **Dioc.Sem.**
Provincial Seminary **Prov.Sem.**
Catholic Institute . **Cath. Inst.**
Young Men's Catholic Association. **Y. M. Cath. A.**
Parochial Library **Paroch. Lib.**
Female Academy, **Fem. Ac.** or **Acad.**
Coadjutor with right of succession . **Coad.** *cum. jure suc.*
Blessed Virgin Mary . **B. V. M.**‖

* The clergy are divided into Secular clergy and Regular clergy. D. D. is generally placed only after the name of a member of the secular clergy; *i.e.*, of one not belonging to a religious order. After the name of a member of a religious community, congregation, or order, it is usual to put the initials only of that com., cong., or order. In all cases, the D. D. precedes any other initials; as, "Very Rev. A—— B——, D. D., V. G."

† Written with a *small c* if after the name; as, "Rt. Rev. A—— B——, coadjutor."

‡ Never in capitals, and always after the name; as, "Rt. Rev. A—— B——, Bp. of —— *in part.*"

§ A kind of religious order.

‖ Frequently found in Catholic Directories, after the name of a church as, for instance, "Church of the Visitation, B. V. M."

ABBREVIATIONS OF THE PRINCIPAL RELIGIOUS ORDERS IN THE UNITED STATES.

Written after the Names of the Members.

ENGLISH.	ABBREVIATION.	LATIN.
Benedictines . .	**O. S. B.**	Ordinis Sancti Benedicti.
Dominicans. . .	**O. P.** or **O. S. D.**	Ordinis Prædicatorum; or Ordinis Sancti Dominici.
Franciscans . .	**O. S. F.**	Ordinis Sancti Francisci.
Augustinians . .	**O. S. A.**	Ordinis Sancti Augustini.
Capuchins . . .	**Cap.** or **O. Min. Cap.**	Capucinus; or, Ordinis Minorum Capucinorum.
Cistercians . . .	**O. Cist.**	Ordinis Cisterciensis.
Jesuits	**S. J.**	Societatis Jesu.
Redemptorists .	**Redempt.**, or **C. SS. R.**	Redemptorista; or, Congregationis Sanctissimi Redemptoris.
Passionists . . .	**Pass.** or **C. P.**	Passionista; or Congregationis Passionis.
Minor Conventuals	**O. M. Conv.**	Ordinis Minorum Conventualium.
Carmelites, Calced.	**O. C. C.**	Ordinis Carmelitarum Calceatorum.
" Discalced.	**O. C. D.** or **Dis.**	Ordinis Carmelitarum Discalceatorum.
Vincentians, or Lazarists	**C. M.**	Congregationis Missionum.
Sulpitians . . .	**S. S.**	(Societatis) Sancti Sulpitii.
Oblates of Mary Immaculate . . .	**O. M. I.**	

Ladies of the Sacred Heart . . . . **Ladies of the S. H**
Nuns of the Visitation . . . . **Nuns of the V.**
Sisters of Charity . . . . **Sisters of Char.**
Sisters of Notre Dame . . . . **Sisters of N. D.**

II. English.

[Owing to our intimate social relations with the people of England, a knowledge of the proper forms and titles to be used in addressing various officers and persons of rank in that country is with many almost a social necessity. To all, indeed, these forms must be a matter of interest, on account of the light they throw on the history and literature, as well as the political and social life, of the Mother Country. We therefore devote two or three pages to a presentation of English Forms of Address and Salutation.]

1. The Royal Family.

The King or the Queen.

To the King's (or Queen's) Most Excellent Majesty. *Sire*, or *Sir* (or *Madam*):— *Most Gracious Sovereign*:— *May it please your Majesty*:—

Sons and Daughters, Brothers and Sisters of Sovereigns.

To His Royal Highness the Prince of Wales. To Her Royal Highness the Duchess of York. *Sir*, or *Madam*:— *May it please your Royal Highness*:—

Other Branches of the Royal Family.

To His Highness the Duke of Cambridge. Or, To Her Highness the Princess Mary of Teck. *Sir*, or *Madam*:— *May it please your Highness*:—

2. The Nobility and Gentry.

A Duke or Duchess.

To His Grace the Duke of Montrose. Or, To Her Grace the Duchess of Montrose. *My Lord*, or *My Lady*:— *May it please your Grace*:—

A Marquis or Marchioness.

To the Most Noble the Marquis (or Marchioness) of Lansdowne. *My Lord* (or *My Lady*):— *May it please your Lordship* (or *Ladyship*):—

An Earl or Countess.

To the Right Honorable the Earl (or Countess) Russell. *My Lord* (or *My Lady*):— etc.

A Viscount and a Baron.

A Viscount (or Viscountess) and a *Baron* (or Baroness) are also addressed as *Right Honorable*, with the salutation, *My Lord* (or *My Lady*):— etc.

Baronets and Knights.

To Sir A—— B——, Bart., Piccadilly. *Sir:*— (Their wives are addressed by the title of *Lady.*)

Esquires.

To James Thomson, Esq. *Sir:*— (In regard to the use of this title in England, see remarks on page 240.)

3. Officers in the Civil Service.

A Member of Her Majesty's Most Honorable Privy Council.

To the Rt. Hon. Earl Granville, Her Majesty's Principal Secretary of State for Foreign Affairs. *Sir:*— *Right Hon. Sir:*— or *My Lord* (as the case may require).

An Ambassador.

To His Excellency the American (or other) Ambassador. *Sir,* or *My Lord,* or *Your Excellency.*

A Judge.

To the Rt. Hon. Sir George Cockburn, Lord Chief-Justice of England. *My Lord:*— *May it please your Lordship:*—

The Lord Mayor of London, York, or Dublin, and the Lord Provost of Edinburgh (during office).

To the Rt. Hon. A—— B——, Lord Mayor of London. To the Rt. Hon. A—— B——, Lord Provost of Edinburgh. *My Lord:*— *May it please your Lordship.*

The *Provost* of every other town in Scotland is styled *Honorable.*

The *Mayors* of all corporations (except the above-mentioned Lord Mayors), and the Sheriffs, Aldermen, and Recorder of London, are addressed *Right Worshipful;* and the Aldermen and Recorders of other corporations, and the Justices of the Peace, *Worshipful.* Salutation, *Sir:*— *Your Worship:*—

4. The Parliament.

House of Lords.

To the Rt. Hon. the Lords Spiritual and Temporal, in Parliament assembled. *My Lords:*— *May it please your Lordships:*—

House of Commons.

To the Hon. the Commons of the United Kingdom of Great Britain and Ireland. *May it please your Honorable House:*—

5. The Clergy.

An Archbishop.

To His Grace the Archbishop of C——. Or, To the Most Reverend Father in God, Archibald, Lord Archbishop of C——. *My Lord:— May it please your Grace:—*

A Bishop.

To the Right Reverend the Lord Bishop of S——. *My Lord.— May it please your Lordship:—*

A Dean.

To the Very Reverend Dean of C——. Or, To the Reverend Dr. Scott, Dean of C——. *My Lord:— May it please your Lordship:—*

Archdeacons and Chancellors in the same manner. *The Rest of the Clergy* as in this country. *If ennobled* to be addressed thus:—

To the Right Honorable and Reverend ——, etc

6. Military and Naval Officers.

In addressing officers in the Army and Navy above the subaltern, their military rank should precede their names and civil positions, thus —

To Field-Marshal His Grace the Duke of W——. *My Lord*, etc.

In the Navy, Admirals are styled Right Honorable, and the rank of the flag follows their names and titles; thus —

To the Right Honorable the Earl of Eglinton. G. C. B., Admiral of the Blue

The other officers are addressed as in the army, with the addition of R. N. (Royal Navy); thus:—

To Captain the Right Honorable the Earl of Egremont, R. N.

Esquire.—This title is now popularly applied to all persons of respectability; but it legally belongs to the following classes only:—

The sons of Peers, whether known in common conversation as Lords or Honorables; the eldest sons of Peers' sons and their eldest sons in perpetual succession; all the sons of Baronets; the Esquires of the Knights of the Bath; Lords of Manors, chiefs of clans, and other tenants of the Crown *in capite* (these are Esquires by prescription); Esquires created to that rank by patent, and their eldest sons in per*petual succession*; Esquires by office, such as Justices of the Peace while on the roll; Mayors of towns during mayoralty, and Sheriffs of counties (who retain the title for life); Members of the House of Commons; Barristers at Law; and Bachelors of Divinity, Law, and Physic.

All who, in commissions signed by the sovereign, are ever styled Esquire, retain that designation for life.

Miscellaneous.—Married women are addressed according to the rank of their husbands.

The widow of a nobleman is addressed in the title of her husband, with the addition of *Dowager;* as, "To the Right Honorable the Dowager Countess of Stanhope."

The title *Lady* is prefixed to the name of any woman whose husband is not of lower rank than Knight, or whose father was a nobleman not lower than an Earl.

The *eldest* sons of Dukes, Marquises, and Earls, bear, by courtesy, the second title in their respective families. Their wives are addressed accordingly.

The *younger* sons of Dukes and Marquises have the title of Lord, and are addressed as Right Honorable Lords,—to which is added the Christian name. Their wives have the title of Lady, and are addressed as Rt. Hon. Ladies; and, except when originally superior in rank, take their husbands' Christian names, not their own. The title Lady, and the address Rt. Hon. Lady, also belong to all the daughters of Dukes, Marquises, and Earls; to which is also added the Christian name.

Classified List of Abbreviations.

(EXCLUSIVE OF THOSE DENOTING TITLES.)

Use.—In formal letters and notes, especially those addressed to persons of high position, few abbreviations, except those of social and scholastic titles, are allowable, as they imply haste, and are therefore not quite respectful (see note on page 217, also on page 235). In familiar and business letters they may be used more freely, but only such as are authorized and will certainly be understood.

Explanations.—The following list does not contain all the abbreviations that are tolerated, but only such as are most frequently used in writing. For others rarely used the reader is referred to the dictionary.

In such lists, the abbreviation is generally given first, and then the explanation of it; but in this list we reverse the order, giving first the word and then the abbreviation,—our object being to assist in writing rather than in reading.

Classification.—For convenience of reference we have divided the following list into seven classes: I. Geographical; II. Chronological; III. Relating to Books and Literature; IV. Relating to Business; V. Relating to Law and Government; VI. Ecclesiastical; VII. Miscellaneous.

☞ *For abbreviations of degrees and other titles, see page 217; for those used especially by Roman Catholics, see page 235.*

I. Geographical Abbreviations.

United States (U. S.).

States.

Alabama	**Ala.**
Arkansas	**Ark.**
California	**Cal.**
Colorado	**Col.**
Connecticut	**Conn.** or **Ct.**
Delaware	**Del.**
Florida	**Fla.**
Georgia	**Ga.**
Illinois	**Ill.**

Indiana	**Ind.**
Iowa*	**Io.**
Kansas	**Kan.**
Kentucky	**Ky.**
Louisiana	**La.**
Maine*	**Me.**
Maryland	**Md.**
Massachusetts	**Mass.**
Michigan	**Mich.**
Minnesota	**Minn.**
Mississippi	**Miss.**
Missouri	**Mo.**
Nebraska	**Neb.**
Nevada	**Nev.**
New Hampshire	**N. H.**
New Jersey	**N. J.**
New York	**N. Y.**
North Carolina	**N. C.**
Ohio*	**O.**
Oregon	**Or.**
Pennsylvania	**Pa.** or **Penn.**
Rhode Island	**R. I.**
South Carolina	**S. C.**
Tennessee	**Tenn.**
Texas*	**Tex.**
Vermont	**Vt.**
Virginia	**Va.**
West Virginia	**W. Va.**
Wisconsin	**Wis.**

Territories and Districts.

Alaska	**Alas.**
Arizona Ter.	**Ariz. Ter.**
Dakota Ter.	**Dak. Ter.**
District of Columbia	**D. C.**
Idaho Territory	**Id. Ter.**
Indian Ter.	**Ind. Ter.** or **I. T.**
Montana Ter.	**Mon. Ter.**
New Mexico Ter.	**N. Mex. Ter.**
Utah Territory	**U. T.**
Washington Territory	**W. T.**
Wyoming Territory	**Wyo. Ter.**

Cities.

[But few abbreviations of cities have more than a local recognition. They are not allowable in superscriptions.]

Baltimore	**Balt.** or **Balto.**
Boston	**Bos.**
Mobile	**Mob.**
New Orleans	**N. O.**
New York	**N. Y.**†
Philadelphia	**Phil.** or **Phila.**
Washington	**Wash.**

Miscellaneous.

Alley	**Al.**
America, -can	**Am.** or **Amer.**
Avenue	**Av.**
Borough	**Bor.** or **bor.**
County	**Co.** or **co.**
Corner	**Cor.**
Court House	**C. H.**
District	**Dist.**
East, **E.**; West, **W.**; North, **N.**; South, **S.**	
Island	**Isl.**
Lake	**L.**
Mountain or Mount	**Mt.** (pl. **Mts.**)
Railroad	**R. R.**
River	**R.**
Street	**St.** (pl. **Sts.**)
Township	**tp.**
Village	**Vil.** or **vil.**

* Such short words as these should rarely if ever be abbreviated.

† *New York*, meaning the city, is rarely abbreviated, except when used adjectively; as, "N. Y. Tribune." The name of the state is generally abbreviated.

Foreign Countries.

[We give but few under this head, as in foreign correspondence names should generally be written in full.]

British America	**B. A.**
Britain, British	**Brit.**
Canada	**Can.**
Canada East	**C. E.**
Canada West	**C.W.**
England, English	**Eng.**
France, French	**Fr.**
Germany, German	**Ger.**
Great Britain,	**G. B.**
Ireland	**Ire.**
Italy, It.; Italian	**Ital.**
Jamaica	**Jam.**
Japan	**Jap.**
Mexico	**Mex.**
New Brunswick	**N. B.**
New Foundland	**N. F.**
Prince Edward's Island	**P. E. I.**
Prussia, Prussian	**Prus.**
Russia, Russian	**Russ.**
Scotland	**Scot**
South America	**S. A.**
Sandwich Islands	**S. Isl**
Spain	**Sp.**
West Indies	**W. I.** or **W. Ind.**

Cities.

Brussels	**Brus.**
Cambridge	**Cam.**
Dublin	**Dub.**
Edinburgh	**Edin.**
(After titles	**E.**)
Glasgow	**Glas.**
Gottingen	**Gott.**
Leyden	**Leyd.**
London	**Lond.**
Leipsic	**Leip.**
Madrid	**Mad.**
Oxford, *Oxonia*	**Oxf.**, **Oxon.**

II. Chronological.

Time of Day.

Hour, **h.**; minute, **min.**; second, **sec.**

Forenoon (*ante meridiem*)	**A. M.**
Afternoon (*post meridiem*)	**P. M.**
Noon (*meridiem*)	**M.**

Days.

Day	**d.**
Sunday	**Sun.**
Monday	**Mon.**
Tuesday	**Tues.**
Wednesday	**Wed.**
Thursday	**Thurs.**
Friday	**Frid.**
Saturday	**Sat.**
Christmas	**Xmas.**

Months.

Month, months	**mo., mos.**
Last month (*ultimo*)	**ult.**
This month (*instant*)	**inst.**
Next month (*proximo*)	**prox.**

The Calendar.—

January	**Jan.**
February	**Feb.**

March* . . . . **Mar.**	
April* . . . . **Apr.**	
May* . . . . ——	
June* . . . . **Je.**	
July* . . . . **Jul.**	
August . . . . **Aug.**	
September . . . . . **Sept.**	
October . . . . **Oct.**	
November . . . . . **Nov.**	
December . . . . **Dec.**	

Years and Eras.

Year, years . . . . **yr., yrs.**
By the year (*per annum*) **per an.**
Before Christ . . . . . **B. C.**
In the Christian Era (*anno Domini*) . . . . **A.D.**
In the year of Rome **A. U. C.**
Century . . . . **Cen.**
Old Style (before 1752) . **O. S.**
New Style (since 1752) . . **N. S.**

III. Relating to Books and Literature.

Abbreviated . . . . . . **abbr.**
Abridged . . . . **abr.**
Anglo-Saxon **A.-S., Ang.-Sax.**
Anonymous . . . . . **Anon.**
Answer . . . . **Ans.**
Article . . . . **Art.**
Appendix . . . . **App.**
Book . . . . . . **Bk.** or **bk.**
Boards (binding) . . . **bds.**
Bound . . . . **bd.**
Half-bound . . . . . **hf.-bd.**
Capital letter. **Cap.** (pl. **Caps.**)
Small Capitals **S. Caps., S. C.**
Chapter . . . . **Chap.**
Compare (*confer*) . . . . . **cf.**
Cyclopædia . . . . . . **Cyc.**
Dictionary . . . . . . **dict.**
Edition. **Edit., ed.**; editor. **Ed.**
Encyclopædia . . . **Encyc.**
Et cætera (and other things) **etc., &c.**
Et sequentia (and what follows) **et seq.**
Example . . . . **Ex.**
Exempli gratia (for example) . **e. g., ex. g.**
Exception . . . . . . **Exc.**
Figure, figurative . . . . **fig.**
History, historical . . . **Hist.**
Idem (same author) . **Id.** or **id.**
Id est (that is) . . . . . . **i. e.**
Introduction . . . . . . **Intr.**
Journal . . . . **Jour.**
Library, librarian . . . **Lib.**
Lower case (type) . . . . **l. c.**
Manuscript . . **MS.** (pl. **MSS.**)
Observation . . . . . . **Obs.**
Page, pages . . . **P., p., pp.**
Paragraph . . . . . **par., ¶.**
Preface . . . . **Pref.**
Postscript . **P. S.** (pl. **P.SS.**)
Publisher, -lication, -lished **pub.**
Question . . . . **Ques.**
Query . . . . . **Qy., qy.,** or **?**
Quod vide (which see) . . **q. v.**
Review . . . . **Rev.**

---

* *May* is never abbreviated; and *March, April, June,* and *July,* being short, should generally be written in full.

Rhetoric	**Rhet.**	Synonyme	**Syn.**
Remark	**Rem.**	Transpose	**tr.**
Section	**Sec.**	Version	**Ver.**
Shakspeare	**Shak.**	Volume	**Vol.** (pl. **vols.**
Supplement	**Sup.**	Wrong font (type)	**w. f.**

Sizes of Books.

A book formed of sheets folded
- in 2 leaves, is a folio = **fol.**
- in 4 leaves, is a quarto = **4to.**
- in 8 leaves, is an octavo = **8vo.**
- in 12 leaves, is a duodecimo = **12mo.**
- in 16 leaves, is a **16mo.**
- in 18 leaves, is an **18mo.**
- in 24 leaves, is a **24mo.**
- in 32 leaves, is a **32mo.**
- in 64 leaves, is a **64mo.**

IV. Relating to Business.

Account	**acct., %**	Ditto (the same)	**do.**
Agent	**Agt.**	Discount	**disc.**
Amount	**Amt.**	Dividend	**div.**
At or to (mercantile)	**@, a.**	Dollar, dollars	**dol., dols., $.**
Average	**av.**	Dozen	**doz.**
Balance	**bal.**	Each	**ea.**
Barrel, barrels	**bl., bbl.** or **bls.**	Foot, feet	**ft.**
Bank	**bk.**	Gross	**gro.**
Brother, Brothers	**Bro., Bros.**	Hundred	**hund.**
Bushel	**bu., Bush.**	Hogshead	**hhd.**
By the	**P., p.,** or **℔.**	Interest	**int.**
Cashier	**Cash.**	Journal	**jour**
Cleared	**cld.**	Measure	**meas**
Company	**Co.**	Number, numbers	**No., Nos.**
Collector	**Coll.**	Ounce	**oz.**
Commerce	**Com.**	Pound, pounds	**lb., lbs.**
Credit, creditor	**Cr.**	Pennyweight	**pwt., dwt.**
Cent, cents	**ct., cts.**	Package	**pkge.**
Clerk	**clk.**	Peck, pecks	**pk., pks.**
Cash on Delivery	**C. O. D.**	Pint, pints	**pt., pts**

Payment	**payt.**	Received	**recd.**
Paid	**pd.**	Schooner	**schr.**
Per annum (by the yr.)	**per an.**	Sailed	**sld.**
Per cent. (by the hund.)	**per cent.**	Tonnage	**ton**
Quart, quarts	**qt., qts.**	Weight	**wt.**
Quarter, quarters	**qr., qrs.**	Yard, yards	**yd., yds.**

V. Relating to Law and Government.

For abbreviations of official titles not here given, see page 219.

Administrator	**Admr.**	His (Her) Majesty	**H. M.**
Advocate	**Adv.**	His (Her) Roy. Highness	**H.R.H.**
Attorney	**Atty.**	House of Representatives	**H. R.**
Against (*versus*)	**v.** or **vs.**	Justice of the Peace	**J. P.**
Alderman	**Ald.**	Legislature	**Leg.**
Assistant	**Asst.**	Member of Congress	**M. C.**
And others (*et alii*)	**et al.**	Non prosequitur (he does not prosecute)	**Non pros.**
Clerk	**clk.**	Member of Parliament	**M. P.**
Commissioner	**Com.**	Notary Public	**N. P.**
Committee	**Com.**	Parliament	**Parl.**
Common Pleas	**C. P.**	Plaintiff	**plff.**
Congress	**Cong.**	Post-Office	**P. O.**
Constable	**Const.**	Post-Master	**P. M.**
County Court	**C. C.**	Public Document	**Pub. Doc.**
Co. Commissioner (or Clk.)	**C. C.**	Queen Victoria (*Victoria Regina*)	**V. R.**
Court of Common Pleas	**C. C. P.**	Right Honorable	**Rt. Hon.**
Court of Sessions	**C. S.**	Republic, Republican	**Rep.**
Defendant	**deft., dft.**	Solicitor	**Sol**
Deputy	**Dep.**	Superintendent	**Supt**
Department	**Dept.**	Surveyor General	**Surv. Gen.**
District Attorney	**Dist. Atty.**		
His (Her) Brit. Majesty	**H.B.M.**		

VI. Ecclesiastical.

For abbreviations of clerical offices and titles, see pages 219, 228.

By God's grace (*Dei gratia*)	**D. G.**	God willing (*Deo volente*)	**D. V.**
Church, churches	**Ch., chs.**	Episcopal	**Epis.**
Clergyman	**Cl.**	Evangelical	**Evang.**
Deacon	**Dea.**	Ecclesiastical	**ecc., eccl.**

Jesus the Saviour of men (*Jesus hominum Salvator*) . **I. H. S.**

Jesus of Nazareth, King of the Jews (*Jesus Nazarenus Rex Judæorum*) . . . **I. N. R. I.**

Methodist . . . . . . **Meth.**

Methodist Episcopal . . **M. E.**

Protestant . . . . . . **Prot.**

Protestant Episcopal . . **P. E.**

Presbyterian . . . . **Presb.**

Reformed, Reformation . **Ref.**

Roman Catholic . **Rom. Cath.**

VII. Miscellaneous.—(*Unclassified.*)

Ad libitum (at pleasure) **ad lib.**

Architecture . . . . **Arch.**

Arithmetic . . . . . . **Arith.**

Astronomy . . . . **Astron.**

Ætatis (of age) . . . **Æt., Æ.**

Botany . . . . **Bot.**

Chemistry . . . . . **Chem.**

College . . . . **Coll.**

Corresponding Sec. **Cor. Sec.**

Delineavit (he drew it) . . **del.**

Errors excepted . . . **E. E.**

Executive Com. . **Exec. Com.**

Fahrenheit (thermom.) . **Fahr.**

For example (*exempli gratia*) **e. g., ex. g.**

Fecit (he did it) . . . . **fec.**

Grammar . . . . . . **Gram.**

Geography . . . . . **Geog.**

Geometry . . . . . . **Geom.**

Handkerchief . . . . **hdkf.**

Horticulture . . . . **Hort.**

Hic jacet sepultus (here he lies buried) . . . . . **H. J. S.**

Hic requiescat in pace (here he rests in peace) . **H. R. I. P.**

Incognito (unknown) . . **Incog.**

In transitu (in the passage) **in trans.**

Junior . . . . . . **Jr.** or **jun.**

Military . . . . **Mil.**

Mythology . . . . . **Myth.**

National, natural . . . **Nat.**

Nemine contradicente (no one contradicting) . **Nem. Con.**

Nemine dissentiente (no one dissenting) . . . **Nem. diss.**

Non sequitur (it does not follow) **non seq.**

Nota Bene (note well) . **N. B.**

Number (*numero*) **No.** (pl. **Nos.**)

Obit (he died) . . . . . . **ob.**

Objection, objective, etc. . **obj.**

Obedient . . . . **obt.**

Optics . . . . **Opt.**

Ornithology . . . . **Ornith.**

Philosophy . . . . . . **Phil.**

Phonography . . . **Phonog.**

Phrenology . . . . **Phren.**

Physiology . . . . . **Phys.**

Pinxit (he painted it) . **pinx.**

Pro tempore (for the time) **pro tem.**

Recording Secretary . **Rec. Sec.**

Regiment . . . . . . **Regt.**

Secretary . . . . . . **Sec.**

Sculpsit (he engr. it) **sc., sculp.**

Senior . . . . **Sr., sen.**

Senator . . . . **Sen**

Servant . . . . . . **Servt.**

Turn over . . . . . . **T. O.**

Videlicet (namely) . . . . **viz.**

Zoology . . . . **Zool**

FOREIGN WORDS AND PHRASES.

For the convenience of writers and readers, we give below a collection of such foreign words and phrases as are most frequently used in letters and conversation by educated people.

(*F.*, French; *L.*, Latin; *It.*, Italian.)

Ab initio [L.], from the beginning.

Ab uno disce omnes [L.], from one you may judge of all.

Ad infinitum [L.], to infinity.

Ad interim [L.], meanwhile.

Ad libitum [L.], at pleasure.

Ad nauseam [L.], to nausea.

Affaire d'amour [F.], a love affair.

Affaire d'honneur [F.], an affair of honor.

Affaire du cœur [F.], an affair of the heart.

Au fait [F.], skilful. expert.

A la bonne heure [F.], in the nick of time.

A la mode [F.], in the fashion.

Alter ego [L.], my other self.

Argumentum ad hominem [L.], argument applied to the person.

Ars est celare artem [L.], the art is to conceal art.

Au revoir [F.], adieu till we meet again.

Bal masque [F.], a masquerade ball.

Bas bleu [F.], blue-stocking—literary woman.

Beau monde [F.], the gay world.

Bete noir [F.], a black beast; a bugbear.

Blasé [F.], worn out by excesses.

Bonne bouche [F.], a delicate bit.

Bon mot [F.], a witty saying.

Bon ton [F.], fashionable society.

Cacoethes loquendi [L.], a rage for talking.

Cacoethes scribendi [L.], a rage for writing.

Cæteris paribus [L.], other things being equal.

Café [F.], a coffee-house.

Carte blanche [F.], a blank sheet; permission to do as one chooses

Chef d'œuvre [F.], a masterpiece.

Chère amie [F.], dear friend (fem.)

Ci-devant [F.], former; formerly.

Comme il faut [F.], as it should be

Compagnon de voyage [F.], a travelling companion.

Con amore [L.], with love.

Contretemps [F.], a mishap.

Corrigenda [L.], words to be altered.

Costume de rigueur [F.], full dress, in character.

Couleur de rose [F.], rose-color; flattering hue.

Coup de grace [F.], finishing stroke.

Coup de soleil [F.], sunstroke.

Coup d'état [F.], a stroke of statecraft.

Coup d'œil [F.], a rapid glance.

Cui bono [L.], for whose benefit? of what use?

Cum grano salis [L.], with some grains of salt—some allowance.

De facto [L.], in reality.

De gustibus non disputandum [L.], there is no disputing about tastes.

De mortuis nil nisi bonum [L.], say of the dead nothing but good.

Demi-monde [F.], depraved females.

Denouement [F.], the ending.

De novo [L.], anew.

Dernier ressort [F.], a last resort.

Dieu et mon droit [F.], God and my right.

Distingué [F.], distinguished.

Dolce far niente [It.], sweet idleness

Double entendre [F.], an ambiguous expression.

Douceur [F.], a bribe.

Dramatis personæ [L.], characters of the drama.

Dulce et decorum est pro patria mori [L.], it is sweet and honorable to die for one's country

Élite [F.], the choice part.

Embonpoint [F.], plumpness.

En déshabillé [F.], in undress, or home dress.

En passant [F.], in passing.

Entrée [F.], admittance; dishes of the first course.

Entre nous [F.], between us.

En ville [F.], in the town or city = E. V.

Ergo [L.], therefore.

Esto perpetua [L.], may it last for ever.

Facile princeps [L.], the admitted chief.

Fait accompli [F.], a thing already done.

Faux pas [F.], a false step; a woman's loss of character.

Fête champêtre [F.], a rural entertainment.

Festina lente [L.], hasten slowly.

Fidus Achates [L.], a true friend.

Fille de chambre [F.], a chambermaid.

Hinc illæ lachrymæ [L.], hence these tears.

Homme d'esprit [F.], a man of genius.

Hors de combat [F.], not in a condition to fight.

Ibidem [L.], in the same place = ibid.

Id omne genus [L.], all of that kind.

In articulo mortis [L.], at the point of death.

In extremis [L.], at the point of death.

In extenso [L.], at full length.

In hoc signo vinces [L.], under this standard thou shalt conquer.

In loco parentis [L.], in place of a parent.

In medias res [L.], in the midst of things.

In memoriam [L.], in memory.

In propria persona [L.], in person.

Inter alia [L.], among other things.

Inter nos [L.], among ourselves.

Inter se [L.], among themselves.

In toto [L.], in the whole.

In vino veritas [L.], in wine there is truth (a drunken man tells the truth).

Ipse dixit [L.], a dogmatic assertion.

Ipsissima verba [L.], the very words.

Jeu de mots [F.], a play upon words; a pun.

Jeu d'esprit [F.], a witticism.

Labor omnia vincit [L.], labor conquers all things.

Lapsus calami [L.], a slip of the pen.

Lapsus linguæ [L.], a slip of the tongue.

Lares et penates [L.], household gods; home.

Lex scripta [L.], the written law.

Lex non scripta [L.], the unwritten law.

Lex talionis [L.], the law of retaliation.

Liaison [F.], an amour.

Libretto [It.], a little (opera) book.

Litera scripta manet [L.], what is written remains.

Locum tenens [L.], a proxy.

Ma chère [F.], my dear (to a woman).

Magnum opus [L.], a great work

Mal à propos [F.], ill timed.

Mauvaise honte [F.], false modesty.

Mens sana in corpore sano [L.], a sound mind in a sound body.

Mésalliance [F.], marrying a person below one's self.

Meum et tuum [L.], mine and thine.

Mon cher [F.], my dear (to a man).

Morceau [F.], a small piece; pl. *morceaux*.

Mutatis mutandis [L.], the necessary change being made.

Née [F.], born—family name.

Ne sutor ultra crepidam [L.], the shoemaker should not go beyond his last (a person should stick to his calling).

Nil desperandum [L.], never despair.

N'importe [F.], it matters not.

Nolens volens [L.], willing or unwilling.

Nom de plume [F.], a writer's assumed name.

Nous verrons [F.], we shall see.

On dit [F.], they say.

Ora pro nobis [L.], pray for us.

O tempora! O mores! [L.], O the times! O the manners!

Otium cum dignitate [L], leisure with dignity.

Par excellence [F.], by way of eminence.
Par nobile fratrum [L.], a noble pair of brothers.
Particeps criminis [L.], an accomplice in the crime.
Peccavi [L.], I have sinned.
Penchant [F.], inclination.
Per se [L.], by itself.
Petitio principii [L.], a begging of the question.
Poeta nascitur, non fit [L.], the poet is born, not made.
Pons asinorum [L.], bridge of asses.
Pour prendre congé [F.], to take leave=P. P. C.
Quantum sufficit [L.], it is enough.
Quid nunc [L.], what now? a newsmonger.
Quid pro quo [L.], an equivalent.
Qui vive? [F.], who goes there? on the alert.
Quondam [L.], former.
Rara avis [L.], a rare bird.
Récherché [F.], rare, exquisite.
Requiescat in pace [L.], rest in peace.
Repondez s'il vous plaît [F.], answer if you please=R. S. V. P.
Resurgam [L.], I shall rise again.
Robe de chambre [F.], a dressing-gown.
Sang froid [F.] indifference.
Sans cérémonie [F.], without ceremony.
Sans culotte [F.], without breeches; a rag-a-muffin.
Scan. mag.—scandalum magnatum [L.], scandal of high personages.
Sic transit gloria mundi [L.], thus passes the glory of the world.
Soi disant [F.], self-called, pretended.
Soirée dansante [F.], dancing party.
Sotto voce [It.], in a low voice.
Suaviter in modo, fortiter in re [L.], gentle in manner, resolute in deed.
Sub rosa [L.], under the rose; *i. e.* secretly.
Sui generis [L.], of a particular kind.
Tableau vivant [F.], a picture represented by living persons.
Tempus fugit [L.], time flies.
Terra firma [L.], firm ground.
Terra incognita [L.], an unknown land.
Tout ensemble [F.], the whole taken together.
Ut infra [L.], as cited below.
Ut supra [L.], as above.
Valet de chambre [F.], a valet, a body servant.
Verbatim et literatim [L.], word for word and letter for letter.
Vis à vis [F.], face to face.
Viva voce [L.], by word of mouth.
Vive la république [F.], long live the republic.
Vive le roi [F.], long live the king.
Vox et præterea nihil [L.], sound and nothing more.
Vox populi, vox Dei [L.], the voice of the people the voice of God

Postal Information.

Condensed from the "United States Official Postal Guide."

Rates of Domestic Postage.

(*For all Places in the United States and Canada.*)

Classes.—Mailable matter is divided into four classes, known respectively as *First-Class*, *Second-Class*, *Third-Class*, and *Fourth-Class* matter.

First-Class Matter.

This class embraces all packages sealed against inspection; also all letters, drawings, plans, designs, diplomas, and other matter wholly or partly in writing, except as stated below. (See *Writing Allowable*, under each of the other classes.)

The rate of postage on matter of the first class is *three cents for every half ounce* or fraction thereof, except drop-letters and postal cards. (*Two* cents for every half ounce, after July 1, 1883.)

Drop-Letters.—The postage on local or drop-letters at letter-carrier offices is *two cents for every half ounce* or fraction thereof; at other offices, *one cent.*

Postal Cards.—Postal cards have the stamp imprinted on them, and require no further postage. They are treated by postmasters the same as sealed letters, except that they are in no case returned to the writers. Unclaimed postal cards, if wholly written, are sent to the dead-letter office; if printed or partly written, they are put with the waste paper. An ordinary business-card may be sent as a postal card if prepaid by a one-cent stamp; but it must contain no writing except the address. Nothing must be written upon the face of a postal card except the address. Anything else so written subjects it to letter postage. Nor is it allowable to paste, gum, or attach anything to a postal card other than a slip containing the printed address.

Second-Class Matter.

This class embraces all newspapers and other periodicals regularly issued from a known office of publication not less than four times a year and numbered consecutively, without addition by writing.

The rate of postage on matter of the second class (except county papers) is *two cents a pound*, in bulk, prepaid by stamps prepared for *the purpose.*

County Papers.—Newspapers are sent—one copy to each actual subscriber living within the county of publication—free of postage.

Writing Allowable.—Bills, receipts, and orders for subscription may be enclosed in second-class matter, but no other writing is allowable except the address of the subscriber.

Third Class Matter.

This class embraces books (printed and blank), transient newspapers and other periodicals, circulars, proof-sheets and corrected proof-sheets and manuscript accompanying the same, valentines, hand-bills, posters, lithographs, engravings, heliotypes, hectograph-prints, photographs, printed blanks and cards, tags, tickets, and other matter the value of which depends on the printing. It must in all cases be so wrapped that the contents may be inspected without destroying the wrapper.

The rate of postage on matter of the third class is *one cent for every two ounces* or fraction thereof.

Writing Allowable.—The sender may correct a typographical error, or mark a passage to which he desires to call attention; may write upon the cover or blank leaves of a book or other printed matter a simple dedication or inscription; and may write upon the matter itself or upon the wrapper his name or address with the word "From" above or before the same. Any other writing subjects the matter to letter postage.

Weight Allowable.—The weight of a single package is limited to *four pounds*. A single volume of a book and public documents may, however, exceed that weight.

Fourth-Class Matter.

This class embraces all articles of merchandise that are mailable, envelopes in quantity with printing thereon, blank bills and letter-heads, blank cards, card-board and other flexible materials, flexible patterns, blank letter-paper and envelopes, models, sample cards, samples, seeds, cuttings, bulbs, roots, paintings in oil or water-color, and all mailable matter not included in the other classes. It must in all cases be so wrapped that the contents may be inspected; otherwise it will be rated as first-class matter.

The rate of postage on matter of the fourth class is *one cent for every ounce* or fraction thereof. To *Canada*, ten cents for every eight ounces, prepaid by stamps.

Writing Allowable.—The sender may write upon the package his own name and address, preceded by the word "From," and also the number and names of the articles enclosed, with a mark or number attached by card or label for identifica-[illegible]. *Any other writing* subjects the package to letter postage.

Weight Allowable.—The weight of a single package is limited to four pounds.

REGISTRY.—First-, third-, and fourth-class matter may be registered for a fee of ten cents in addition to the regular postage.

RATES AT LETTER-CARRIER OFFICES.—The postage on newspapers (except weeklies) deposited in a letter-carrier office for local delivery is as follows:—

On *newspapers* (except weeklies), whether regular or transient, and without regard to weight or frequency of issue, *one cent each.* On *periodicals* (other than newspapers) not exceeding two ounces in weight, *one cent each;* exceeding two ounces in weight, *two cents each.*

Weekly Newspapers (excepted above) to regular subscribers, *two cents per pound,* whether delivered through carriers, boxes, or general delivery.

(For drop-letters, see under *First-Class Matter.*)

UNMAILABLE MATTER.—Liquids, poisons, explosive and inflammable articles, fruits or vegetable matter, confectionery pastes or confections, substances exhaling a bad odor, and every letter or postal card upon which indecent delineations or language is written or printed, and all matter relating to lotteries, gift concerts, and other fraudulent schemes, also anything that would cut or injure the mail-bag, are unmailable.

Rates of Foreign Postage.

Most of the civilized nations of the world have formed themselves, for postal purposes, into an association known as the *Universal Postal Union.* Mailable matter may be sent to the principal cities and towns of all the countries and colonies embraced in this Union, at the following rates: *Letters*, five cents for each half ounce, prepayment optional; *Postal Cards*, each two cents; *Newspapers* and other printed matter, one cent for every two ounces; *Samples of Merchandise*, one cent for every two ounces. The *Registry* fee for letters and packages is uniformly ten cents in addition to postage.

Among the countries in the Universal Postal Union, besides the United States and Canada, are the following: Argentine Republic, Austria-Hungary, Belgium, Brazil, British India, Bulgaria, Ceylon, Chili, Denmark, Egypt, France and Colonies, Germany, Great Britain and Ireland, Greece, Hong Kong (China), Italy, Jamaica, Japan, Mexico, Netherlands and Colonies, Newfoundland, Norway, Persia, Peru, Portugal and Colonies, Russia, Spain and Colonies, Sweden, Switzerland, Turkey, Uruguay, Venezuela.

For rates of postage to other countries, see *Postal Guide,* or inquire of a postmaster.

Sending Money.

There are two safe ways of sending money by mail, viz.: 1. By *Registered Letter;* 2. By *Money Order.*

1. By Registered Letter.—A letter to any part of the U. S., containing money or other mailable matter of value, may be registered at any office on the payment of a fee of 10 cents in addition to the usual postage.

The rate of registry to foreign countries is 10 cents in addition to the regular postage (see table on page 255).

A letter to be registered should be sealed by the sender, and the postmaster has no right to inquire as to the contents.

The P. O. Department is not legally liable for the loss of registered matter; but owing to the extraordinary safeguards thrown around such matter its safe delivery is almost certain.

2. By Money-Order.—The best and safest way to send small sums of money is by a postal money-order, which may be obtained at any "money-order office," payable at any other such office. (A list of such offices may be seen at any post-office.) Indeed money so sent is absolutely safe, as the Post-Office Department is liable for the amount.

Domestic Money-Orders.—The charges for orders on United States offices are as follows:—

For orders not exceeding $15	10 cents.
Over $15 and not exceeding $30	15 cents.
Over $30 and not exceeding $40	20 cents.
Over $40 and not exceeding $50	25 cents.

When a larger sum than fifty dollars is required, additional orders to make it up must be obtained. But postmasters are not allowed to issue on the same day to the same remitter, and in favor of the same payee, more than *three* money orders payable at the same office.

If a money-order is lost, another may be obtained free of charge on application.

The given names of both the remitter and payee should be given in an application for a money order; and married women should be described by their own *names, not those of* their husbands.

Foreign Money-Orders.—Money may be sent in the same manner to and from the following countries: Great Britain and Ireland, Germany, and Switzerland. This exchange of money-orders is effected through the agency of "International Exchange Offices," of which New York is the office on the part of the United States. Hence an international money-order is not drawn by a postmaster in one country directly upon a postmaster in the other, but must be drawn upon the "International Exchange Office." The offices at which foreign money-orders may be obtained may be ascertained by inquiry of any postmaster. The charges are as follows:—

On British, Swiss, and Italian post-offices:—

For orders not exceeding $10	25 cents.
Over $15 and not exceeding $20	50 cents.
Over $20 and not exceeding $30	75 cents.
Over $30 and not exceeding $40	$1.00
Over $40 and not exceeding $50	1.25

On Canadian post-offices:—

For orders not exceeding $10	20 cents.
Over $10 and not exceeding $20	40 cents.
Over $20 and not exceeding $30	60 cents.
Over $30 and not exceeding $40	80 cents.
Over $40 and not exceeding $50	$1.00

On German post-offices —

For orders not exceeding $5	15 cents.
Over $5 and not exceeding $10	25 cents.
Over $10 and not exceeding $20	50 cents.
Over $20 and not exceeding $30	75 cents.
Over $30 and not exceeding $40	$1.00
Over $40 and not exceeding $50	1.25

One pound sterling (£1) is equal to $4.86 in gold, and one thaler (German) is equal to 71 cents in gold. One dollar (gold) is equal to 5 francs 15 centimes (Swiss).

Stamped Envelopes and Wrappers.

Stamped envelopes, letter-size, may be obtained of postmasters at various prices, according to quality and denomination. Three cent envelopes cost from 80 to 83 cents per pack (25), or $32 to $33.20 per thousand.

Special Request Envelopes.—When ordered in quantities of 500 and upward, the Department will, if desired, print on the upper left-hand corner, *without additional charge*, the name and residence of the parties ordering, with a request to return if unclaimed in a certain time These "Special Request Envelopes" must in all cases be ordered from the postmaster, and not from the Department.

Stamped *newspaper wrappers* may also be obtained at a cost a little more than the value of the stamps printed on them.

The postage on *stamped envelopes and wrappers spoiled in directing* will be refunded in stamps by a postmaster, if he is satisfied that they have never been sent by mail, and if presented in a whole condition.

Miscellaneous Facts and Suggestions.

Observe carefully the following facts and suggestions, in addition to those given above:—

1. See that every letter and package sent by mail is securely folded and fastened. Use only good strong envelopes and wrappers. Heavy articles should be secured with a string.

2. Never send money (except in very small amounts) or other articles of value in an unregistered letter.

3. See that every letter contains your full name and directions (inside), as advised in Part I. of this work.

4. See that the outside address is full and plainly written, as advised on pages 57–63. On foreign letters, not only the name of the town or city, but also the name of the *country*, should be written. Letters directed to "*London*" are often sent to London, Canada.

5. When dropping a letter or paper into a street letter-box, see that it does not stick fast.

6. Cut stamps, stamps cut from stamped envelopes, mutilated postage stamps, and internal revenue stamps, cannot be accepted in payment of postage.

7. To use or attempt to use a stamp that has already been used, is punishable by a fine of fifty dollars.

8. To insure the forwarding of a letter, it must have not less than three cents affixed in postage stamps. Always be sure to affix stamps enough. In doubtful cases put on another.

9. A double rate of six cents for each half ounce is chargeable on every letter that reaches its destination without having been fully prepaid—deducting the value of the stamp affixed.

10. To enclose any written matter in printed matter subjects the mailing party to a fine of five dollars, unless the party addressed pays letter postage on the package.

Business Forms.

In this article we give forms of the following business papers which are in general use, and are intimately connected with the subject of letter-writing, viz.: I. Receipts; II. Notes; III. Due Bills; IV. Drafts; V. Orders.

Receipts.

A receipt should always be given and required for any money or other article of value paid or deposited. Many misunderstandings, losses, and lawsuits may thus be prevented.

1. Money on Account.

Received, Philadelphia, April 1, 1875, of John Paywell, One Hundred and Fifty $\frac{25}{100}$ Dollars on account.

\$150$\frac{25}{100}$ *John Wilson & Co.*

The above form is used when money is paid on an unsettled account. When the money closes an account, substitute for "on account," the words, "in full of balance on settlement," as in (2). If the payment is in discharge of *all* indebtedness, use the words, "in full of all *demands*," or simply "in full."

In all business papers, the number should always be expressed *in words.* The number of cents is generally expressed fractionally. The entire amount should also be expressed in figures, above or below.

2. Receipt in Full.

Philadelphia, May 5, 1875.

Received of P. W. Hiestand, Treasurer of the State Normal School, Millersville, Pa., Two Hundred and Seventy-Five Dollars, in full of balance on settlement.

\$275. *Murray & Brown,*
per J. B.

The date may be written at the top as in (2), or be incorporated in the sentence as in (1). In written receipts the latter practice is preferable.

The account on which the money is paid may be stated, as in the following:—

3. On Account of Sundries.

Received, Millersville, Dec. 4, 1875, of A—— B——, Treasurer of the Board of School Directors, One Hundred Dollars, on account of salary as teacher (or as the case may be).

$100. *John Williams.*

4. Receipt endorsed on a Note.

Received, April 1, 1876, on the within note, One Hundred and Seventy-five Dollars.

$175. *Charles Carroll & Co.*

5. Receipt for Merchandise.

Received, Millersville, Pa., Feb. 7, 1876, of Carbon & Co., per John Smith, teamster, two tons of coal.

S. G. Behmer, Steward.

Promissory Notes.

1. Individual (on Demand).

$250. *Indiana, Pa., June 5, 1876.*

On demand I promise to pay to A—— B——, or order, Two Hundred and Fifty Dollars, without defalcation, for value received.

James Westfall.

A note payable to "A—— B—— or order," as above, is *negotiable;* that is, it may be transferred to another by the person named in the note, by his writing his name across the back. This is a general endorsement. It may be endorsed, "Pay to C—— D—— or order (or bearer)." A note payable "to A—— B—— or *bearer*," may be transferred without endorsement

In Pennsylvania and New Jersey the words, "without defalcation," are required; and in Missouri, the words, "negotiable and payable without defalcation or discount." In other states these phrases are unnecessary, though not detrimental.

2. Principal and Surety Note (time, with interest).

$1500. *Boston, July 4, 1876.*

Sixty days after date, I promise to pay to James Livingston, or order, Sixty-five Hundred Dollars with interest, value received.

Surety *Amos Lawrence.*

James Livingston.

A surety note should be made payable to the order of the surety, who should endorse it on the back to the order of the endorsee or creditor. It is held that a note made in favor of the creditor and endorsed by the surety does not bind the latter to the payment of the debt.

3. Joint Note (time, payable at Bank).

$500. *Chicago, Jan. 26, 1876.*

Thirty days after date, we promise to pay Richard Cox, or order, at the First National Bank of Chicago, Five Hundred Dollars, for value received.

John Wentworth.
Albert Ramsay.

4. Joint and Several (demand, with Interest).

$7525 $\frac{75}{100}$. *Philadelphia, January 1, 1876.*

On demand, for value received, we jointly and severally promise to pay John Brown & Co., or order, Seventy-five Hundred and Twenty five $\frac{75}{100}$ Dollars with interest, without defalcation.

Wm. Lincoln.
Charles Collins.
John Wilkins.

Due Bills.

A due bill should always be given and required for money lent and for any business accommodation or indebtedness, unless a promissory note or other obligation is used, as a memorandum of the transaction. The consideration for which a due bill is given should always be stated in the paper itself.

1. For Money.

$100. *Millersville, Pa., Apr. 1, 1875.*

Due Richard Ross, on demand, One Hundred Dollars, for value received (or for labor done, or for cash borrowed, or as the case may be).

John Duncan.

2. For Merchandise.

$25 $\frac{50}{100}$. *Albany, July 1, 1874.*

Due John Smith, or bearer, Twenty-five $\frac{50}{100}$ Dollars for work done, payable, on demand, in Merchandise at our store.

Robert Johnson & Co.

Drafts.

(Sometimes called "Inland Bills of Exchange.")

1. Time Draft.

$125 $\frac{25}{100}$. *Philadelphia, Nov. 25, 1876.*

At ten days' sight pay to the order of William Wheeler One Hundred and Twenty five $\frac{25}{100}$ Dollars, value received, and charge to our account.

Jones, Jenkins & Co.

To James Carrington,
Lancaster, Pa.

The signer of a draft is the *drawer*, the one to whom it is directed is the *drawee* the one to whom the money is payable is the *payee*.

A draft payable *at sight* must be paid when presented. If it is payable *at ten days' sight* (as above), it is due ten days (with three days grace added) after it has been *accepted* by the drawee. In the case supposed in the above form, the payee (Wheeler) takes the draft to the *drawee* (Carrington); and if the latter honors it, he writes "accepted" across the face, with his name and the date, and the paper is then known as *an acceptance*, and is in effect a promissory note payable in ten days. Time drafts may be made payable a certain number of days after *date* as well as after sight.

2. Check.

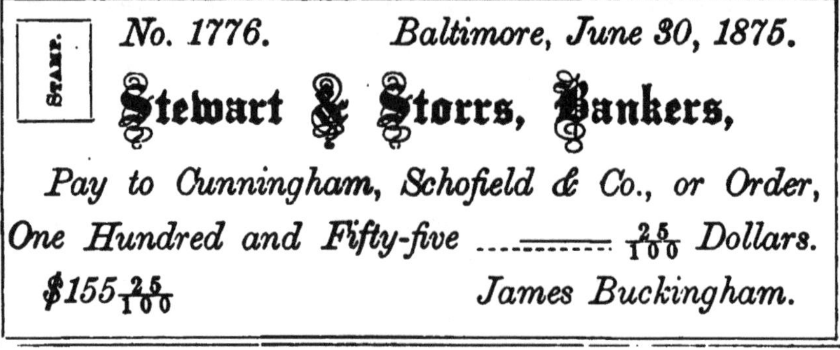

STAMP.

No. 1776. Baltimore, June 30, 1875.

Stewart & Storrs, Bankers,

Pay to Cunningham, Schofield & Co., or Order,

One Hundred and Fifty-five ———— $\frac{25}{100}$ Dollars.

\$155 $\frac{25}{100}$ James Buckingham.

A check is essentially a kind of draft, and is here so regarded. A check must have affixed to it a two-cent revenue stamp, cancelled by the drawer. Checks should invariably be dated on the day on which they are drawn. Unless the check is to be presented immediately and in person, it should not be made payable *to bearer*. Most checks are now printed "Pay to the order of ——," etc.

Orders.

1. For Money.

Troy, N. Y., May 1, 1875.

Mr. John Hoover,

Please pay John Brown One Hundred and Thirty Dollars on my account

\$130. Wm. Carter.

2. For Merchandise.

Trenton, N. J., Oct. 12, 1875.

Mr. Wm. Wilkins,

Please pay John Myers One Hundred and Fifty $\frac{25}{100}$ Dollars in Merchandise and charge to my account.

\$150 $\frac{25}{100}$. Thomas Miller.

General Index.

Always be in a hurry
but never show it.

IA.

S.

s in
aized
most
the
volu-
y for
aken
, the
chers
made

M.
log-

BY WM. FEWSMITH, A.M., AND EDGAR A. SINGER.

The uniform testimony of teachers who have introduced these grammars is, that they have been most agreeably surprised at their effects upon pupils. They are easy to understand by the youngest pupil, and the lessons before dreaded become a delight to teacher and *pupils. Extraordinary care* has been taken in grading every lesson, modeling rules and *definitions after* a definite and uniform plan, and making every word and sentence an *example of grammatical* accuracy. They only need a trial to supersede all others.

Lightning Source UK Ltd.
Milton Keynes UK
UKHW02f1040300118
317057UK00006B/453/P

9 780282 004132